STRESS AND STABILITY IN LATE EIGHTEENTH-CENTURY BRITAIN

STRESS AND STABILITY IN LATE EIGHTEENTH-CENTURY BRITAIN

Reflections on the British Avoidance of Revolution

The Ford Lectures
Delivered in the University of Oxford
1983–1984

IAN R. CHRISTIE, FBA
Astor Professor of British History,
University College London

CLARENDON PRESS · OXFORD

Oxford University Press, Walton Street, Oxford OX2 6DP
Oxford New York Toronto
Petaling Jaya Singapore Hong Kong Tokyo
Nairobi Dar es Salaam Cape Town
Melbourne Auckland
and associated companies in
Beirut Berlin Ibadan Nicosia

Oxford is a trade mark of Oxford University Press

Published in the United States
by Oxford University Press, New York

© Ian R. Christie 1984
First published 1984
Reprinted (new as paperback) 1986

British Library Cataloguing in Publication Data
Christie, Ian R.
Stress and stability in late eighteenth-
century Britain.
1. Great Britain—Social conditions
—18th century
I. Title
941.07'3   HN385
ISBN 0-19-820064-1
ISBN 0-19-820108-7 (pbk)

Typeset by Joshua Associates, Oxford
Printed in Great Britain
at the University Press, Oxford
by David Stanford
Printer to the University

To the memory of my father
John Reid Christie

Preface

Lectures 1, 2, 4, and 5 remain substantially as delivered, apart from the addition of some minor detail. Lecture 3 now appears in considerably lengthened form, and the sixth has been expanded into two chapters embodying additional material which it was impossible to deploy within the confines of a single lecture.

Various acknowledgements are due. I am particularly grateful to the University of Oxford for giving me the occasion to write this book by honouring me with the invitation to deliver the Ford Lectures. I must recall a debt to the late Dr George Kitson Clark. A seed planted almost twenty years ago originated in one of our conversations at a Cumberland Lodge Historians' Conference, during which he expressed his grave misgivings about the turn taken by recent interpretations of British social history in the period of the Industrial Revolution.

My sense of various problems connected with the themes of these lectures has been sharpened by discussions with my colleagues, Mr R. S. Craig, Mr N. B. Harte, and Dr M. J. Daunton. Dr R. J. B. Knight and Dr R. A. Morriss, former research students of mine, kindly allowed me to draw upon their doctoral theses for points relating to labour in the royal dockyards. At various times I have gleaned suggestive comments, advice, and pieces of information from Professor Eric Hobsbawm, Professor Olwen Hufton, Mr E. A. Smith, Mrs Patricia Storrar, and Dr Stephen Conway. To all of them I am exceedingly grateful.

I. R. C.

Contents

Introduction

At the time I was invited to deliver the Ford Lectures, I was working on the later chapters of my general history of Great Britain in the reign of George III, recently published under the title *Wars and Revolutions*. One major unanswered question was emerging—and one with which I could not deal within the scope of that work—namely, how should we account for the fact that this country avoided a revolution during the 1790s? According to long-standing traditional interpretation, at that time the revolutionary contagion was widespread. The first seeds had been sown in the English-speaking world: Americans had asserted their independence from Britain during the 1770s. By the 1790s important areas of western Europe were undergoing what has commonly been considered by historians as a revolutionary experience, and the British faced a barely suppressed revolt in the sister kingdom of Ireland. How, in this age of turbulence, did Britain itself escape? These were the considerations which led me to take for the theme of these lectures 'Stress and Stability in late eighteenth-century Britain'. It appeared to me that although no one had so far propounded a comprehensive answer to this question, many hints could be drawn from the monograph literature which I was combing for a different purpose, and that an attempt to establish one would be worth while.

Accordingly, the theme of these lectures, while in one respect taking a wide chronological sweep, on the other focuses attention on the few years either side of 1789. I shall be drawing upon evidence relating to the condition of Great Britain from the 1760s up to a few years after 1800, but the main preoccupation is with the state of affairs in the last two decades of the eighteenth century. Within this general framework I propose first to review the key problem of concepts. What is a revolution? Was there an 'Age of Revolution' in the late eighteenth century? How do answers to these questions relate to our understanding of the situation in Britain? I shall next consider the British scene as one in which factors of stress were undeniably present. In the remaining five chapters I propose to consider various aspects of British society, which may have contributed to national stability. A number of questions suggest themselves. Was the general economic situation favourable or unfavourable? Was society close-knit, or was it fragmented? How far did forms of self-help and popular organization create a sense of confidence and security? Was social support a significant factor in fending off discontent. Did prevailing intellectual and religious attitudes contribute to a satisfaction with or a defence of the status quo? Obviously, there are limits to the significance of the material presented in argument. It is hard enough for a historian to assign causes for events. It is even harder—almost to the point of impossibility—to identify with confidence causes for the non-occurrence of events; and revolution was a non-event, so far as eighteenth-century Britain was concerned. But despite these difficulties I hope that at least some suggestive conclusions may emerge from the discussion that follows.

I

An Age of Revolution?

Can we discern a pattern of revolution in the abstract, which might provide a key to the history of Britain in the late eighteenth century? Was there a general age of revolution at that time that provides a meaningful context for events in Britain?

I

The study of revolutions in the abstract has been a respectable theme for political scientists since ancient times. More recently, from Karl Marx onwards, the nineteenth and twentieth centuries have witnessed a steady stream of literature on the subject.[1] Numbers of authors have attempted to propound some sort of general theory of the nature of revolutions, working on the assumption that such social phenomena can be treated as subjects for scientific investigation and that models of cause and effect can be established. A first drawback of all this work, from the viewpoint of my present theme, is that most of it is concerned with revolutions which took place rather than with situations in which they did not. Even so, a science of revolutions might be helpful if it were, for example, to establish a set of necessary conditions and determining causes leading to revolution, which would enable one to pursue the question, how far were these conditions present in late eighteenth-century Britain?

[1] For an excellent summary and discussion, see Perez Zagorin, 'Theories of Revolution in Contemporary Historiography', *Political Science Quarterly*, 88 (1973), 23-52. Also useful are Lawrence Stone, 'Theories of Revolution', *World Politics*, 18 (1966), 159-76, and Henry Bienen, *Violence and Social Change: a review of current literature* (Chicago, 1968). An important starting-point for the more recent discussion of the subject was provided by Crane Brinton, *The Anatomy of Revolution* (New York, 1938, 2nd edn., 1952). For other attempted formulations, see Chalmers Johnson, *Revolution and the Social System* (Stanford, 1964), and *Revolutionary Change* (Boston, 1966); Harry Eckstein, 'On the Etiology of Internal Wars', *History and Theory*, 4 (1965), 133-63; J. C. Davies, 'Towards a Theory of Revolution', in *When Men Revolt and Why*, ed. J. C. Davies (New York, 1971); Ted Robert Gurr, *Why Men Rebel* (Princeton, 1970); Mark N. Hagopian, *The Phenomenon of Revolution* (New York, 1975).

Alas, it turns out that dialogue between historians and political scientists is not so easy to establish, at least not in this field, and the possibility of progress along these lines seems distinctly limited. By and large historians studying revolutions have viewed the approach of the political scientist with considerable reserve and have found attempts at the formulation of scientific models of revolutions unrealistic. Set at its crudest, the conflict of the two disciplines is extreme. The American historian turned political scientist, Crane Brinton, in a book which commands respect as opening a new modern stage of debate in this field—his study, *The Anatomy of Revolution*—posed it thus:[2]

We shall have to be content with the crude assertion that the doctrine of the absolute uniqueness of events in history seems nonsense. History is essentially an account of the behaviour of men, and if the behaviour of men is not subject to any kind of systematization, this world is even more cockeyed than the seers would have it. History at least gives us case histories, is at least material for the clinician.

Brinton obviously thought that with this trumpet-blast he had solved the methodological problem. This was far from being the case. Even setting aside the assumption that historians have provided adequate firm case histories for clinical study, which I doubt, at least three formidable objections can be raised.

The first is that not only men but also circumstances are inextricably intertwined in historical events, and chains of circumstances leading to an event can never be exactly repeated. Another very able political scientist, Mark Hagopian, has thus posed the problem for his discipline:[3]

Critics of the concept of cyclical processes of change point out that since history never repeats itself, what appears to be a re-edition of a familiar cycle or a simple recurrence is itself so peculiar and unprecedented that essentially it is something entirely new. But when pushed too far this thesis imperils the very basis of social science by denying the degree of commonness necessary to both comparison and subsequent generalization. Recurrences of a cyclical nature are the social scientist's surrogate for the natural scientist's laboratory experiment.

[2] *The Anatomy of Revolution*, p. 20.
[3] *The Phenomenon of Revolution*, p. 133.

The historian, conscious of the linear one-way process of the human story throughout the past, can but reflect sympathetically, that this denial is unavoidable, and that the social scientist's surrogate for the laboratory experiment does not exist.

Moreover, it is not only that the events are not the same a second or third time round; neither are the perceptions in the minds of the men experiencing them. This leads on to a second objection, that the social scientists fail to allow for the potentially almost infinite diversity of human perception, reaction, and behaviour.

Now it is true that neuropsychologists investigating the elementary levels of sense perception postulate a basic uniformity of human responses.[4] But *pace* their findings or the thrust of the theories of early exponents of psychology like Freud and Jung, it is far from evident that all human reaction can be deduced from such a narrow foundation, for instance, as the sexual drive, or that the principle of uniformity can be extended to cover the realm of imaginative concepts on which individual behaviour may be based. Here almost infinite variety seems possible—a circumstance which, biologically speaking, is both the great strength and, possibly, the great weakness of the human species. Think only of the multitude of different forms of religious belief which have determined the actions of individuals in numerous different societies all over the world during the four thousand or so years for which we have any written record of them—beliefs which have carried some groups to success and others to utter disaster. Brinton's seers are far outpaced by reality.[5] The

[4] This general approach is apparent in such works as D. O. Hebb, *The Organization of Behaviour: A Neuropsychological Theory* (1949), and *Textbook of Psychology* (3rd edn., 1972); and J. Z. Young, *Programs of the Brain* (1978).

[5] The most disastrous apocalyptic vision known to me, which nearly destroyed the Xhosa nation of South Africa, is thus described under the heading 'Cattle Killing Delusion' in *The Encyclopaedia of Southern Africa*, comp. Eric Rosenthal (5th edn., 1970): 'In 1856 a young Xhosa woman ... Nongquase, preached that the day was approaching when Europeans in their country would be driven into the sea. Dead chiefs would arise, kraals would be filled with cattle and grain-pits with new harvests. Upon that day the sun would rise blood-red, fields would stand ready for reaping, illness would disappear, as would old age. All white people and those who had disobeyed orders from the other world would be carried into the sea by a great wind. To make these things possible it was necessary to kill every head of livestock in the hands of the Xhosa nation, and to destroy all grain and

way the brain processes involved in such mental phenomena operate is—at least at present—far beyond the capacity of neuropsychological science to explain, but their unpredictability seems beyond question.[6] The American scientist Carl Sagan has pointed out that the immense number of potential functionally different configurations in the human brain, based on the count of neurones and the synapses connecting them, is far greater than the total number of elementary particles (electrons and protons) in the entire universe. His conclusion offers nothing but gloom and despondency to the social scientist:[7]

In the face of these numbers [writes Sagan] the wonder is that there are regularities at all in human behaviour. The answer must be that all possible brain states are by no means occupied; there must be an enormous number of mental configurations that have never been entered or even glimpsed by any human being in the history of mankind. From this perspective, each individual human being is truly rare and different.

A vast unexplored mental territory lies open to continued gradual penetration by mankind. Here is the biological basis of what Jacob Talmon, writing before Sagan's scientific insights were stated in print, has described as 'the uniqueness and the unpredictability of human nature and human conduct, which result either from the irrational elements in our being, or from men's egotism'.[8]

A third difficulty springing from the first and the second is, that the factual and the mental patterns of the past are simply too intractable to be forced into a general mould. Mark Hagopian's able study, *The Phenomenon of Revolution*,

garden produce.' In the hope of this miracle the Xhosa people stripped themselves of every source of food, and in consequence suffered 'a nightmare of starvation and despair.' In the first seven months of 1857 the population of British Kaffraria fell from 104,721 to 37,229, and the military power of the Xhosa was broken for ever. I am indebted for this reference to Mrs Patricia Storrar.

[6] 'Scientists . . . do not know . . . how the brain works even in the simplest animal, let alone in man.' Max Perutz, in a probing review essay on Liebe F. Cavalieri, *The Double-Edged Helix* (1981), *Times Literary Supplement*, 6 Nov. 1981, p. 1287.

[7] Carl Sagan, *The Dragons of Eden. Speculations on the Evolution of Human Intelligence* (1978), p. 42. In this view the totalitarian passion for total uniformity in thought and action is in conflict with the fundamental biological facts of human nature.

[8] J. L. Talmon, *The Origins of Totalitarian Democracy* (1952), p. 136.

is punctuated by despairing acknowledgements of this fact; thus (p. 52): 'Revolutions are too complex and too unique to be reducible to a facile formula such as bourgeois or proletarian'; (p. 112): 'It seems then that revolutions are more responses to indigenous patterns of social conflict than manifestations of a transnational wave'; (p. 123): 'Unfortunately, there is no simple law of revolution under which we can subsume particular instances with their set of appropriate initial conditions, and accordingly explain past or predict future revolutions.; (p. 185): 'While each revolution is unique, certain causal features are common enough to merit special comparative emphasis'; (p. 363): 'If one thing has clearly emerged from our comparative survey of revolutions, it is the complexity and particularity of each historical revolution.' Years ago Crane Brinton attempted to apply a general pattern to four revolutions, the Great Rebellion in England, the American, the French, and the Russian Revolutions. He emerged with a model which fitted many of the known facts about the French Revolution but conformed much less with any of the others. Harry Eckstein has drawn up a classified list of commonly advanced hypotheses dealing with the causes of revolutions, but the degree of correspondence of this list with particular revolutions is highly variable: a uniform model fails to emerge.[9]

There is yet another difficulty: historians and political scientists do not necessarily agree on what their definition of a revolution should be. This is evident, for instance, from the work of Mark Hagopian. 'A revolution', he writes, 'is an acute, prolonged crisis in one or more of the traditional systems of stratification (class, status, power) of a political community, which involves a purposive élite-directed attempt to abolish or to reconstruct one or more of the said systems by means of an intensification of political power and recourse to violence.'[10] This definition, which in many respects has

[9] Perez Zagorin, article cited, pp. 30-1, 44. Cf. Alfred Cobban, *The Social Interpretation of the French Revolution* (Cambridge, 1968), pp. 8-14, and especially pp. 13-14: 'In practice, general social laws turn out to be one of three things. If they are not dogmatic assertions about the course of history, they are either platitudes, or else, to be made to fit the facts, they have to be subjected to more and more qualifications until in the end they are applicable only to a single case.'   [10] *The Phenomenon of Revolution*, p. 1.

a great deal to commend it, nevertheless abstracts the subject from the phenomena which historians find worthy of consideration under such descriptions. If one turns to the late eighteenth century, for example, Hagopian's definition excludes the American Revolution, which he classes as a non-revolutionary movement for secession.[11] More broadly, on this basis he finds no ground for accepting the idea of a general revolutionary crisis in Europe either in the seventeenth or the eighteenth century.[12] I am slightly sceptical about the grounds of Hagopian's judgement about the American Revolution, since I think one can discern a regionally orientated crisis within the systems of stratification he posits if one looks at the British Atlantic Empire as a single political unit.[13] But, as will appear, I agree with his assessment of the American Revolution on rather different grounds, and also with his scepticism about a revolutionary age in the eighteenth century.

Most if not all the foregoing considerations tend to support the practical conclusions of the historian that, to quote Perez Zagorin, 'nothing has appeared that qualifies as a general theory of revolution', and that, 'above a certain level of generality social science theory is too remote from reality to be either very interesting or useful'.[14] To a limited extent, however, the probings of the social scientists may be suggestive. Eckstein, for instance, has put forward an explanatory model at a high level of abstraction, incorporating eight variables which in combination establish the presence and extent of the preconditions for revolution. The negative variables working against revolution are the facilities (especially for coercion) available to the men in power,

---

[11] *The Phenomenon of Revolution*, pp. 33–4, 45.

[12] Ibid., pp. 107–12.

[13] While the point must not be pressed too far, a sense of a confrontation between a hitherto dominant (landed) élite centred in Britain and a new mercantile élite centred in the peripheral region of the American Atlantic coastline seems to ring through some of the ministerial speeches on the Massachusetts Charter Act of 1774; for example, Lord North: 'I propose, in this Bill, to take the executive power from the hands of the democratic part of government'; Lord George Germain: 'I would not have men of a mercantile caste every day collecting themselves together, and debating about political matters.' *The Parliamentary History of England . . . to 1803*, ed. William Cobbett and T. C. Hansard (36 vols., 1806–20), xvii, cols. 1193, 1195.

[14] Zagorin, article cited, pp. 29, 52.

effective repression, adjustive concessions, and diversionary mechanisms. The positive variables working in favour of revolution in this analysis are the inefficiency of élites, disorienting social processes, subversion, and the facilities for violence available to insurgents.[15] Hagopian presents a different model (though there are some common features) in which he distinguishes seven long-term causes, some of them economic or intellectual in nature, and five 'middle-term' causes, including 'economic depression', 'alienation of the intellectuals', 'division and ineptitude in the ruling class', war, and 'government financial crisis'. The possible permutations and combinations among all these factors are obviously exceedingly numerous.[16] Now, a survey of the factors of stress and stability in British society in the late eighteenth century can indeed be organized in some degree according to the sorts of categories suggested by Eckstein and Hagopian, and to this extent the political scientist's approach may suggest useful lines of investigation; but it is doubtful whether this process carries us very far and I think it will appear in the end that the actual picture is more complex than they would suggest. Such categories are, as Zagorin indicates, so rarefied, so abstracted from reality, as to be of only minimal help to a historical enquiry.

II

If overviews of revolution in general do not help very much, neither, I suspect, do attempts to make generalizations about the limited series of 'revolutions' which occurred or threatened in the western world during the later part of the eighteenth century, beginning with the American assertion of independence. The title of that splendid *tour de force* by Professor R.R. Palmer, *The Age of the Democratic Revolution*,[17] implies that within this confine of time and space a number of countries were affected by a common experience, and that

[15] Ibid., p. 45.

[16] *The Phenomenon of Revolution*, pp. 135–66. It is not wholly clear how far these circumstances might be regarded as necessary conditions rather than causes.

[17] R. R. Palmer, *The Age of the Democratic Revolution. A Political History of Europe and America, 1760–1800.* Vol. i: *The Challenge*; Vol. ii: *The Struggle* (Princeton, 1959, 1964).

democracy was a common theme running through them all. While the American Revolution initially appeared as an isolated event, its sequel in France kindled anticipations of a different sort. To some enthusiastic contemporaries the French Revolution appeared at the outset to offer a Utopia of potentially universal extent and not confined to the French state, 'a fraternal association . . . above the inherited anachronisms of race and language'. It was an expectation from which these optimists were all too soon disabused.[18] No doubt in certain limited respects, depending on one's definitions, the concept of a revolutionary movement overleaping national boundaries may have an element of truth; and yet, I have a suspicion that, through the coining of a ringing phrase, historians have become stuck with a label for this particular age which in some respects is profoundly misleading.[19] A consideration of general characteristics of the American and of the French Revolutions points to this conclusion. The situation in near-revolutionary Ireland, which has a special relevance to the British situation, also seems to suggest this. Accordingly, if we abandon generalization, and consider separately certain salient features of the American, the Irish, and the French situations, we may lay a ground for both context and contrast which will help to explain the British escape from revolution.

Inspired by the bicentenary of 1776 there has been a flood of writing about the American Revolution, but this has brought little agreement about its essential nature. The Revolution has variously been seen as a crusade in defence of liberty; as the triumph of a new nation freeing itself from constitutional or economic bonds; as a colonial struggle for independence; as a democratic revolution against an *ancien régime*, or as a civil conflict followed by secession. The models favoured have perhaps to some extent been determined for particular historians by their area of scholarly interest, their particular intellectual tradition, or even their emotional involvement. In the present state of learning, one

---

[18] Simon Schama, *Patriots and Liberators. Revolution in the Netherlands, 1780–1813* (1977), pp. 6–9, quotation at p. 7.

[19] Cf. George Rudé, *Revolutionary Europe, 1783–1815* (1964), pp. 65, 220–2.

or two of these models appear to be more plausible than others, but the debate over their respective merits is by no means over.[20]

Perhaps the most critical attack on this problem has been mounted by Jack P. Greene. His favoured line of argument leads away from concepts of democratic revolution and in the direction of an explanation in terms of a civil conflict followed by secession.[21] He notes that various sorts of social stress did exist in the American colonies before 1776, but that no one has been able to link them effectively with the overall causal pattern of the revolution. Such discontinuities as did occur in American life after 1776 are to be explained not in terms of the internal circumstances but on the basis of the conflict with Great Britain. That conflict was concerned with the nature of the imperial system of which Britain formed the centre and the colonies a large section, though not the whole, of the outlying periphery. During the 1760s and 1770s both the colonial and the home British political nations were increasingly racked by anxiety over what each side took to be a series of fundamental and menacing violations of the established imperial order by the other. As Edmund Burke phrased it in 1769: 'The Americans have made a discovery, or think they have made one, that we mean to oppress them: we have made a discovery, or think we have made one, that they intend to rise in rebellion against us. . . . We know not how to advance; they know not how to retreat.'[22] These tensions had arisen out of the

[20] For surveys of these differences of interpretation, see Esmond Wright, *Causes and Consequences of the American Revolution* (Chicago, 1966); Jack P. Greene, *The Ambiguity of the American Revolution* (New York, 1968), and *The Reinterpretation of the American Revolution* (New York, 1968); Ian R. Christie, 'The Historians' Quest for the American Revolution', in *Statesmen, Scholars and Merchants: Essays in eighteenth-century History presented to Dame Lucy Sutherland*, ed. Anne Whiteman and others (Oxford, 1973), pp. 181–201. Cogent presentations of particular viewpoints are given in W. H. Nelson, 'The Revolutionary Character of the American Revolution', *American Historical Review*, lxx (1964–5), 998–1014, and T. C. Barrow, 'The American Revolution as a Colonial War of Independence', *William and Mary Quarterly*, 3rd ser. xxi (1968), 452–64.

[21] Jack P. Greene, 'The Social Origins of the American Revolution: an Evaluation and an Interpretation', *Political Science Quarterly*, 88 (1973), 1–22.

[22] *Sir Henry Cavendish's Debates of the House of Commons*, ed. J. Wright (2 vols., 1841–3), i. 348–9.

circumstance that by the middle years of the eighteenth century most of the American mainland colonies had come to possess 'virtually all of the conditions necessary for self-governing states', which the signatories of the Declaration of Independence later declared them to be. They had evolved 'stable, coherent, effective, and acknowledged local political and social elites', practised in government and assured of broad public support; effectively functioning organs of local legislation and administration, from colony to district level; and a flexible political system which satisfied local aspirations and channelled conflict into political terms. The civilized arts were well established and their economic potential was becoming substantial. By the 1770s colonists had developed a series of complex assumptions about the working of the imperial relationship, any violations of which raised serious alarm. At the heart of the conflict which thereafter developed lay a British assumption of a 'perpetual dependency of the colonies upon the mother country, while the colonial [emphasis] suggested an eventual equivalence'. In these conditions the decisions of British administrations to reaffirm and make effective their assumptions about the imperial relationship had catastrophic results.[23] As a confrontation led on the one hand by the merchant and planter aristocracy of the colonies and on the other by the aristocracy, gentry, and a minority of politically active merchants in Britain, with dissident minorities from the same sections of society in both countries, the American Revolution does not appear to offer any sort of model for a development of tensions within Britain itself.[24]

It is true that the same style of 'Commonwealth' rhetoric was employed on both sides of the Atlantic during the 1760s and 1770s. American patriots emulated the language of British oppositionists and political reformers.[25] But this

[23] Jack P. Greene, 'An Uneasy Connection. An Analysis of the Preconditions of the American Revolution', in *Essays on the American Revolution*, ed. S. G. Kurtz and J. H. Hutson (Chapel Hill, NC, 1973), pp. 35 ff.

[24] For a powerful, full-scale interpretation along these lines, see Robert W. Tucker and David C. Hendrickson, *The Fall of the First British Empire. Origins of the War of American Independence* (Baltimore and London, 1982).

[25] Bernard Bailyn, *The Ideological Origins of the American Revolution* (Cambridge, Mass., 1967); *The Origins of American Politics* (New York, 1969).

perhaps reflected an old-fashioned rather than a new-fangled theme. The American events fit ill into the picture of an age of democratic revolution. In fact, a strong case can be argued that the American Revolution, sometimes taken as having set the whole sequence in motion, was a revolution concerned far less with democracy than with the issue of a government of laws. The British Parliament was seen as acting in arbitrary fashion in its relations with the colonies. The constitution-making which followed the Declaration of Independence, not least the construction of the federal system, and still more especially the adoption of declarations of rights culminating in the first ten amendments to the constitution of the United States, was intended to impose checks upon any further such development. The method adopted was to give special sanction to basic rules, in accordance with which the exercise of political power was to be conducted. Furthermore, far from acting on what the twentieth century would regard as the democratic message of the dictum in the Declaration of Independence—'all men are created equal'— the revolutionary generation in America was deeply committed to the principle of political inequality. Americans, one scholar has written, 'displayed little disposition to abandon the traditional British insistence upon personal independence and virtue as the criterion for citizenship'.[26] Property and the vote were still coupled after 1776, as they had been before.

The American emphasis on the rule of law provides an important commentary on theories of general revolution at this time, because it underlines the cleavage between an Anglo-Saxon political tradition shared by Britain and America on the one hand and on the other the form in which democratic revolution emerged in France. To the powerful legal fraternities among the English-speaking peoples on both sides of the Atlantic, the most important repository of knowledge, apart from the Bible, was Sir William Blackstone's *Commentaries on the Laws of England*.[27] Law and precedent were,

[26] Cf. Hannah Arendt, *On Revolution* (1965), pp. 92, 147-8; Jack P. Greene, *All Men are Created Equal. Some Reflections on the Character of the American Revolution* (Oxford, 1976), pp. 4, 32, and see the whole lecture for the exposition of this point.

[27] In March 1775 Edmund Burke told the House of Commons: 'I hear that they have sold nearly as many copies of Blackstone's *Commentaries* in America as

or should be, paramount, and in the British tradition the word 'revolution', far from carrying its present-day meaning of 'violent change', represented a profoundly conservative concept. Originally used by astronomers to describe the circular motions of the heavenly bodies, to the contemporaries of George III and of George Washington the term 'revolution' as applied to politics retained its cyclical connotation and implied 'restoration', a return to a desirable state of affairs previously experienced in the past: it did not signify the creation of a new political or social order.[28]

III

Revolutionary tendencies in Ireland towards the end of the eighteenth century sprang from factors which had little or no parallel in Britain. A series of complex and sometimes mutually frustrating lines of cleavage divided Irish society.[29]

The ruling minority—the 'Protestant Ascendancy'—united by its loyalty to the episcopal Church of Ireland and by its role as the landowning class, was divided within itself between those who sought a greater degree of political independence from London and those who believed that their security depended upon the perpetuation of the existing relationship. The activists in the former camp, men like Lord Charlemont and Henry Grattan, partly inspired by the stand taken by the American colonists over their constitutional rights, had also taken up the slogans and myths of the Rockinghamite opposition in Britain. They had won limited political emancipation in 1782, but in doing so had kindled aspira-

---

in England' (*The Parliamentary History of England*, xvii, col. 495). The importance of Blackstone to the Americans of the revolutionary generation is discussed in Gerald Stourzh, 'William Blackstone: Teacher of Revolution', *Jahrbuch für Amerikastudien* (Heidelberg, 1970), 184–200. An example of the far-flung distribution of Blackstone's work appears from the surviving legal library of George Rex, the first marshall of the British court of vice-admiralty at Cape Town (in post, 1797–1803): it consists of a set of the *Commentaries* (information from Mrs Patricia Storrar, author of *George Rex. Death of a Legend*, Johannesburg, 1974).

[28] Arendt, *On Revolution*, pp. 42–3; Perez Zagorin, article cited, p. 26.

[29] For a general survey, see R. B. McDowell, *Ireland in the Age of Imperialism and Revolution, 1760–1801* (Oxford, 1979). The Irish revolutionary movement is given detailed treatment in Marianne Elliott, *Partners in Revolution. The United Irishmen and France* (New Haven and London, 1982).

tions for political reforms of a more sweeping kind than they themselves were prepared to countenance. The extrapolation of political dissent into programmes of parliamentary reform, as championed by sections of the Volunteer movement during the early 1780s, carried a threat to the power of the oligarchy of landowners. It also threatened the 'Protestant Ascendancy'; for in Ireland, the logic of parliamentary reform—of the widening of the extent of participation in public life—carried with it ineluctably the implication of Catholic emancipation, indeed the grant of political rights to men of all denominations. Such an outcome held out the prospect of the swamping of a Protestant minority by the Catholic majority. In the 1780s even a leading Irish patriot like Grattan found this overmuch to swallow.

Some progress in this direction was eventually made nevertheless. But the few tentative concessions gradually extended to Catholics—the abandonment of various civil disabilities and penal laws in 1778 and 1782, admission to the legal profession in 1792, entry into the army and the grant of the parliamentary franchise in 1793—raised hopes of full participation in public life, which those in power in Dublin flatly rejected. Hopes deferred made many Catholics sick with their situation. In the city environments the points of friction and the animosities between the denominations were less, common interests were more obvious, and educated circles, touched by the more ecumenical and also secular outlook of the age, looked forward to a sinking of differences and full political co-operation. Yet, in the early 1790s, the legitimate aspirations of many Catholics of the middling and professional classes, represented through either the Dublin Catholic Committee or the more radical Dublin Society of United Irishmen, remained blocked by the 'Ascendancy'. By that time leaders of the United Irishmen in Dublin, and also in Belfast, where they drew substantial support from the Presbyterian element of the population, were alike moving towards the view that the internal conflicts in Ireland, and the real interests of what they felt to be an Irish nation, would never be settled by the British-backed oligarchy, but only by a more enlightened, independent Irish government provided by themselves. Many of these leaders were drawn from the legal profession. They belonged to the Church of Ireland but did not share its religious exclusiveness, and they sought to draw people of all denominations into a movement which increasingly they identified as a national cause.[30]

This religious and political movement coincided with one of the most divisive cleavages in Irish rural society, that between Protestant landowner and Catholic tenant.[31] This itself was a fusion of several distinct causes of conflict. Over several generations a fundamental lack of sympathy had prevented the growth of a civilized relationship between landlord and tenant. Although there were some exceptional landlords, like Lovell Edgeworth, driven by a social conscience and anxious to promote the welfare of those dependent upon them, too many were absentees, indifferent to the proper management of their estates, and leaving them to the oppressive regime of rack-renting agents.[32] The fierce competition for land caused by an expanding population, by the development of capitalist farming, and by the widespread sense of insecurity arising from these conditions, intensified peasant unrest and hostility. These were also fuelled by ancient national animosities. Irish peasants of native descent nursed old traditions of common clan ownership of the land and dreamed of one day dispossessing the landowning group first imposed on the country in the period of the Elizabethan and Jacobean plantations. Among none did this spirit burn more strongly than the descendants of the old clan chieftains, who retained a keen sense of their being the rightful gentry of the land, and whose memories of lineage and inheritance were carefully preserved. 'The lower orders or old Irish consider themselves as plundered and kept out of their property by the English settlers and on every occasion are ready for riot and revenge', the Lord-Lieutenant wrote in 1793.[33]

This discontent was further inflamed by the confrontation in Ulster of Catholic and Presbyterian competitors for farm tenancies. The Ulster Presbyterians gave strong support to radicalism in the early 1790s and were then regarded by the

---

[30] Elliott, *Partners in Revolution*, pp. 24–34.

[31] Marianne Elliott, 'The Origin and Transformation of Early Irish Republicanism', *International Review of Social History*, 23 (1978), 405–28.

[32] Michael Hurst, *Maria Edgeworth and the Public Scene* (1969), pp. 16–21.

[33] Elliott, 'Early Irish Republicanism', p. 411.

government as the most dangerous republican element in the country. But the land question opposed an insuperable obstacle to what might have been a formidable national Catholic–Presbyterian alliance. The conflict between the two groups came to a head during the 1790s. The operations of the Catholic Defenders ultimately provoked the foundation of the Orangist movement in 1795 and the serious outbreak of sectarian violence directed against Catholics commonly known as the Armagh outrages. Large numbers of Ulster Catholics took refuge in the south of Ireland, where they helped to kindle a fierce anti-Protestant sentiment. The consequent dread of Catholic insurrection pushed the Dublin administration into a ruthless repression which did much finally to create the very situation it was intended to prevent.

This chain of circumstances was more immediately responsible than anything else for the outbreak of rebellion in Ireland in 1798, while at the same time it spelled the breakdown of the nationalist, non-sectarian solution to Irish problems sought by the United Irishmen. A revolutionary leadership had developed among the Defenders even earlier than among the United Irishmen. As early as 1792, before the involvement of Britain in the war against revolutionary France, the Defenders tried to interest French agents in a rising, which would have a redistribution to the native Irish of Protestant-owned estates as one of the objects.[34] Such a social revolution was by no means to the taste of the United Irishmen. Their movement, like that of the Americans, reflected a sectional or national interest seeking independence from a political superior. Although they also sought help from France, they did not want the French Revolution exported to Ireland. They disliked its atheism. They failed to capture and to channel to their own purposes the Defender movement, for its hostility to Protestantism as well as to Protestant landlords was fatal to their hopes of getting all religious groups to work together. The anti-Protestant manifestations of the southern Irish rising in 1798 drove the hitherto discontented and republican Presbyterians of the north-east suddenly and decisively on to the opposing side and cemented their attachment to the established order.

[34] Elliott, 'Early Irish Republicanism', pp. 417, 420–1.

In sum, the abortive Irish revolution of the late eighteenth century was largely due to two different national movements, working at different social levels, between which a full understanding and alliance was impossible, and it arose out of acute religous animosities with which one of these national movements, but not the other, was intimately linked. Nothing in all this paralleled the situations in America, in France, or in Britain itself.

IV

If the American Revolution and the abortive revolution in Ireland present their own unique features with little relevance to conditions in Britain, what then of France? The French Revolution was certainly the key event of that period in the history of the West. There is no doubt that it was a real revolution, by any standards. People in Britain were intensely interested in it.[35] Some interaction at least took place across the Channel after 1789, and but for events in France it is most unlikely that there would be any such problem as these lectures set out to discuss.

And yet, to the searcher for parallels the French Revolution is equally unhelpful. Studies of its nature and causes present an even more confused picture than in the case of the revolution in North America. It has been variously attributed to the economic conditions in France before 1789, to stresses produced by various aspects of social structure, to political conflict between the monarchy and the aristocracy or between the monarchy and a body of Jacobin conspirators. Some writers have blamed it on the intellectual demolition of the premises of the *ancien régime* by the *philosophes* during the forty years preceding 1789. And then there is the question of the responsibility of the old order itself. Harry Eckstein comments that 'scarcely anything in the French *ancien régime* has not been blamed by one writer or another for the revolution'. He adds, perhaps rashly: 'All of their

[35] The enterprise of the partners of the *Morning Chronicle* in arranging first-hand reports of events in France during 1791-2 sent the sales of this journal rocketing to unprecedented heights. ('James Perry of the *Morning Chronicle,* 1756-1821', in Ian R. Christie, *Myth and Reality in late eighteenth-century British politics, and other papers* (1970), pp. 344-5.)

interpretations, however contradictory, are based on solid facts'—which looks a little like an example of the way political scientists trying to use historians' materials may venture into quicksands without fully realizing that they are there.[36] The view has recently been put forward by François Furet that it was the virtually spontaneous demise of the *ancien régime*, after it had destroyed the cohesive forces of the old political and social order, that created a power-vacuum into which the Revolution flowed.[37]

For much of the present century French historians have tended to view their revolution as a working out of the Marxist dogma of social evolution, and have professed to see in it a successful overthrow of a feudal system by the bourgeoisie. If there were any degree of universalism in such a theory, this could imply that certain elements of a parallel process might also be found north of the Channel, and the question could then arise, why did a revolution mature in the one country but not in the other? But not only is that universalism itself highly debatable. In fact this traditional interpretation of the revolution in France is now largely exploded, although it will be no doubt an unconscionable time a-dying.[38]

During the last thirty years various writers on this subject have shown the inadequacy of the Marxist analysis. France could not in any real sense of the term be described as 'feudal' in the late eighteenth century. True, one of the great grievances among the farmer class was the existence of a wide range of seignorial dues of medieval feudal origin, for which no parallels had survived in Britain; but these had long since become converted into forms of property right, often alienated quite independently of the landownership with which they had originally been associated. To a large

---

[36] Alfred Cobban, *Historians and the Causes of the French Revolution* (1958), *passim*; Eckstein, article cited, pp. 137–8.

[37] François Furet, *Interpreting the French Revolution*, trans. Elborg Forster (Cambridge, 1981), pp. 113–14.

[38] For a survey of the recent literature, see Part I of William Doyle, *Origins of the French Revolution* (Oxford, 1980), pp. 7–40. Alfred Cobban, *The Social Interpretation of the French Revolution* (Cambridge, 1968), was an early onslaught on the Marxist view. The recent comprehensive attack by Furet (*Interpreting the French Revolution*, pp. 81–131) provides further compelling reasons for the condemnation and evacuation of this intellectual slum-block.

extent they had passed into the hands of individuals who belonged to the Third Estate, some of whom were prepared to exploit them much more ruthlessly than members of the old nobility would have thought to do. One writer has suggested that, far from being considered as in any sense 'feudal', they were much better described, in more modern idiom, as 'a commercial racket'.[39] In many areas they were only a minor burden, and they formed only a small part of landowners' income.[40]

There are other difficulties in the projection of a conflict between a feudal nobility and a bourgeoisie at the commencement of the French Revolution. On the one hand, the nobility in France had ceased to be a clearly defined socio-economic category. Those who were described as noble represented all levels of wealth and poverty, with widely differing sources of income and social status.[41] On the other, neither is it possible to classify as bourgeois the men in the National Assembly in 1789, predominantly of the Third Estate, who were to emerge as leaders of the revolution. They came from the ranks of minor officials and the liberal professions, were owners of property, and were concerned about property rights: they did not belong to or represent a rising commercial, financial, and industrial class.[42] Their ambition for a larger share of political power was a major driving force behind the revolution, one which drew in support from sections both of the clergy and of the nobility. This ambition entailed conflict with the monarchy, which was loath to accept the change in the power-balance effected after the establishment of the National Assembly.[43]

Abandoning explanation in Marxist determinist terms, the historian must look in other directions; and there seems to be a fair degree of consensus that the origins of the Revolution lay in a complex of circumstances which had no parallels

[39] Cobban, *Social Interpretation of the French Revolution*, p. 51.
[40] Furet, *Interpreting the French Revolution*, p. 93.
[41] Cobban, *Social Interpretation of the French Revolution*, p. 32. Cf. J. McManners, 'France', in *The European Nobility in the eighteenth century*, ed. A. Goodwin (1953), pp. 22–42.
[42] Cobban, *Social Interpretation of the French Revolution*, pp. 61–80.
[43] Ibid., p. 81; Doyle, *Origins of the French Revolution*, pp. 91–4, 120, 168–71, 204–8.

in Britain. Gwyn A. Williams conveys something of this when he writes that 'The Ancien Regime seems to have reached the point of breakdown almost simultaneously in social, political, economic, and intellectual terms. From 1787 a chain of "revolutions", royal renovation, aristocratic reaction, bourgeois revolution, popular rebellion, Great Fear, hunger riots, municipal coups, peasant revolts, swept to a climax in 1789.'[44] William Doyle points to the alienation of the French political nation by the total ineptitude of the monarchy and its failure to avoid bankruptcy, on top of which came the intervention of a meteorological disaster that increased the endemic disorder among the poor.[45] Furet stresses the degree to which the Bourbon monarchy had atomized French society, drained all natural resilience out of any corporate bonds making for social cohesion, and had created numerous damaging divisions within the nobility itself.[46] Whereas the British political system was a vigorous going concern in the late eighteenth century, run by a broad propertied oligarchy, affairs in France were in a unique state of confusion at the commencement of the Revolution and gave rise to a unique train of events in the years that followed. Despite the ingenious and interesting attempt by Dr Jarrett to suggest parallels in the situations of France and Britain in the late eighteenth century, it is, I believe, far more fruitful to consider the contrasts between them.[47]

This difference between a solid political system on one side of the Channel and a state of disorganization and decay on the other is one of two salient contrasts which I think are crucial for my theme. The second contrast is to be found in the style and conceptual nature of the approach to change in

[44] Gwyn A. Williams, *Artisans and Sansculottes* (1968), p. 9. Cobban has suggested that the factors in the transformation of one enormously complex and changing historic situation into another, equally complex and changing, are so complicated, that the results of an investigation may well be something 'which it is difficult to list as a series of causes in a text-book, and in this sense the search for causes of the . . . Revolution may well be at an end'. (*Historians and the Causes of the French Revolution*, p. 39. See also his treatment of the subject in his *A History of Modern France*, vol. I: *Old Regime and Revolution, 1715-1799* (Harmondsworth, 1957), *passim*.

[45] Doyle, *Origins of the French Revolution*, Part II, *passim*.

[46] Furet, *Interpreting the French Revolution*, pp. 100-16.

[47] Derek Jarrett, *The Begetters of Revolution. England's Involvement with France, 1759-1789* (1973).

France. Essentially the French Revolution was an attempt to substitute a new state authority for one which had already collapsed. What form was this to take? Initially the revolutionary movement was ambiguous on this point.[48] Janus-like, it looked in two directions. One face appeared to point in the direction of representative government in a mould familiar to both British and American experience. For some time this profile concealed from most Englishmen the implications of the other. But very soon the Revolution was advancing down a very different path, heading in the direction of political apocalypse. Whereas the American Revolution was 'a classic contest for political liberty secured by constitutional complexity', leaders of the Revolution in France moved towards 'a totally new and entirely man-made order', and did so with a horrifying excess of certitude.[49]

Numbers of writers have stressed this new departure in France. To Crane Brinton an outstanding character of revolutions, as seen in the French experience, was the way in which the idealist was enabled to break out of the established framework of social ideas in order to realize his dreams. 'What differentiates this ideal world of our revolutionaries', he wrote, 'from the better world as conceived by more pedestrian persons is a flaming sense of the immediacy of the ideal, a feeling that there is something in all men better than their present fate, and a conviction that what is, not only ought not, but need not, be.'[50] Hannah Arendt and Jacob Talmon have pointed to the process by which the unleashed revolutionary, in his emotional response to the needs of categories of people as he envisages them, becomes entirely ruthless towards individuals and falls into the principle that the end justifies the means. In this process, 'pity, taken as the spring of virtue, has proved to possess a greater capacity for cruelty than cruelty itself'. In the French Revolution, for the first time, revolutionaries, through the 'boundlessness of their sentiments', became 'curiously insensitive to reality in general and to the reality of persons in particular', whom they felt

---

[48] Furet, *Interpreting the French Revolution*, pp. 182–90, especially pp. 182–3; Cobban, *A History of Modern France*, vol. i, pp. 160–2.

[49] James H. Billington, *Fire in the Minds of Men. Origins of the Revolutionary Faith* (1980), pp. 3–10 (quotations at pp. 9–10).

[50] Crane Brinton, *The Anatomy of Revolution*, pp. 50–1.

no compunction in sacrificing to their 'principles', or to the course of history, or to the cause of revolution in general.[51] James Billington writes of the revolutionaries seeking a new reality which was 'radically secular and stridently simple'. 'Most revolutionaries', he concluded, 'viewed history prophetically as a kind of morality play. The present was hell, and revolution a collective purgatory leading to a future earthly paradise.'[52] For the French revolutionaries the new reality was simple: there developed a 'tremendous cultural drive for equality'; and with the over-simplification of objective came a corresponding over-simplification of difficulties. The inertia and obstinacy of facts and circumstances became personified as the wrongheadedness and sin of human opponents. One may envisage this development as the emergence of a Manichaean view of the world, or perhaps as a form of acute and aggressive paranoia—whichever figure is adopted, the ultimate result was the same: the Terror.

It is small wonder that historians grappling with the problem of defining the French regime which culminated in the Terror have sometimes been forced back on metaphor. The presentation of a rational description is inherently difficult because the thing at its heart was so fundamentally irrational. The groups of intellectuals who stepped into the power-vacuum left by the collapse of the French monarchy had a vision before them which they believed to be held by the nation as a whole: they themselves were merely its instruments. It was as if the 'general will' postulated by Rousseau were being materialized in their will and action.[53] François Furet writes that 'the Jacobin creed was indeed founded on immanence in history, on the realization of values in and by

---

[51] Arendt, *On Revolution*, pp. 80-1, 90; Talmon, *Origins of Totalitarian Democracy*, pp. 38-164; Alfred Cobban, *In Search of Humanity. The Role of the Enlightenment in Modern History* (1960), pp. 181-93.

[52] Billington, *Fire in the Minds of Men*, p. 8. Alexis de Tocqueville was shocked and repelled by the transcendental element he detected in Jacobinism: 'A party that openly attacked the very notion of religion and of God and yet derived from its debilitating doctrine the ardour needed for proselytizing and even for martyrdom, which hitherto only religion seemed able to impart. At least as inconceivable as it is frightening, such a sight is capable of unsettling the most stable intelligence.' Quoted in Furet, *Interpreting the French Revolution*, p. 197.

[53] I use Rousseau's general will merely as an illustration. It has been emphasized by both Cobban and Furet that there are no grounds for presuming that Rousseau had any direct influence on the men in the National Assembly.

political action'. There was 'a kind of spontaneous equivalence between the values of revolutionary consciousness
—liberty and equality—the nation that embodied these
values, *and the individuals charged with implementing or
defending them*'. This assumption postulated a collective
entity, the people, which constituted 'the supreme source
of political legitimacy.'[54] In the words of the Abbé Sieyès,
who gave verbal definition to this inchoate idea: 'The Nation
exists before all things, and is the origin of all things. Its
will is always legal, it is the law itself. It is sufficient that its
will is manifested for all positive law to vanish before it.
In whatever manner a Nation wills, it is sufficient that it
does will: all forms are valid, and its will is always the
supreme law.'[55]

But if the nation was to act—and to act simply in its
collective capacity—representation was ruled out. Such an
assumption constantly raised the insoluble problems of what
forms the Revolution should take and of who was speaking
in its name. To quote Furet again, 'Politics was a matter of
establishing just *who* represented the people, or equality, or
the nation: victory was in the hands of those who were
capable of occupying and keeping that symbolic position.'[56]
Since the achievement of the central revolutionary ambition
of a total identification between society and power was in
practical terms impossible, the price exacted by 'the fiction
of pure democracy' was an inner circle which 'prefabricated
consensus' and sought to exercise exclusive control over it.
Yet there were no ground rules by which the competing
knots of revolutionary leaders could compose differences of
opinion either between themselves or between them and their
constituency, a situation leading to what Furet called 'a
cascade of usurpations'. Legitimization of authority was
sought through 'a series of imaginary equations in which the
people became identified with the opinion of the clubs, the
clubs with the opinion of their leaders and these leaders with

[54] Furet, *Interpreting the French Revolution*, p. 29.
[55] From *Qu'est-ce que le tiers état?* quoted Cobban, *In Search of Humanity*,
p. 189. Furet notes that the concept of 'The Nation' was articulated in 'hundreds'
of pamphlets in France in the years immediately preceding the Revolution.
(*Interpreting the French Revolution*, p. 33 and notes).
[56] Furet, *Interpreting the French Revolution*, p. 48.

the Republic'.[57] In this chaotic situation the man could win who could succeed best in branding his critics as enemies of the nation, of the general will, of the revolution in action; who could smell out deviance and bring it to destruction. No longer were there any legal or constitutional certainties, no longer any safety of person or property; and the logical conclusion of the process was an arbitrary dictatorship in the name of the people—totalitarian democracy, in Talmon's phrase. Whether in the hands of one man, or of a few, such a dictatorship was the ultimate negation of the democracy for which it claimed to act, the fundamental contradiction at its heart. It was a blueprint for enslavement and aggression: in the phrase of William Pitt, 'a species of tyranny, which adds insult to the wretchedness of its subjects, by styling its own arbitrary decrees the voice of the people, and sanctioning its acts of oppression and cruelty under the pretence of the national will'.[58] It was utterly alien to British tradition and British experience.

The main thrust of this discussion has been to suggest, that whatever happened in France, it is doubtful if British history in the late eighteenth century should be viewed in a context of an 'age of revolution'. Such a proposed context creates expectations about the British experience, a presumption that a revolution might have occurred but somehow did not. These expectations, I think, are not justified. What this survey also suggests is that, in considering stress and stability in late eighteenth-century Britain, and in speculating about the country's escape from revolution, relatively little help is to be expected from either models of revolutionary situations set up by political scientists or comparisons with revolutionary America, France, Ireland, or any other political community. It is worth while to consider whether Britain displayed any of the features of the theoretical models, or any of the features supposed to contribute to the American or French Revolutions. Parallels or contrasts which may emerge may be instructive. It may be possible to conclude, perhaps, that some limited elements of a revolutionary pathology were present. But in the main, the situation

[57] Ibid., pp. 176, 178, 190, 201.
[58] Quoted in Cobban, *In Search of Humanity*, p. 191.

in Britain needs to be treated as unique, and to be explored from that point of view, with the object of discovering what circumstances provided a bonding which kept society together and counteracted the strains which undoubtedly existed.

II

Britain under Strain

I

Many forms of stress can be seen in British society in the late eighteenth century. This is a situation which no human community can escape: it would be unrealistic to think otherwise. It is, I suppose, just possible to imagine a closed society in which tensions were virtually eliminated; but this would be one in which all life was guided by habitual rule and custom. No change of any kind could ever be envisaged, and so no improvement in the conditions of individuals or of the society as a whole could be capable of realization. Utopians dream up such systems, but the whole tide of human affairs since the dawn of agriculture and the first urban settlements, perhaps ten thousand years ago, bears witness to their unnatural character.

Such a theoretical model was about as far removed as could be from the actual state of Great Britain in the second half of the eighteenth century. From the 1750s onwards, the nation was moving with increasing momentum into decades of dynamic flux and rapid change. Some of the changes experienced were sought deliberately, as energetic individuals pursued ambitions for the improvement of their lot, or the lot of their fellows, in one way or another, material, intellectual, or spiritual. Others were the unforeseen consequences of human endeavour. Men's circumstances and men's aspirations created a complex web of frictions, tensions, and strains, at many different levels of society, and in many different social, economic, and political contexts.

External pressures contributed to this state of affairs to a significant degree. A survey of international affairs gives ground for the conclusion that the British people were harshly buffeted by fate in the long generation between 1760 and 1800. This circumstance in itself might be expected to set up tensions, as indeed it did. The diplomatic counters were stacked against Great Britain. Save for a brief fragile recovery in the 1780s, the country remained in far from splendid diplomatic isolation. After their humiliation in the Seven Years War the two enemies, France and Spain, were irreconcilable. The Prussians sought safety in neutrality. So did the Dutch. The Austrians considered the French, not the British, to be the most effectual support for their pretensions. The Russians enigmatically pursued their own eastern designs. No European state had any motive, arising for instance out of considerations of the balance of power, for supporting and preserving the strength of Great Britain. On the contrary there was irritation at the way the British appeared to presume on their mid-century victories. When war broke out against the rebellious American colonies in the 1770s, far from finding friends, the nation rapidly acquired further enemies and ended by facing four, not one. Even the explosion of hostilities in Europe provoked by the course of the French Revolution did not produce any durable, effective, and cordial alliance system. In the 1790s the safety of Britain at sea seemed more than once at hazard. The French found it not impossible to mount raids on the British Isles, and it was luck rather than defensive capability that preserved George III's realms from the most formidable of these thrusts—the Hoche expedition to Ireland at the end of 1796. After eight years of expensive and exhausting warfare, the British could do no more than fight to a draw, and conclude an uneasy truce, leaving the French still poised as a menace to their shores, to their trade, and—prospectively at any rate—to their overseas possessions. If success in war and diplomacy are among the means by which governments disarm opposition and foster internal stability, then scarcely any British government after 1763 up to the end of the century could claim much credit of this kind.

In 1763 the British state stood at the hub of what appeared to be a highly successful imperial system, its tentacles far outstretched to both east and west. Across the Atlantic lay the highly prized West Indies and the great mainland empire comprising the thirteen old and the four newly aquired North American colonies. Halfway further round the globe the servants of the East India Company were in the process of consolidating their quasi-sovereign position in Bengal, and, with government assistance, had established an ascendancy over their French rivals in other parts of the Indian sub-continent. Nearer at hand, the subordinate kingdom of Ireland appeared firmly subject to British political control, a strategic asset in the eastern Atlantic, an additional reservoir of manpower, and a valuable source of foodstuffs, sailcloth, and other materials required by the navy and by overseas bases.

Yet here too disappointment and disaster lay in store. Matters went sadly awry with this splendid inheritance during the four last decades of the eighteenth century. The thirteen American colonies broke away into independence in the 1770s, and a significant element in Ireland sought to do so in the 1790s. The American War of Independence, like the French Revolutionary War two decades later, created a crisis of conscience for many individuals in Britain. Both wars produced serious differences of opinion about external policy which, to some extent, were linked with strongly held views about the domestic situation, and they thus contributed to the tensions which were developing in internal politics.[1] Both wars were opposed by significant minorities of dedicated and principled, highly articulate politicians and intellectuals.

II

External events thus afforded no means of relief for internal tensions of various kinds which were becoming more marked between 1760 and 1800.

During this period the British nation faced the problems caused by a rapidly growing population. In the 1750s the number of people in England and Wales was about six and a half million, and in Scotland another million and a quarter; and in the south of England, at any rate, the pace of growth was small. But this did not remain the case for long. Before the end of the 1770s the evangelical preacher John Wesley was remarking in his journal on the hordes of young children

[1] See pp. 37–46 below. But opposition to war did not necessarily mean sympathy with radical or revolutionary ideas (J. E. Cookson, *The Friends of Peace: Anti-War Liberalism in England, 1793–1815*, Cambridge, 1982, *passim*, and esp. p. 148).

encountered on his travels; local censuses were confirming his conclusions; and by the end of the century it was clear that more people were marrying early, more infants were born to them, and fewer children were succumbing in their early years to epidemic illnesses. By 1800 the age structure of the population had changed. A larger proportion of it was composed of children and of people in early adult life. And it had become far more numerous. The seven and three-quarter million Britons of 1750 had become ten and three-quarter millions by the time of the first national census in 1801.

Nor was this the only change. By 1801 an appreciably larger proportion of the population were urban dwellers, and the inhabitants of a certain number of very large towns were losing contact with a rural environment. In half a century Greater London had increased in population from about 700,000 to 900,000, and eight other British towns and cities each housed over 70,000 people in 1801. In the Midlands and parts of the north of England and the Scottish lowlands, small urban centres and villages were developing into sizeable industrial towns. During the third quarter of the century the proportion of the population living in towns of over 2,500 people had remained fairly constant at about 25 per cent. Thereafter the increase was perceptible, and by 1801 the proportion stood at slightly over a third. In some localities a striking change in environment and style of life had taken place: for instance, according to one assessment, the traditional, fairly even balance between farming and manufacturing had been so far upset in the Black Country by the 1780s that no more than one-sixth of the population were by then gaining their living from agriculture.[2] A large proportion of the people living in the new urban centres were immigrants, involved in creating a new social milieu for themselves, exploiting for this purpose both associations in their place of work and societies based on local, religious, cultural, or philanthropic interests of one kind or another.[3]

[2] C. M. Law, 'Some notes on the Urban Population of England and Wales in the eighteenth century', *The Local Historian*, 10 (1972-3), 18, 22; Witt Bowden, *Industrial Society in England towards the end of the eighteenth century* (New York, 1925), p. 99.

[3] For the bewildering variety of such enormously valuable social connections in one area, the West Midlands, see John Money, *Experience and Identity*.

Hand in hand with urbanization went economic development; and the economic changes sweeping over the country at this time were destroying traditional patterns of life for numbers of people in both country and town. Among the rural populations, especially in the Midlands, two groups were particularly affected by the increasingly rapid progress of agricultural enclosure: the squatters who had no property rights in the commons; and the poorer commoners, whose resources were insufficient to meet the costs of fencing and whose awards were inadequate in acreage to provide a livelihood. Although the enclosures did not reduce the overall number of small freeholders, considerable changes in landownership took place, with numbers of formerly independent cultivators being thrown into direct dependence on wage earning of one kind or another.[4] In a few areas enlightened landowners eased their difficulties by the creation of allotments, but many people in this group tended to become a burden on the Poor Law as the century drew towards its close. Increasingly harsh enforcement of the game laws further reduced the possibilities of an independent livelihood, and added to the discontent and social tension between landowner and labourer caused by enclosure. But by its nature this was a dispersed, unfocused discontent, and the dependence of such men on the good will of those in charge of the Poor Law and of local charity acted as a further brake on any active show of resentment. The worst problems of rural poverty, however, were not the result of enclosure, which often provided compensations of other kinds; they arose out of local overpopulation in rural areas, and were associated largely with districts in the south-east of the country where enclosure had taken place a century or more ago.

Outside the agricultural sector industrial enterprise was superseding old by new forms of earning on a scale greater than the country had previously known, and in doing so it

Birmingham and the West Midlands, 1760-1800 (Manchester, 1977), pp. 98-105, esp. pp. 98-9 and note 6; and 136-41.

[4] J. D. Chambers and G. E. Mingay, *The Agricultural Revolution, 1750-1880* (1966), pp. 86-99; G. E. Mingay, *Enclosure and the Small Farmer in the Age of the Industrial Revolution* (1968).

acted as a force for social as well as economic change. Entrepreneurs set in motion waves of change and imitation which
rendered obsolete existing plant and methods of production,
replacing them with something much superior: progress in
capitalism proceeds in 'a gale of creative destruction'.[5] Such
was the work of the Wilkinsons and Matthew Boulton in iron
production; of Josiah Wedgwood in pottery; of James Watt
in the manufacture of power plant; of the elder Sir Robert
Peel in textile-printing; of Arkwright in cotton-spinning; of
men like Metcalf, Smeaton, Brindley, and Telford in the
development of road and water communication; and of
numbers of men whose names are unfamiliar or quite unknown to us. To a limited extent the threat of technological
redundancy was beginning to hang over the heads of people
engaged in traditional cottage industries, though this did not
yet show itself as a serious threat to livelihood.

Old and new forms of economic activity alike were affected
by the commercial uncertainties due to war. In the mid
1770s the expansion of markets on the Continent more than
compensated for the losses due to the break with the American colonies, but after 1778 trade was badly hit by the entry
into the American war of France, Spain, and the Netherlands.
A decade of buoyant prosperity followed that war, but this
was succeeded by similar problems during the 1790s. The
trade partnership with France established by the Eden commercial treaty of 1786 came to an abrupt end in 1792, with
a loss of direct export trade worth over £500,000 a year.
Before long the Netherlands markets were also closed by
French military action. Textiles dependent on export outlets
suffered severely; so did consumer hardwares; and there was
a surge of unemployment in the Black Country, the East
Midlands, Norwich, and the Clyde Valley. An uncomfortable
period of readjustment followed, until some of the industrial
slack was taken up by war demands. But there were areas of
the economy which got little help in this way, notably the
producers of fine woollens in the west of England and in
East Anglia. In both these districts commercial depression
fuelled anti-war sentiment.

Apart from these unsettling experiences, the British people

[5] Quoted in J. K. Galbraith, *A Life in our Times. Memoirs* (1981), p. 49.

were finding that the bounty of nature no longer seemed so certain as it had been in previous decades. Among the uncertainties of life created by the growth of population after 1750 was a fluctuation in the level of food prices, especially grains, superimposed upon a slower secular increase. The old policy of subsidizing exports and maintaining an output of grains surplus to the country's normal requirements no longer achieved its purpose. In years of poor harvest domestic demand—at least locally—tended to outrun supply. The situation was never desperate. Improved agriculture was perfectly capable of meeting the increased demand, and a secular rise in grain prices by about a third over the half century both stimulated production and helped to provide the capital for improvement. But a natural time-lag in the response meant the existence of a situation in which a slight shortfall due to poor yields could and did lead periodically to speculation on shortages, to high prices, and to popular tumults. Occasionally, especially in the 1790s, dearth seriously affected the lives of numbers of people and created considerable hardship.[6] The country experienced outbreaks of food riots in the late 1760s, in the early 1770s, in the mid 1780s, in the mid 1790s, and again at the turn of the century.

Indeed, popular turbulence was a fact of life which the ruling classes in Britain had learned to put up with as a matter of course. Dearth was not the only spark to the tinder. There were formidable riots against the reorganization of the militia in the 1750s and the early 1760s. Unemployment and wage disputes caused others in London in 1765 and in 1768-9. Political excitement could give rise to intimidating disturbances. Threats of mayhem contributed to break the nerve of the Earl of Bute in November 1762: it was thought that but for his rescue from rioters by a troop of the guards he would hardly have escaped with his life. The high points of John Wilkes's career in the 1760s were punctuated by tumultuous demonstrations. In March 1784 William

---

[6] For example, on the situation in the West Riding at that time, see R. A. E. Wells, *Dearth and Distress in Yorkshire, 1793-1802* (Borthwick Papers, no. 52, York, 1977). For other discussion of food riots, and references to the literature, see pp. 150-5 below.

Pitt the Younger, newly become Prime Minister, was caught at the centre of a desperate mêlée between Pittite and Foxite mobs in Westminster, the latter egged on by one or two Foxite MPs, and was lucky to escape without serious injury: his carriage was virtually demolished.[7] Religious bigotry was a powerful motive in the Gordon Riots of 1780, when numbers of Roman Catholic chapels and other property, including Langdale's distillery, were destroyed, and in the antiradical riots aimed against Nonconformists in Birmingham and Manchester a decade later. At Coventry, at the general election of 1780, anti-Catholic rioting at one time led to the suspension of the proceedings: voters were stripped naked and their clothes torn to pieces by a hired mob of local colliers.[8]

The possible implications of this propensity of Englishmen to riot often worried members of the ruling class and had done so long before the accession of George III. In 1743 John Perceval, Earl of Egmont, had considered a 'republican spirit' to be much the most serious threat to the balance of the constitution.[9] But the anti-militarist spirit of the nation forbade any effective police organization to curb it. In the last resort the guards were available in London, and slender military resources could be used in extreme need elsewhere. However, those in authority were exceedingly loath to employ them. Rioters often behaved—and with much good reason—as if they had nothing to fear from soldiers even if these were present. There were occasional tragic incidents, when outrages against property proceeded too far, but the only really ugly confrontation between army and mob during the second half of the century came at the tail end of the Gordon Riots, when plundering crowds swollen with criminal

---

[7] Wilkite riots can be followed in Horace Bleackley, *The Life of John Wilkes* (1917). For the Bute episode, see *The Correspondence of the Fourth Duke of Bedford*, ed. Lord John Russell (3 vols., 1842-6), iii. 160. The description of Pitt's ordeal, written by his brother who was present, is printed in John Ehrman, *The Younger Pitt, the years of acclaim* (1969), pp. 140-1. Pitt's brother thought there was a deliberate scheme to trap them.

[8] Sir Lewis Namier and John Brooke, *The History of Parliament, The House of Commons, 1754-1790* (3 vols., 1964), i. 402.

[9] See Linda Colley, 'Eighteenth-century English Radicalism before Wilkes', *Transactions of the Royal Historical Society*, 5th ser. 31 (1981), 1-19 *passim*; quoting at p. 1, [Egmont], *Faction detected by the evidence of Facts*, 2nd edn., 1743, p. 134.

elements got completely out of hand and military firing by volley caused the deaths of several hundreds.[10] Riots by the Spitalfields weavers in 1765 panicked Horace Walpole into the comment that there was 'such a general spirit of mutiny and dissatisfaction in the lower people' as to create danger of rebellion and civil war 'in the heart of the capital'.[11] A more experienced and level-headed observer, Viscount Barrington, the secretary-at-war, deplored in 1776 the dispatch of troops to fight the Americans, on the ground that they might be needed to quell insurrection at home. London, he believed, particularly required attention, 'on account of the many actively desperate and ill-affected people . . . in it'. It was not merely crime or mayhem that he feared but a challenge to the social order from the discontented and underprivileged. 'The present apparent quiet', he wrote, 'should not make it forgotten, that there is a very levelling spirit among the people.'[12]

Nevertheless, even after the traumatic experience of the Gordon Riots, the ruling class preferred to live with the situation rather than attempt to establish any effective system of police. The Earl of Shelburne found himself wholly unsupported in Parliament, when he suggested at the outset of the Riots that the government ought on this occasion to borrow from French example and create a metropolitan civil police.[13] The idea was not to be taken seriously for half a century. Such an indifference suggests that, apart from the scaremongers, there was a general awareness among the political class that occasional violent demonstrations should not be taken too seriously, that they usually arose over particular material grievances, and that they were not directed against the social system in general. In a real sense oligarchical government in late eighteenth-century Britain stood foursquare on its foundations in the tacit consent of the people.

[10] Tony Hayter, *The Army and the Crowd in Mid-Georgian England* (1978), pp. 9–19, 147–59, 166, 177–86.
[11] Horace Walpole to the Earl of Hertford, 20 May 1765, to Sir Horace Mann, 25 May 1765, quoted Hayter, p. 130.
[12] Shute Barrington, *The Political Life of William Wildman, Viscount Barrington. Compiled from Original Papers* (1814), pp. 154–6.
[13] Lord Edmond Fitzmaurice, *Life of William, Earl of Shelburne* (2 vols., 1912), ii. 60–1.

For much the same reason, up till the 1780s, little heed was paid to the effusions of radical authors and propagandists, since they did not challenge the social order, and could not seriously be regarded as giving cause to incite the populace to insurrection. What changed this situation to some extent was the breadth of the political and social criticism contained in Thomas Paine's *Rights of Man*, and the broadcast nature of its appeal and of the response, set against the background of the French Revolution. In 1794, reflecting on the nature of the public debate let loose by Edmund Burke's *Reflections on the Revolution in France* and Paine's famous riposte,[14] the editor of the *Annual Register* declared that violent divisions had returned to British politics for the first time for a century:

These two famous performances revived, as it were, the royal and republican parties that had divided this nation in the last century, and that had lain dormant since the Revolution in 1688. They now returned to the charge with a rage and an animosity equal to that which characterized our ancestors during the civil wars in the reign of Charles I.

The writer went on to suggest that there was much greater apprehension after 1790 that sections of the populace were ceasing to be swayed by the habit of deference.[15] The ruling class responded in part with the repressive legislation that has sometimes, in a gross exaggeration, been described as Pitt's 'reign of terror'. But it is notable that, so far as police was concerned, the regime continued to depend largely on voluntary action, in the Loyalist Associations of 1792-3, and in the Volunteers formed for home defence after the outbreak of war with France in 1793.[16] Thus at the time of greatest strain the forces of law and order drew upon the strength

[14] For the nature, and the context, of this debate, see pp. 170-8 below.

[15] *The Annual Register for 1794*, p. 267.

[16] On the Loyalist Associations see: Eugene Charlton Black, *The Association. British Extra-Parliamentary Political Organization, 1769-1793* (Cambridge, Mass., 1963), chapter VII; Austin Mitchell, 'The Association Movement of 1792-3', *Historical Journal*, 4 (1961), 56-77; D. E. Ginter, 'The Loyalist Association Movement of 1792-3 and British Public Opinion', ibid. 9 (1966), 179-90; and on the Volunteers, J. R. Western 'The Volunteer Movement as an anti-Revolutionary Force, 1793-1801', *English Historical Review*, lxxi (1956), 603-14. For a sober assessment of the repressive action taken by the authorities, see Clive Emsley, 'An Aspect of Pitt's "Terror": prosecutions for sedition during the 1790s', *Social History*, 6, no. 2 (1981), 155-84.

to be derived from popular spontaneous support but also at the same time rested upon a foundation reflecting a broad-based moderation.

III

So far I have been considering possible disruptive pressures among the lower orders of society. But what of the people above? It is an acknowledged fact that usually, if insurrections prosper, they do so because a discontented mass finds a leadership formed by a part of the social élite, that is, by men who may be regarded as renegades by the rest of their group, because they have turned against the regime with which the group is identified.

From one violent form of political schism of this kind the British nation had been safely delivered by 1760—a conflict of loyalty over the succession. In hindsight there has usually been a tendency to dismiss the threat of Jacobitism in the early Hanoverian period. I have my own personal reasons for doubting the soundness of this view—an English ancestor born in Wiltshire, one of the Tory heartlands of the early eighteenth century, who was baptized in the Stuart name of Charles about the time the Young Pretender was storming south out of Scotland on his way to Derby.[17] More seriously, there is a certain amount of scholarly work indicating that Jacobite loyalties were not finally quenched even by the disaster of the Forty-five, nor until the last hopes of a French invasion on behalf of the Stuart line were finally destroyed with the annihilation of French fleets at the battles of Lagos and Quiberon in 1759.[18] After 1760, although the clergy of the Scottish Episcopalian Church still professed loyalty to the Stuarts, it is doubtful if anyone else in Britain did. Whatever

[17] Charles Whatley, born at Wilton in 1745, seems not to have shared the apparent sympathies of his parents, or else sensibly abandoned them: in 1783 he named his only son George, after 'the best of Kings'. Wilton Parish Registers, Wiltshire CRO.

[18] See: Eveline Cruickshanks, *Political Untouchables. The Tories and the '45* (1979), pp. 104-13; David Daiches, *Charles Edward Stuart. The Life and Times of Bonny Prince Charles* (1973), pp. 283-8, 290-1; Claude Nordmann, 'Choiseul and the last Jacobite Attempt of 1759', in *Ideology and Conspiracy: Aspects of Jacobitism, 1689-1759*, ed. Eveline Cruickshanks (Edinburgh, 1982), pp. 201-17; P. D. G. Thomas, 'Jacobitism in Wales', *Welsh History Review*, 1 (1962), 279-300.

use was made of the bogey of Stuart absolutism in political propaganda during the 1760s, it was not in connection with any idea of Jacobite restoration. Old Toryism was dying very swiftly in the early 1760s, and no distinct party of that name or colour existed after about 1765. Its remnants became scattered right across the political spectrum, and a significant proportion of former Tories became firmly attached to groups which asserted most vehemently the purity of their Whig principles.

This did not mean an end to political divisions within the country. It would have been naïve on anyone's part to think that it would. While Parliament acted on the one hand as a grand council of the nation, frequently accommodating sectional interests by means of local legislation, on the other it constituted an arena for political conflict. Divisions between the politicians, no longer complicated by overtones of Jacobite disloyalty, now tended to appear most simply and clearly as contests for office and power. After a period of flux in the early years of George III's reign, ministerial stability was re-established, and this in itself helped to promote a corresponding stability in the political opposition. In a general pattern broken only by the political crisis of 1782-4, the ministerial politicians favoured and employed by George III were opposed by a phalanx which was headed successively by the Marquis of Rockingham and then by Charles James Fox, and which was held together by a combination of dynastic landed interest, ideological commitment, and personal loyalties.

From the mid 1760s onwards, a question of crucial importance for the political stability of the nation was, could the duel between Government and Opposition be contained within the framework of the existing parliamentary system —could it be carried on without danger to the political fabric? Looking back with hindsight historians can, of course, give an affirmative answer to this question: yes, the political contest was contained. But it would be wrong to conclude that the situation was wholly without strain.

Over the whole period from the late 1760s till 1801 political conflict took on a slightly menacing tone. The major issue at stake between government and opposition was not just, which groups of politicians should enjoy office; though that point was also in dispute. It was not a matter of which policies should be adopted in given situations, though policy did come into the argument. The fundamental under-lying question in debate related to constitutional propriety. By 1769, if not before, the Rockinghamite Opposition had begun to project itself as the sole champion and guardian of the constitution and of English liberties, against sub-version by a supposed secret junto working behind the scenes in court and Parliament. This group was assumed to be using government patronage to overcome parliamentary resistance to its nefarious activities, manipulating and coercing the ostensible ministers, and thus gradually asserting autocratic power without responsibility. It was accused of a settled and systematic design to destroy the rule of law and erect a new form of arbitrary power based on corruption. While, at first both the ministers and the king were described by the pro-ponents of this theory as dupes rather than participants, by 1780 these assumptions were being abandoned and their association with the conspiracy taken for granted. Various individuals were at different times cast for the central role in such a conspiracy—initially George III's early favourite, the Earl of Bute; later, the eminent lawyer Lord Mansfield, chief justice of the king's bench, who, like Bute, could be made the target of English prejudice against the Scots; later still the able under-minister Charles Jenkinson, subsequently created Lord Hawkesbury and first Earl of Liverpool. Once a myth of this kind had been developed, it could be adapted and used to explain and condemn almost every circumstance its champions wished to censure.

I have discussed elsewhere the growth of this quite baseless political myth up to 1782.[19] Here I have to emphasize its perpetuation into the decades of the French Revolution and the French wars. Edmund Burke's correspondence is sprinkled with references to it during the 1780s. In 1780 he is to be found deploring 'the power and prostitution of the faction, which has long dominated and still does domineer in this country'. In March 1782 Rockingham's plans for a close-knit

[19] Ian R. Christie, *Myth and Reality in late eighteenth-century British Politics, and other papers* (1970), pp. 27–54.

cabinet based on his party associates met with his approbation, and he urged Rockingham: 'It is on that Cabinet you
must rely for the utter destruction of the Cabinet that has
destroyed everything else, and which is equally mischievous
in the highest as in the lowest hands.' In December, using the
word 'court' in the sinister connotation his party had given
it, he observed that Lord North's party thought 'the Court'
looked with more favour on them than on any other of the
political parties. Pitt's Bill of 1783 to reduce Customs sine-
cures he dismissed as 'a scheme to set up another treasury
board in the hands of mean subservient people to act under
Secret Cabinet influence'. Alerting a friend at Bristol in
January 1784 to the possibilities of a general election, he
wrote: 'There is no doubt that many [candidates] are ready
to begin an attack under the guidance of the secret influence
upon every member of Parliament who is resolved to assert
the privileges and dignity of the two Houses.' And when the
elections had brought disaster to his party, he commented:
'The people did not like our work; and they join'd the court
to pull it down.' In January 1789 he described Pitt's Regency
Bill as 'the monstrous proceedings of the Cabal', and in the
following November, in a letter to Earl Fitzwilliam, he
referred to Pitt, in the same sort of terms that he and his
friends had formerly used of North, as 'the ostensible
minister'.[20]

After 1789 the theme of 'secret influence' disappeared
from Burke's correspondence, as the nightmares of French
revolutionary democracy laid hold of his mind. But it remained a reality for others in opposition. It was aired in a
pamphlet of 130 pages shortly after the general election of
1790, in which the 'faction' was described as a 'set or junto,
said to have the power of guiding and controlling administrations'. The Prime Minister was written off as its puppet:
'Mr Pitt may affect what he pleases, but Lord Hawkesbury
can dismiss him whenever it suits his purpose.' Belief that

[20] *The Correspondence of Edmund Burke*, ed. T. W. Copeland and others
(9 vols., 1958-70), iv. 296, 423, v. 57, 94, 121-2, 154 (and cf. 294-5), 445,
vi. 35. For similar allegations by Charles Fox, see L. G. Mitchell, *Charles James
Fox and the Disintegration of the Whig Party, 1782-1794* (1971), pp. 75, 76, 78,
84, and by Earl Fitzwilliam, E. A. Smith, *Whig Principles and Party Politics,
Earl Fitzwilliam and the Whig Party, 1748-1833* (Manchester, 1975), p. 49.

Pitt's tenure of office was thus not legitimate, and must be destroyed, countered for some time the inclinations of the two Foxite magnates, the Duke of Portland and Earl Fitzwilliam, to give him countenance, although by 1792 their hostility to the French Revolution was even stronger than that of Pitt himself. Fox remained obdurately committed to the view that George III and his ministers were set on undermining the constitution. In an argument with Fitzwilliam over policy early in 1792 he made this plain: 'Our apprehensions are raised by different objects; you seem to dread the prevalence of Paine's opinions (which in fact I detest as much as you do) while I am much more afraid of the total annihilation of all principles of liberty and resistance.' Portland, expostulating with Fox the following November, found him totally hostile to the cause of kings.[21] The involvement of Britain in war with France in 1793 seemed to Fox—as two decades before the American war had seemed to the Rockinghamites—a commitment to the destruction of liberty everywhere. King, ministry, and secret junto were inextricably jumbled up in this vision of a sinister plot, and remained so until the end. Only three weeks before Pitt's death (and nine months before his own), Fox remarked of Pitt that he had 'for the sake of office, surrendered himself up entirely into the hands of the court'; and when Pitt died he opposed a Commons address for a public funeral, on the ground that Pitt 'had countenanced and supported a system of government which had unfortunately prevailed through the whole of the present reign, that of invisible influence, more powerful than the public servants of the crown'.[22]

This superstition about 'secret influence' provides an

[21] Review of *Faction unmask'd by the Evidence of Truth. In a letter from an Old Member of the late to a New Member of the Present Parliament* (1790), in *The Monthly Review; or, Literary Journal Enlarged*, vol. iv (1791), pp. 99–100; H. Butterfield, 'Charles James Fox and the Whig Opposition in 1792', *Cambridge Historical Journal*, ix (1949), 293–330, quotation at p. 296.

[22] For charges that the ministry wished to impose despotic rule over the Americans, see *The Parliamentary History*, xix. 543, 679, xx. 51, 399, xxi. 387, 1103, xxii. 612, 695, 823; for Fox and the French war, Mitchell, *Fox and the Whig Party*, pp. 217–18. Fox to Thomas Coutts, 1 Jan. 1806, quoted ibid., p. 217; *The Diary and Correspondence of Charles Abbot, Lord Colchester*, ed. Charles, Lord Colchester (3 vols., 1861), ii. 31.

indispensable key to understanding. For the tension at the heart of late Georgian politics lay in the fact that the Opposition could not give whole-hearted loyalty to the system within which they were operating. Or perhaps it would be more correct to say that their beliefs continually edged them in the direction of refusing that loyalty, although at the same time they resisted this tendency by holding out the hope that somehow they would be able to rectify the system. The men of Rockingham's generation were the more successful in keeping the tension under control in this way. As one of them, Lord John Cavendish, put it towards the end of his life, in a letter to Burke, acknowledging a copy of his *Reflections on the Revolution in France*: 'Though some of our allies have now and then run wild, our original sett have allways contended for that temperate resistance to the abuse of power, as should not endanger the public peace, or put all good order into hazard.'[23] Everything that we know about the Rockinghamite Opposition confirms this statement. Although these men saw themselves as defending the constitutional settlement of 1689 against renewed attack, they never contemplated an appeal to force, or a violent or extensive alteration of the political system. Their practical programme was confined to 'economical reform', which was little enough; parliamentary reform they shunned. In the last resort their conduct seems to have been shaped largely by their calm confidence in the massive inertia of the society of which they constituted the élite, and in its capacity to absorb and to neutralize any blows that might be struck against it.

The younger generation of parliamentary politicians in opposition—the generation of Charles James Fox—dealt less effectively with this tension at the heart of the opposition, and it was perhaps as well for the peace of the country that their numbers remained few and their following in the constituencies limited. Fox was their star. Much of the style of opposition politics in the 1790s must be attributed to him, and that style was not wholly reassuring.

Sir Herbert Butterfield long ago suggested that Fox stood out, 'in what might be called the "set" of his personality, the fact that, deeper than any political theory, was a kind of instinct for liberty, which ... tended to make him impetuously anti-government'. A more cynical commentator might suggest that Fox was an impetuous young egoist, who had never since infancy been subjected to any form of discipline, and who was bitterly resentful when he did not get his own way.[24] The personal hostility he developed for George III after 1780 —in 1782-3 he was going about referring to him as Satan and openly speculating that he might die before long and then matters would mend—introduced a jarring note, which augured ill for future political relationships. Burke absolved him of any taint of republicanism in 1791, but a year or two later one or two of his greatest admirers were developing qualms about where his hostility to the king and to Pitt might be leading. In November 1792, after two conversations with him, the Duke of Portland reported that he seemed indifferent to the levelling influence in Britain of events in France, and wrote: 'I am sorry to say, that I fear I observed symptoms of no very strong indisposition to submit to the experiment of a new and possibly a Republican form of government.'[25] Little over a year later Fox appeared to have moved still further in this direction, telling a shocked supporter that 'the sovereignty was absolutely in the people, that the monarchy was elective, otherwise the dynasty of Brunswick had no right, and that when a majority of the people [thought] that another kind of government [was] preferable, they undoubtedly had a right to cashier the king'. At the time of the final breach between Fox and Portland, in the summer of 1794, the Foxites' faithful organ, the *Morning Chronicle*, made the forthright assertion that all men were now to be divided into two classes, 'Royalists and Republicans'.[26]

The impression given here of a facile tendency to slip into

[24] Butterfield, 'Fox and the Whig Opposition', p. 298; Christie, *Myth and Reality*, pp. 133-44.

[25] Mitchell, *Fox and the Whig Party*, pp. 10, 59; *Burke Correspondence*, vi. 316-17, vii. 316 n. 2.

[26] Mitchell, *Fox and the Whig Party*, pp. 218, 237, and cf. comments at pp. 201, 233. On the party connection of the *Morning Chronicle*, see Ian R. Christie, *Myth and Reality*, pp. 334-58, and I. S. Asquith, 'James Perry and the *Morning Chronicle* 1790-1821', Ph.D. thesis, University of London, 1973.

a posture of at least theoretical disloyalty is buttressed by other incidents. In 1791 Fox took steps to traverse the government's foreign policy in a manner which skirted very near if not over the line of treason: Burke at any rate thought it a 'high treasonable misdemeanour'. At a time when Pitt was trying to hold an alliance with Prussia together by exerting pressure on Russia to yield back the conquered fortress of Ochakov to the Turks, Fox's friend, Robert Adair, went to Petersburg, conducted with Fox from there a secret correspondence in cipher, and apparently gave the Russian court information which encouraged the Empress to defy a British ultimatum. Six years later he seems to have acted at least as unscrupulously in connection with the activities of his cousin, the leader of the United Irishmen, Lord Edward Fitzgerald. Knowing Fitzgerald was in contact with France, then a hostile power, over the question of Irish independence, Fox counselled caution but seems neither to have protested nor to have taken any steps to stop him. This action certainly skirted the crime of misprision of treason, and it undoubtedly gave heart to forces inimical to Britain. The most recent scholarly investigator of this episode has commented that 'a widespread belief in the tacit support of the parliamentary opposition fortified the United [Irish] campaign in Ireland, in England, and above all in France'.[27]

What should we make of all this? Not too much, perhaps. There can be no question of regarding Foxite disaffection in the 1790s as a danger in any way comparable with the Jacobites during the early eighteenth century. Most, if not all, were perfectly loyal. In August 1791 Burke's sober assessment in a letter to his son—which of course differed from the scare-tactics he was mounting in print and in private letters to the party magnates—was, 'that the whole of those who think with the French Revolution (if in reality they think at all seriously with it) do not exceed half a score in both Houses'; and he did not then regard Fox as one of them.[28]

---

[27] Adair's intrigue at Petersburg was first publicly exposed in 1793 by Burke in *Observations on the Conduct of the Minority* (*Works*, iii. 472-3). The episode is discussed in John Ehrman, 'The Younger Pitt and the Ochakov affair', *History Today*, 9 (1959), 462-72. On Fox and Fitzgerald see Marianne Elliott, *Partners in Revolution. The United Irishmen and France* (1982), pp. 211-12.

[28] *Burke Correspondence*, vi. 316-17.

What worried Burke was Fox's refusal to come out firmly against French principles and against ideas of remodelling the British parliamentary system. The more Burke attempted to force him in this direction, the more he became associated with the opposing viewpoint. He remained a symbol, perhaps slightly more than a symbol, of national disunity and stress after the outbreak of the French war, and became naturally a target of mistrust. This culminated in his expulsion from the privy council in 1798, after continued public demonstrations of attachment to the 'sovereignty of the people'. Fox had given that toast in 1789. It had then meant little, and could be taken as within the context of conservative political philosophy, as represented for instance by Paley or even by Burke himself. But in the context of seven years of chaotic revolutionary violence in France, of five years of unsuccessful war, and of a threatening popular rising in Ireland in which his own cousin was deeply implicated, the striking of such attitudes was foolish even if it was not sinister. Doubts about the degree of his loyalty and of his commitment to the established order in Britain were understandable.[29]

Before concluding discussion of the dissonant attitudes to be found among the political élite, one other suggestion needs to be dismissed. Despite the posturings of Portland, British politics had not become polarized in a conflict between king and aristocracy. This theme was overworked by R. R. Palmer in his work *The Age of the Democratic Revolution*, in his attempt to draw parallels between British and Continental situations. A very brief examination of the facts disproves it. In 1782 the memoir writer Horace Walpole gibed at the pretensions of 'two or three great families' in opposition;[30] and if this is an unfair exaggeration, it is nevertheless the case that Palmer's so-called 'magnates' in the Opposition never amounted to more than about one-fifth of the total lay membership of the House of Lords. And

[29] For the toast in 1789, Mitchell, *Fox and the Whig Party*, p. 155. The events leading to the expulsion from the privy council are most fully detailed, though without understanding of the context, in Loren Reid, *Charles James Fox. A Man for the People* (1969), pp. 354, 356. See also J. Ann Hone, *For the Cause of Truth. Radicalism in London, 1796–1821* (Oxford, 1982), pp. 42–7.

[30] For Portland's view, see for example Mitchell, *Fox and the Whig Party*, p. 229, and for Palmer's too ready acceptance, *The Age of the Democratic Revolution*, i. 151, 285. Walpole's remark is quoted in Mitchell, p. 32.

there were magnates enough on the other side. The Duke of Bridgewater and Earl Gower were men of enormous wealth. The Spencers of Blenheim, the Yorkes, the Grenvilles of Stowe, not to mention others, disposed of great fortunes. Even the Earl of Bute might be ranked in this class during his brief period of political prominence, on the strength of the immense fortune he controlled after his wife's inheritance of the Wortley-Montagu estate. In sum, in the upper reaches of society most opposition politicians were satisfied with the political system, and were prepared to work within it; they had no desire to reform it radically or to destroy it. Under pressure from the French Revolution, there was eventually a flight from opposition on the part of many of Fox's aristocratic political friends. These deserted him during 1793 and 1794, to join or to give support to a national war coalition headed by William Pitt.

IV

What of those people of the middling and lower classes who became involved in movements for constitutional reform during the late eighteenth century? Did they constitute a danger to the state? Some of them were motivated by the same fears about dangers to the constitution that coloured the thinking of the parliamentary opposition; and as we have seen, this attitude involved at least a latent danger of the development of assumptions that the system might be incorrigible and intolerable and fit only for destruction.

There is little sign of stress of this kind in the earlier years of George III's reign, despite the furore created by John Wilkes. The alarmists were members of a fairly restricted circle of young lawyers and intellectuals, some of them also caught up in the development of Unitarianism at this time. Their influence was strictly limited: indeed it was clear that in the eighteenth-century British context intellectuals could neither make nor sustain a revolution. The publications of Obadiah Hulme, James Burgh, Major John Cartwright, Richard Price, and Joseph Priestley, between them provided ample blueprints for an extensive remodelling of the constitution—some of this on conspicuously anti-aristocratic lines—and nothing could be more revolutionary than the ideas developed by Hulme and Burgh for a national association, in effect an anti-Parliament, which would dictate reforms to the existing legislature.[31] But it was more practical issues arising out of the adventures of Wilkes which gave rise to metropolitan political dissonance in the period around 1769 to 1774. There was certainly an appreciable body of middle-class opinion in the greater London area at that time which felt itself under-represented in the national councils and wanted a redistribution of constituencies to put this right, but much of the Wilkite effort was spent on other, more limited objectives. The movement showed no signs of revolutionary intent.[32]

Ideas about reform and an anti-Parliament surfaced again at the beginning of the 1780s. In 1949 Sir Herbert Butterfield committed himself to the view, pursued further by R. R. Palmer in 1959, that 'our French Revolution is in fact that of 1780—the revolution that we escaped'. He pressed this view on the ground that the county association movement launched in Yorkshire in December 1779 was quasi-revolutionary. He judged it to be so because it proceeded on the assumption that assemblies of private persons, forming spontaneously throughout the country, were more representative than Parliament itself, both in being truer spokesmen of the people's wishes and in having power to take binding action in their name.[33] Now, there is no doubt that both before and during the year 1780 one or two radical writers nursed this vision. But to assume that the county association movement came near to fulfilling it is a misjudgement. The country gentry who formed the core of the

[31] On Burgh in particular, see H. Butterfield, *George III, Lord North and the People, 1779-80* (1949), pp. 259-62; Ian R. Christie, *Wilkes, Wyvill and Reform. The Parliamentary Reform Movement in British Politics, 1760-1785* (1962), pp. 53-7.

[32] Christie, op. cit., pp. 1-67; George Rudé, *Wilkes and Liberty. A Social Study of 1763 to 1774* (Oxford, 1962); John Brewer, *Party Ideology and Popular Politics at the Accession of George III* (Cambridge, 1976), and, especially, 'The Wilkites and the Law', in *An Ungovernable People. The English and their law in the seventeenth and eighteenth centuries*, ed. John Brewer and John Styles (1980), 128-71.

[33] Butterfield, *George III, Lord North and the People*, p. vi; Palmer, *The Age of the Democratic Revolution*, i. 294-7.

movement gave virtually no support to any such idea, and the leader of the Yorkshire Association, Christopher Wyvill, was quick to issue a public repudiation of it.[34] In 1780 Charles James Fox talked wildly about the delegate character of members of Parliament (in a strain very different from the one he was to adopt in 1784), but members of the Rockinghamite Opposition recoiled from the notion. Even very moderate schemes of reform of the representation made so little appeal at that time to members of the political class or to the interested public at large (either in Britain or in Ireland) that the issue was dead by the summer of 1785.

Its resuscitation in the opening period of the French Revolution proved scarcely any more threatening to the established order in Britain.[35] One or two of the contributors to the extensive and growing literature on radicalism in the 1790s have envisaged the movement variously as presaging late nineteenth-century British democracy or as encapsulating a revolutionary threat which was successfully contained by a ruthlessly repressive governing class.[36] These views need to be treated with reserve. It is appropriate to distinguish three broadly different phenomena: the aristocratic reform movement headed by the Society of the Friends of the People; the popular reform movement organized in the corresponding societies; and a revolutionary residue lurking behind the second of these groups.

The Friends of the People—the Earl of Lauderdale, Charles Grey, and the rest of the Foxite party who took up parliamentary reform—were in a real sense 'neo-Rockinghamites'. They took up reform where Burke and his friends

[34] Christie, *Wilkes, Wyvill and Reform*, p. 73. Sir George Onesiphorus Paul, the leading personality in the Gloucestershire Committee, fumed about 'reformation urged in the language and tabled in the guise of revolution': Esther Moir, *Local Government in Gloucestershire, 1775–1800* (Bristol and Gloucestershire Arch. Soc. Records Section, vol. 8, 1969), p. 70.

[35] In Ireland, however, a more threatening situation developed: see pp. 14–18 above.

[36] For a selection of the large bibliography on this subject see Lucy M. Brown and Ian R. Christie, *Bibliography of British History, 1789–1851* (Oxford, 1977), entry 95; and in addition, E. P. Thompson, *The Making of the English Working Class, 1790–1830* (1964), chapters 4 and 5; Albert Goodwin, *The Friends of Liberty. The English Democratic Movement in the age of the French Revolution* (1979); J. Ann Hone, *For the Cause of Truth. Radicalism in London, 1796–1821* (1982).

had dropped it in 1782, and for the same purpose. 'Economical Reform', passed into law in 1782, had clearly not achieved its object. To save the constitution from the evil fate threatened by 'secret influence', the representative system itself must also be reformed. But Grey and his friends envisaged this being done in a way which perpetuated, did not destroy, aristocratic rule, while reducing the opportunities for the use of crown influence in elections, and also disarming some at least of the critics to the left of them in the political spectrum who wanted a more extreme democratic and republican system. Conservative criticism of the Friends fastened upon the fact that, much as they might wish it, their own campaign could not be disentangled from the more revolutionary one being mounted by the corresponding societies—and so both alike threatened the destruction of the established order.

Outside parliamentary circles popular interest in radical reform in the 1790s was undoubtedly more widespread than a decade before. Equally certain, it was stimulated by popular discussion of Thomas Paine's *Rights of Man*, with its strong pro-French, and anti-monarchical, anti-aristocratic tone. This movement involved numbers of people in the social levels of the minor professions—including Nonconformist ministers—and the skilled craftsmen, many of whom were both literate and articulate. It attained a degree of organization in local corresponding societies and constitutional societies, of which the London Corresponding Society, though not the first, is the most familiar. Much of its propaganda was disseminated by the little group of intellectuals gathered together in the Society for Constitutional Information, in which John Horne Tooke and John Thelwall were leading spirits. This movement, coinciding as it did, in 1792 and 1793, with the drift into war against revolutionary France, was thought sufficiently dangerous to warrant a series of government measures against it, beginning with the Proclamation against sedition in May 1792, the calling out of the militia in December 1792, the treason trials of 1793 and 1794, the suspension of the Habeas Corpus Act in 1794, and the Treasonable Practices and Seditious Meetings Acts of 1795—leading up eventually to the Corresponding

Societies Act of 1799. Clearly ministers during those years thought that there was something to fear. Were they justified?

In the sense that the societies represented the germ of a revolutionary plot, the answer is almost certainly no. It is easy to exaggerate the scale of the movement. In few cases are reasonably precise figures or even approximate figures of the strengths of reform societies available. But such as they are, they indicate that total membership should probably be reckoned in thousands, but not in tens of thousands or any larger figure. Burke's suggestion that the whole estimated three-quarters of a million Dissenters constituted a potential revolutionary force was gross exaggeration, intended for effect but actually defeating its object. Exaggeration reached its peak in descriptions of the open-air meetings organized by the London Corresponding Society during 1795. Rumours of huge numbers attending first reached the public in broadsheet puffs. The wildest reports presuppose attendance by nearly a third of the population of the metropolis. This evidence is quite worthless. The profound silence about these meetings in the correspondence of people like Edmund Burke, William Windham, Lord Grenville, William Pitt, and the home secretary, the Duke of Portland, is evidence that they did not raise even a slight ripple in the life of the capital. Furthermore we have direct evidence to the same effect. A young visitor to London, who wrote an account of one of the autumn meetings, made it clear that this was a Hyde Park Corner type of occasion, with a few hundred people round the rostra at any one time and no more than a few thousand present during the course of the day.[37] The idea that there was any mass support in London for the London Corresponding Society may be consigned to oblivion.

[37] These open-air meetings took place on 29 June, 26 October, and 12 November 1795. G. S. Veitch, noting the first two, wisely made no reference to the numbers rumoured to attend (*Genesis of Parliamentary Reform*, 2nd edn., 1964, pp. 322–3). A. Goodwin (in *The Friends of Liberty*) mentions, without endorsement, that estimates of the crowds on 29 June ranged from 10,000 to 100,000 (p. 372), on 26 October from 100,000 to 200,000 (p. 385 and n.), and on 12 November, between 300,000 and 400,000 (p. 391). Less cautiously E. P. Thompson wrote of the meeting of 26 October: 'The claim that 100,000 to 150,000 attended cannot be dismissed', and cited the claim of 200,000 present on 12 November (*The Making of the English Working Class*, pp. 144–5). A Mr Frankland wrote

The popular radicalism of the early 1790s was deliberately directed to seeking its objectives by peaceful and constitutional means. Mass support was to be achieved by propaganda and persuasion. Its proponents were quite sincere in their disavowals of any intention to promote revolutionary violence. Nevertheless, from the point of view of the political establishment, their intentions were implicitly revolutionary. Universal male suffrage, equal electoral districts, and annual parliaments would have led to the establishment of a political system resting on democratic control and incompatible with aristocratic dominance. Property owners believed that under such a system property rights would no longer be honoured. The Painite inspiration was clear; and some of Paine's writings—and not his alone—threatened at least a limited attack on property rights which, if once admitted, might have no logical stopping point.[38] It might be true, as James Watt junior once expressed it in a private letter, that the radicals were appealing only to 'the thinking and sensible part of the nation', and had not sought 'to tamper with the lower orders of the people'.[39] But the mob violence in Paris suggested only too vividly that radical reformers might unleash forces they could not control. The general disbandment of the reformers in face of the government's repressive measures in 1794 and 1795 confirms the peaceful, law-abiding outlook that prevailed among most of them, but that of course was no guarantee as to what might have happened had the floodgates of reform once been opened.

Given the general commitment throughout the country to the established order, the popular radicals scarcely constituted

on 16 November to his sister about the last of these meetings, which he had attended out of curiosity, that at the best-attended time there were about 500 people in the field. A turnover of this number every half hour for eight hours would give a total of 8,000, but some of these, like the witness, were uncommitted or hostile sightseers (A. D. Harvey, *Britain in the early nineteenth century*, 1978, p. 82). This evidence is supported by James Gillray's cartoon, 'Copenhagen House', depicting the meeting of 12 November, in which each of the three orators in action appears to have an audience of between thirty and fifty.

[38] The point is briefly outlined in M. I. Thomis and P. Holt, *Threats of Revolution in Britain, 1789–1848* (1977), pp. 5–20. It is a major theme in an as yet unpublished monograph by Mrs Jennifer Graham: her analysis of the stance and the evasive tactics of Horne Tooke is of particular interest.

[39] Eric Robinson, 'An English Jacobin: James Watt, junior, 1769–1848', *Cambridge Historical Journal*, 11 (1953–5), pp. 354–5.

a serious threat, save perhaps in one respect—this was, that their denunciations of the existing parliamentary system and their advocacy of change helped to create a sense of legitimacy in the minds of a small minority of revolutionaries who wished for the total overthrow of the system. Recent work by a number of scholars has emphasized the presence of a revolutionary fringe in eighteenth-century British radicalism. These people were republican, anti-aristocratic, and to some extent levelling in their aspirations, and their movement was linked to and in some degree fomented by men involved in the Irish nationalist movement which was to culminate in the rebellion of 1798 and the Emmet conspiracy.[40] They represented some sort of threat, however tenuous, to the safety of the state.

In Britain the most dangerous manifestations of this revolutionary element, part Irish, part British, were the naval mutinies of 1797. In the main these mutinies were provoked by genuine grievances about conditions of service, but they were fomented to some extent by an insurrectionary element in which individuals linked with the United Irishmen played an appreciable part. In the late 1790s, nuclei of revolutionaries under the names of United Scotsmen, United Britons, and United Englishmen were known to exist in London, in the West Midlands, in the Manchester area (where Irish influence was strong), and in parts of the North, and these were later to surface again in the Despard Conspiracy. But it seems clear that their numbers and their power to do damage were small. The treasonable intent of a small rump of the London Corresponding Society is, however, beyond doubt. Its characteristic activities included support for the United Irishmen and attempts to encourage disloyalty in the armed forces.[41]

[40] M. I. Thomis and Peter Holt, *Threats of Revolution in Britain*, pp. 5–27; Goodwin, *The Friends of Liberty*, chapter 11; E. P. Thompson, *The Making of the English Working Class*, chapter 5; Marianne Elliott, 'The "Despard Conspiracy" Reconsidered', *Past and Present*, 75 (1977), 41–61, and *Partners in Revolution. The United Irishmen and France* (1982); J. Ann Hone, *For the Cause of Truth*, pp. 11–117; Roger Wells, *Insurrection. The British Experience, 1795–1803* 1983), pp. 69–78.

[41] Conrad Gill, *The Naval Mutinies of 1797* (Manchester, 1913), pp. 299–347; Elliott, *Partners in Revolution*, pp. 134–50, 175–6. According to some data, about 9,600 United Scotsmen were enrolled in September 1797, ibid.,

In the nature of things, it is difficult, for lack of clear evidence, to judge the extent of an abortive underground revolutionary movement. To some degree the conclusions of historians may be subjective. But for the most part scholars have concluded that the 'revolutionary experience' affected only a small minority and offered little threat to the safety and stability of the British state in the late eighteenth century.[42] Nevertheless the brand was smouldering. The lectures which follow will present some possible explanations why the stubble did not take fire.

pp. 144–5; Wells, *Insurrection*, pp. 78–109, 121–8, 151–3, 166–7, 168–70, 188–94.

[42] The strongest arguments against underestimating the dangers of a revolutionary outbreak have been presented in connection with the food crisis of 1800–1 by Roger Wells. He adduces evidence of a loss of nerve among the magistracy, and of a degree of apprehension in governing circles (*Insurrection*, chapter 12). However, I suggest that there are two considerations which tend against his conclusion. One is, that the ruling class in Britain, in its dealings with the 'lower orders' had always shown a degree of pliability and not relied as a matter of course in all circumstances upon assertions of authority by force. The other is the existence of many elements of a social consensus in Britain, which are examined in the chapters that follow.

III

Factors of Social Cohesion

I

Whether considered from the viewpoint of political, social, or economic interconnections, British society in the late eighteenth century displayed a sort of disordered cohesion —the force of that paradoxical description will soon appear —which owed little to the bonds of authority. The very liberty on which the British people prided themselves helped to generate it. The theologian and philosopher William Paley, who often showed himself a shrewd observer, remarked that political conditions of the kind found in Britain were peculiarly conducive to harmony between the different elements in society. This, he thought, was especially true of the parliamentary electoral system:[1]

Popular elections [he wrote] procure to the common people courtesy from their superiors. That contemptuous and overbearing insolence, with which the lower orders of the community are wont to be treated by the higher, is greatly mitigated where the people have something to give. The assiduity with which their favour is sought upon these occasions, serves to generate settled habits of condescension and respect; and as human life is more embittered by affronts than injuries, whatever contributes to procure mildness and civility of manners towards those who are most liable to suffer from a contrary behaviour, corrects, with the pride, in a great measure, the evil of inequality, and deserves to be accounted among the most generous institutions of social life.

It seems probable that, though they might sometimes deplore the fact, few ambitious members of the late eighteenth-century political class would have questioned the reality of this diagnosis—whether it were Edmund Burke, constantly, if resentfully, toiling in London for the Bristol constituents whom he represented between 1774 and 1780, or his patron, the Marquis of Rockingham, obliged to

---

[1] *The Works of William Paley, DD, and an account of the life and writings of the author*, by the Rev. Edmund Paley, AM (4 vols., 1838), iii. 258.

remain in a state of intoxication for hours on end while cultivating his interest among the electors of York.[2]

In fact, Paley's description hardly did justice to the weight of obligations and the degree of management, in which members of the parliamentary class might find themselves involved as a result of attempts to nurse an electoral interest. In larger urban constituencies this entailed constant effort to win the goodwill of leading local personalities and also to establish among the wider body of the electors a reputation for generosity and willingness to serve local interests. There was no substitute for the establishment of harmonious personal relationships, and this could be costly both in time and money: 'where there were real voters, they had to be wooed and cajoled; the patrons had to show concern for their material welfare and respect their political and social prejudices'.[3] This could entail offers of hospitality at regular intervals, the giving of custom to local tradesmen, often on terms distinctly unfavourable to the customer, the forgoing of economic rents on properties occupied by voters, and support for local public works and charity, and other acts of benevolence towards the community. At Aylesbury when John Wilkes was seeking to build up his interest, he threw his park open as a recreation ground for the inhabitants; and Sir William Lee, another landowner with an interest in the borough, who happened to be a trained doctor of medicine, gave medical service free to those who needed it.[4] In all this the patron suffered the effects of what Lord Shelburne once termed 'insensible perspiration', a constant, wearing, if inconspicuous financial drain. The burden could be severe. The patron of the twin boroughs of Launceston and Newport in Cornwall estimated the cost of nursing an interest among the two hundred or so electors at over £4,000 per annum. And in the end, the favours gained were often precarious: in

[2] P. T. Underdown, 'Edmund Burke as Member of Parliament for Bristol', Ph.D. thesis, University of London, 1954, and 'Edmund Burke, the Commissary of his Bristol Constituents, 1774-1780', *English Historical Review*, lxxiii (1958), 252-69; HMC, *Savile-Foljambe MSS*, p. 146.

[3] Sir Lewis Namier and John Brooke, *The History of Parliament. The House of Commons, 1754-1790* (3 vols., 1964), i. 47, and see pp. 46-52.

[4] Richard W. Davis, *Political Change and Continuity, 1760-1885: A Buckinghamshire Study* (Newton Abbot, 1972), p. 21; *The Diary and Letters of . . . Thomas Hutchinson*, ed. P. O. Hutchinson (2 vols., 1883-6), i. 250.

a number of boroughs electors were becoming increasingly independent as the century drew towards its close.

This interaction of the social orders noted by Paley was not confined to politics, and it was a product of a long trend of political and social evolution which had given rise to consequences rarely to be found elsewhere than in England.

One was that there was no distinct social caste of nobility, claiming its own extensive, separate legal privileges as against the rest. Professor Habakkuk has rightly suggested that the nearest British analogy to the European structure of aristocracy—and it is by no means close—was the class of families entitled to armorial bearings.[5] These were broadly speaking the landowners, and they included the peerage. But while the members of this social order enjoyed prestige and career advantages, and the peers could claim the right of trial for crimes before the House of Lords, they had no special rights in respect of law, taxation, the ownership of land, or the public service, nor were they in any way set apart from their fellow-subjects who engaged in trade or industry. Landowners formed a class in society the main body of which in one sense was perfectly distinct and identifiable, but which was not sharply cut off from the rest of the nation, and which in important ways merged with it. Not the least important consequence of this absence of any element of caste was the preservation among the landowners of a sense of common humanity, human responsibility, and common interest with other elements in society. Moreover, a fair degree of social mobility helped to preserve them from social isolation. While primogeniture secured the continuity of landed estate, the younger sons of gentry and even of titled nobility sometimes moved out into business and the professions, especially the law; and the expansion of the commercial and professional classes added to this trend. Members of the professional groups also acquired land and entered landed society. The Cumbrian family of Robinson of the White House, Appleby, perfectly illustrates how a local legal family might gradually entrench itself among the gentry, profiting from the favour

---

[5] H. J. Habakkuk, 'England', in *The European Nobility in the eighteenth century: Studies of the Nobilities of the major European States in the pre-Reform Era*, ed. A. Goodwin (1953), pp. 1 ff.

and protection of great men, while still retaining links with lower levels of society. Over three generations the Robinsons and their connections in marriage, including the Wordsworths, provided an almost unbroken series of clerks of the peace for Westmorland, a succession of senior administrators in the Post Office, and eventually a county MP, himself the son of a tradesman, who inherited an estate, moved into the centre of politics as Lord North's patronage secretary, and married his daughter and heiress to the heir of the earldom of Abergavenny.[6] At the other end of the country, a chairman of quarter sessions in Gloucestershire, at the turn of the century, remarked on this supple quality of British society, observing that honour and dignity were 'open to all who have energy to pursue them'; a fact 'confirmed by daily instances of persons raising themselves from the most humble to the most elevated stations, by means honourable to themselves and useful to the community'.[7]

Men who can rise to the proper level indicated by their abilities are the less likely to feel the bitter frustrations and discontents which can lead to resentment against the established order. Such forces of disruption were also defused by another quality of society to which this relative degree of mobility gave rise. Distinctions between one grade in society and another were slight. Another Gloucestershire justice explained this in felicitous phrase, when he remarked that, 'One of the most agreeable circumstances of this happy country arises in my opinion from that imperceptible gradation of the different orders of society which puts every person at his ease with the person who is a little above or a little below him; and for this reason, that no man can put his finger on any particular point of separation betwixt the one and the other.'[8] The importance of this phenomenon was not, perhaps, quite what this observer supposed. Slight

---

[6] Ian R. Christie, 'John Robinson, MP', in *Myth and Reality in late eighteenth-century British Politics, and other papers* (1970), pp. 145–50. See also the case of William Masterman, MP, ibid., pp. 232–43. Further examples are given in G. E. Mingay, *English Landed Society in the eighteenth century* (1963), pp. 92–103.

[7] Quoted in Esther Moir, *Local Government in Gloucestershire, 1775–1800* (1969), p. 73.

[8] Thomas Estcourt to Lord Verulam, 18 March 1796, HMC, *Verulam MSS*, p. 164, quoted in Moir, op. cit., p. 73.

gradations did not banish the desire to emulate: they encouraged it, because they made it very much easier to attempt emulation with success; and these attempts brought social satisfaction as well as being a significant force stimulating industrial development by creating demand.[9]

Extremes of difference of rank and wealth existed, but those who belonged to what were described as 'the lower orders' nursed as strong a sense of their rights as any men, and claimed and exercised not merely liberty but licence within the protection of the law. Eighteenth-century society included many folk who were materially underprivileged, and numbers against whom the scales of authority were weighted; but nevertheless, the people of the lower orders knew that they had a standing at law, and one in theory equal to that of any other men, however exalted in rank and dignity. 'The sentiment of liberty', wrote the German visitor, von Archenholz, 'and the ever-active protection of the laws, are the causes why the common people testify but little consideration for persons of quality, and even for persons in office, except they have gained their affection by affable and popular manners.'[10] There was no deference—nor was there any sense of repression—among the Wilkite mobs which, amidst other horseplay in 1768, pulled the Austrian ambassador out of his coach and paraded him in a prone position shoulder-high after chalking the symbolic number 45 on the soles of his shoes.[11] Men and women who engaged in food riots during the late eighteenth century stretched their British freedom to the limit, in the full knowlege of the formidable moral and legal impediments against the use of force to suppress them, and often in the confident assumption that it was the social duty of the gentry in authority as magistrates to uphold the cause in which they rioted.[12]

Overseas visitors to Great Britain were struck by the

[9] Cf. Harold Perkin, *The Origins of Modern English Society, 1780–1880* (1969), pp. 90–5.

[10] J. von Archenholz, *A Picture of England* (2 vols., London, 1789–91), quoted in Roy Porter, *English Society in the eighteenth century* (1982), p. 273.

[11] *Horace Walpole's Memoirs of the reign of George III*, ed. G. F. R. Barker (4 vols., 1894), iii. 130–1.

[12] For the inhibitions on the use of force, see Tony Hayter, *The Army and the Crowd in Mid-Georgian England* (1978), pp. 9–19.

freedom with which persons of different ranks associated in the clubs and coffee houses of the metropolis and by the openness and familiarity which prevailed among them. In 1775 the Irish traveller Thomas Campbell was perfectly amazed to observe a craftsman enter the Chapter Coffee House laden with the tools of his trade, sit down, and call 'for his glass of punch and the paper, both of which he used with as much ease as a lord'. In Dublin—a reminder, this, of the more Continental-type tensions which beset that country—such a sight would have been unthinkable. 'Such a man', Campbell reflected, 'in Ireland (and I suppose France too or almost any other country) would not have shown himself with his hat on, nor any way, unless sent for by some gentleman.'[13] The significance of this absence of caste distinction strikes home perhaps all the more if the effects of the converse situation elsewhere are noted—as it struck home to young James Watt, the son of the inventor, during a visit to Paris in 1784. Coming from a milieu where such behaviour would have been condemned at once as outrageous, he was horrified at the aristocratic disregard of the safety of the populace on the public highways. 'One would think', he wrote to his father, 'that the common people here were looked upon as different creatures, for the coachmen have full liberty to drive close to the houses, so that the foot passengers must make the best of the road into the next house or shop, to escape being run over.'[14] Such behaviour in London would have brought immediate retribution from the crowd.

In this and in other ways the king's subjects claimed and exercised their rights as members of the community, including the right to be as outspoken as they pleased about those responsible for the conduct of public affairs. An interest in and at least a smattering of knowledge of political affairs percolated far down the social scale. Visiting London in 1774, the young Irish lawyer John Philpot Curran reported: 'Every coal-porter is a politician and vends his maxims in

[13] H. C. Van Schaak, *The Life of Peter Van Schaak* (New York, 1842), p. 26; *Dr Campbell's diary of a visit to England in 1775*, ed. James L. Clifford (Cambridge, 1947), p. 58.

[14] Eric Robinson, 'An English Jacobin: James Watt Junior, 1769–1848', *Cambridge Historical Journal*, 11 (1953–5), 350.

public with all the importance of a man who thinks he is
exerting himself for the public service; he claims the privilege of looking as wise as possible, of talking as loud, of
damning the ministry and abusing the king, with less reason
than he would his own equal.'[15] To an English traveller
abroad the contrast with French apathy over such matters
was extreme. Arthur Young spent some days in mid August
1789 at Clermont, at a time when stirring revolutionary
events were in train in Paris. He was amazed to find not a
word of politics being mentioned in the company of merchants, tradesmen, and officers among whom he dined. 'The
ignorance or the stupidity of these people must be absolutely
incredible', he commented. 'Not a week passes without their
country abounding with events that are analyzed and debated
by the carpenters and blacksmiths of England. The abolition
of tythes, the destruction of the *gabelle*, game made
property, and feudal rights destroyed, are French topics that
are translated into English within six days after they happen,
and their consequences, combinations, results, and modifications, become the disquisition and entertainment of the
grocers, chandlers, drapers and shoemakers of all the towns
of England; yet the same people in France do not think them
worth their conversation, except in private.'[16] Continental
visitors to Britain were equally amazed. The uninhibited way
in which the British indulged in political comment and
criticized king, ministers, or anyone else set in authority
astonished foreigners, and forcibly impressed upon them
a sense of a society apart and strange from anything they
knew.[17] Not only in London but in the growing provincial
towns also, these vigorous assertions of freedom of discussion
were conducted and sustained through an enormous network of clubs, societies, associations, trade combinations,
and other organizations, which were spawned in increasing
numbers as the century wore on.[18] Connections already
established through such bodies rendered relatively easy the

[15] W. H. Curran, *The Life of . . . John Philpot Curran* (2 vols., 1818), i.
67-8.

[16] Quoted from Young's *Travels in France*, in *The Monthly Review, or
Literary Journal Enlarged*, x (1793), 159-60.

[17] Porter, *English Society in the eighteenth century*, pp. 119, 271-3.

[18] For an excellent account of the spread of such a network in the Birming-

presentation of statements of public opinion on particular major issues by way of petitions to king or Parliament, or in addresses to the throne. Sometimes, as with the widespread campaign against the Fox–North Coalition in 1784, the effects were evident. But even if the political results of such efforts were often disappointing, nevertheless numbers of those in the lower orders of society could have their say, and political tension was thereby eased.

II

The numerous narrow, often imperceptible gradations between the different elements in British society and the bridges established between them by associations of various sorts were a significant element making for social stability. Also important were numbers of socio-economic interconnections which bound the upper ranks to those below them.

Since 'servants' constituted a major element, perhaps as large as a twelfth of the working population, an important bond between landowners and the inhabitants of the countryside came from the service given in the household. Great houses might have a combined indoor and outdoor staff of a hundred or more, wealthy gentry from a dozen upwards to twenty-five to thirty, small squires perhaps half a dozen.[19] Such staff was drawn from the families of farmers and labourers on the estate, and bonds of personal contact and obligation were thus established not merely between the master and his servants but between him and their families, that is, with the whole surrounding community. While the social gulf between high and low in the household was invariably marked, the master of the house might often generate

ham area, see John Money, *Experience and Identity: Birmingham and the West Midlands, 1760–1800* (Manchester, 1977), pp. 99–149.

[19] The following are some examples of middling-sized households. T. W. Coke of Holkham was employing in 1801 twenty-six indoor servants and at least fifteen in the stables, garden, and game coverts (Susanna Wade Martins, *A Great Estate at Work. The Holkham Estate and its Inhabitants in the nineteenth century*, Cambridge, 1980, pp. 49–50). Incomplete lists of servants' sleeping quarters at Erddig House in the early eighteenth century point to a staff of twenty-five to thirty (Waterson, *The Servants' Hall*, p. 30). At Audley End in Essex a staff of sixteen increased to 28 between 1764 and 1791 (A. F. J. Brown, *English History from Essex Sources, 1750–1900*, Chelmsford, 1952, p. 42).

wholesome and pleasant human relations with those who served him. There is less evidence available on this point for the eighteenth century than there is for the nineteenth, but examples can be adduced which provide a caution against assumptions that the master-servant relationship was necessarily one of friction.

In the summer of 1781 the budding law reformer Jeremy Bentham was inveigled by the Earl of Shelburne into a visit to Bowood House in Wiltshire. This was a world hitherto entirely beyond his ken. He searchingly observed the manners of it and wrote a detailed account in a series of letters to one of his closest friends. Among the many things which impressed him was the relationship of Lord and Lady Shelburne with their servants:[20]

The master of the house [he wrote] to judge from everything I have seen yet is one of the pleasantest men to live with that ever God put breath into: his whole study seems to be to make every body about him happy / servants not excepted /: and in their countenance one may read the effects of his endeavours: in his presence they are as cheerful as they are respectful and attentive; and when they think they are alone you may see them merry; but at all times as quiet as so many mice. . . . The mistress has more reserve and less conversation, but as much mildness as the master.

Evidence of a different kind about these sorts of relationships comes from the history of the Yorke family of Erddig, near Wrexham. The eighteenth-century masters of this household were not unique, though they were unusual, in commissioning portraits of a number of their domestic and estate staff. Indeed they had more portraits of servants painted than of members of the family. The student of this subject has remarked that,[21]

One of the striking things about the portraits . . . is that with [one] single exception . . . they are all so very informal: woodmen, gardeners, carpenters and maids are depicted quietly going about their business or casually sitting at home. There is no suggestion of their being

---

[20] Bentham to George Wilson, 24 Aug. 1781, *The Correspondence of Jeremy Bentham*, vol. 3: *January 1781–October 1788*, ed. Ian R. Christie (1971), pp. 57–8.

[21] Merlin Waterson, *The Servants' Hall. A Domestic History of Erddig* (1980), pp. 2, 170. Waterson notes that such portraiture seems to have been typical of an area including Hawarden, Chirk, Dudmaston, Lyme, and Chatsworth.

paraded as a household. Clearly it was their individuality, their personal quirks, which the Yorkes wanted to see recorded.

The family letters of the Yorkes contain frequent references to the faithful services of various members of the staff at Erddig;[22] and both from these family records and from other accounts, one can gather evidence of the sense of obligation which heads of households felt towards their servants. One much valued lady's maid at Erddig received an annuity of £100 after she left the family's service. A housemaid was kept on the strength for nearly eighty years, though for much of her latter time she can hardly have been active; and this record was perhaps surpassed by the veteran family butler whom the tourist Colonel John Byng noted as still retained on the staff at the time he visited Battle Abbey: this venerable servitor's age was 103.[23]

At a different level, the evolution of the English system of land-tenure and land-use—a system which was being rapidly extended through many parts of Scotland during the last thirty years of the eighteenth century—created a harmony of enlightened self-interest between the two most important groups within the agricultural interest, the landowners and the farmers.[24] Landowners were certainly not oblivious of the main chance: they were anxious to maximize rent yields from their estates. A few took an enlightened professional interest in agriculture and used their home farms to provide a model for improvements. But more were concerned chiefly to find go-ahead professional farmers who, by the use of modern methods, would improve the productivity of their farms and so ultimately the rents. Once found—and it was not always easy to find them—such tenants were treasures to be cultivated and preserved, and the situation of mutual

[22] Waterson, p. 101.

[23] Waterson, *The Servants' Hall*, pp. 12, 24 (the housemaid, Jane Ebbrell, was brought by John Mellor when he bought Erddig in 1716, and continued in the service of his nephew and heir, Simon Yorke, and of Simon's son Philip: her portrait was commissioned in 1793, when presumably she was in her late eighties). E. W. Bovill, *English Country Life, 1780–1830* (1962), p. 107. For other instances on the Myddelton estate at Chirk, see G. E. Mingay, *English Landed Society in the eighteenth century* (1963), p. 275.

[24] This subject is ably discussed in Mingay, *English Landed Society*, pp. 60, 166–72, 186–8, 271–2. Cf. Martins, *A Great Estate at Work*, pp. 105–6, 126, 143.

dependence and assistance that developed formed at least part of the basis for the amicable relationships and the business conventions which arose between landlord and tenant.

The landlord's role was essentially to provide the plant: the farmhouse, the outbuildings, and other major capital assets such as hedging after enclosure. The farmer's role was to stock the farm and pursue his craft so as to produce both profit for himself and rent for the landlord. The landlord–tenant relationship appears to have rested on an implicit assumption that the ratio of farmer's profit and of rent was about 2:3.[25] Profit advanced as well as rent, if the farm yield increased. In practice the farmers often did better than this. Some were protected from rent increases by leases for a term of years. As the century wore on, there was an increasing tendency for landowners to replace long leases by tenancy-at-will renewable year by year, but this made much less difference than might have been expected. It had become a generally accepted convention on the greater estates that no radical revision would be made in the terms of a tenancy during the lifetime of an established tenant, especially if his family had a long-standing connection with the estate. Moreover, respect for such family ties led to tenancies being allowed to pass as a normal practice to sons, or widows, or even to daughters of deceased tenants. At a time of rising farm yields and also of rising prices for produce, this created a situation in which additional earnings from a farm often passed mainly to the farmer and were not partly creamed off in the form of a proportionately higher rent.[26] Such a practice also tended to shelter the farmer from increases in taxation and poor-law assessment, in the latter case at least until the re-negotiation of leases at higher rents.[27] With all these advantages, nevertheless in bad times the farmer might benefit by the landlord agreeing to temporary abatements of rent and perhaps assistance with current expenses. On the landlord's part, prestige, popularity, influence, self-respect, and political interest were all served by the policy of con-

[25] Mingay, *English Landed Society*, p. 253.

[26] F. M. L. Thompson, *English Landed Society in the nineteenth century* (1963), pp. 218–20.

[27] F. de la Rochefoucauld, *A Frenchman in England, 1784*, trans. and ed. J. Marchand and S. C. Roberts (1933), pp. 194–9.

sideration for tenants. The continuity of tenancy avoided the risks of acquiring unsatisfactory tenants, or of having farms left vacant which could mean both loss of rents and the diversion of resources and labour into stocking and working. Some major landowners, at least, cemented their relationships by means of cordial personal contacts with their tenants. The system operated to create and sustain a highly prosperous class of farmers, whose conservative interests in the maintenance of the established order were obvious; in this it compared favourably with the often more tense relationships between landlords and cultivators which obtained in France and in Ireland. Arthur Young, during his tour of France, noted that, whereas in England, had he visited a nobleman's house, 'there would have been three or four farmers asked to meet me, who would have dined with the family amongst ladies of the first rank', such a thing was impossible 'in the present manners of France'—a pregnant indication of the greater degree of integration of British rural society.[28]

It is impossible to generalize for the whole country about the state of housing of farmers and of the agricultural population in general during the late eighteenth century. The literature suggests that both very bad and very good conditions could be found. During the 1780s and the early 1790s Colonel John Byng traversed large areas of the country on his vacation tours. He was quick to disparage mean and squalid places when he saw them, and sometimes to condemn landowners whom he thought responsible; but he also frequently praised the neatness and cleanness of English villages, and the balance on the whole tilts to the latter.[29] Thus, for example, 'the road from Farnham to Alton', he noted, 'is very beautiful, the country so rich and neat in cottages, and so well filled with gentlemen's seats'. Approaching Reading, 'the country is rich in trees, cottages and neat farm houses'. Relatively rarely did he report, as on Langford in Bedfordshire, 'a place of misery, of ruined cottages (and where the house

[28] Quoted in Roy Porter, *English Society in the eighteenth century*, p. 79.

[29] *The Torrington Diaries*, ed. C. Bruyn Andrews (4 vols., 1934–8): critical remarks at i. 46, 51, 107, 144, 154, 160, 232, 252, ii. 293, 342, iii. 12, 154–5, 202; favourable comments at i. 38, 47, 77, 78, 89, 108, 130, 192, 223, 227, 228, ii. 18, 22, 174, 194–5, iv. 78, 108, 109.

of God is as wretched as the house of man)', or, more generally, on the small huddles of 'vile cottages' round the churches in east Lincolnshire.[30] In parts of Essex and of Norfolk also, cottage accommodation was primitive,[31] and this also seems to have been characteristic of parts of the far west and the north. The Swedish traveller Svedenstierna, touring England during 1802–3, thought the 'cobhouses' commonly inhabited by the poorer classes in Devon and Cornwall 'the most miserable dwellings which one can see', and he found wattle-and-daub cottages common along the way between Preston and Liverpool.[32] On the other hand, foreign visitors travelling up to London from Dover frequently commented on the neatness and cleanness of English farm-houses and cottages, as compared with the tumbledown accommodation of their own peasant communities. 'In a word', lamented the Marquis de la Rochefoucauld in 1784, 'there is always a marked superiority in the houses of the common people of England over those of the poor peasants in France, which it often pained me to observe.' Another traveller noted in 1802 that the dwelling of a plain farmer might well be mistaken for the residence of an independent gentleman.[33]

Much rebuilding of farms was going on during the late eighteenth century, with older farmhouses replacing still ruder cabins as homes for labourers, and in some rural areas the quality of labourers' housing was being more directly transformed, sometimes as an immediate result of enclosure. Perhaps few parishes were so fortunate as Cardington in Bedfordshire, where the brewer Samuel Whitbread and the prison reformer John Howard, in constant rivalry, vied with each other to create a well laid-out village of neat and comfortable cottages.[34] But other landowners were also busy, and even in cases where their primary concern was the

---

[30] *The Torrington Diaries*, i. 78, 108, ii. 293, 342.

[31] A. F. J. Brown, *Essex at Work, 1700–1815*, pp. 129–30; Martins, *A Great Estate at Work*, pp. 137, 208–16, 236–7, 255.

[32] *Svedenstierna's Tour of Great Britain, 1802–3*, ed. M. W. Flinn (1973), pp. 36, 119.

[33] Rochefoucauld, *A Frenchman in England, 1784*, pp. 158, 172, 180, 213; Christian A. G. Goede, *The Stranger in England* (3 vols., 1807), i. 16.

[34] *The Torrington Diaries*, iv. 109.

improvement of their own amenities, the local population also benefited. For instance, between 1790 and 1820 about thirty major rebuilding programmes were undertaken on the Holkham estate, many taking several years to complete. Fifteen of these involved the complete rebuilding of farmhouses and premises at costs ranging from £1,500 to £3,500.[35] The Oxfordshire village of Nuneham Courtenay was rebuilt with good brick houses during the 1760s by Earl Harcourt in the course of improving his park amenities. In 1785, for similar reasons, the community of Milton Abbey was reconstructed as a model village on a site further away from the big house.[36] In Scotland, this was the era of the 'planned village'; and as it has been calculated that Scottish landlords were responsible for the re-creation of at least 150 such communities between 1760 and 1800, historians may at present be rather underestimating the extent of similar developments in the much larger national community south of the Border.[37]

The landed class was less closely linked with the commercial and industrial sections of the community than with the rural elements so far described, but its contacts in these spheres were by no means negligible. In numbers of instances the interests of landowners themselves often involved an intelligent and sympathetic appreciation of the interests of entrepreneurs. There is plenty of evidence to confirm a conspicuous degree of involvement in the promotion of industrial development on the part of members of the aristocracy and gentry whose estates included mineral resources. Such involvement might mean the leasing on progressive terms of mines and quarries—the undertakers thus sometimes occupying a situation vaguely comparable to a tenant farmer —the promotion of canals to be used for the movement of minerals and manufactures, and the provision of housing for industrial populations. Sometimes, but rarely, it entailed

[35] Martins, *A Great Estate at Work*, p. 143.

[36] André Parreaux, *Daily Life in England in the reign of George III*, trans. Carola Congreve (1969), p. 22.

[37] T. C. Smout, 'The Landowner and the Planned Village in Scotland, 1730–1830', in *Scotland in the Age of Improvement*, ed. N. T. Phillipson and Rosalind Mitchison (1970), pp. 73–106. So far as I know there has been no such systematic examination of this question for England.

direct investment in industrial undertakings.[38] To the familiar
name of the Duke of Bridgewater, for whom coal-mining and
canal construction were two complementary enterprises, can
be added, for instance, those of his brother-in-law, Earl
Gower, later first Marquis of Stafford, and the north Warwickshire baronet Sir Roger Newdigate, who were both
similarly engaged in exploiting the resources of their estates.
In West Shropshire and the Welsh border area near Chirk and
Llangollen the canal construction by Telford, including the
still imposing viaducts across the valleys of the Ceirogg and
the Dee, was carried on under the patronage of the wealthy
Sir William (Johnstone) Pulteney. Other magnates who took
a direct interest in the exploitation of their coal measures
included Viscount Dudley and Ward in the West Midlands,
Lords Middleton and Manvers in the counties of Derby and
Nottingham, and the second Marquis of Rockingham in
Yorkshire. Viscount Dudley exploited both his personal
authority and his legislative influence to push through
between 1774 and 1788 a co-ordinated policy of enclosure,
road and canal construction, estate minerals undertakings,
and the granting of leases to iron and coal masters. He
invested over £6,000 in turnpike construction and some
£4,500 on the Dudley canal, and engaged directly in the
quarrying and mining of coal and limestone: his mines
department had expanded into a supervisory staff of thirty-
three by 1804. Rockingham, who deserves remembrance for
more than just his political career, opened up an industrial
complex of collieries, ironstone mines, and blast furnaces
around the Wentworth Woodhouse estate, and these undertakings were further expanded during the last years of the

---

[38] Detail in the following paragraph is drawn from: *Land and Industry. The
Landed Estate and the Industrial Revolution*, ed. J. T. Ward and R. G. Wilson
(Newton Abbot, 1971), pp. 70, 78-9, 88, 93-4, 100, 145-72; Mingay, *English
Landed Society in the eighteenth century*, pp. 191-6; Perkin, *Origins of Modern
English Society*, pp. 71, 74-6; Money, *Experience and Identity*, pp. 2, 9-10, 58,
60, 89, 91, 164, 198-202, 207, 211; Trinder, *The Industrial Revolution in
Shropshire*, pp. 42, 210; Eric Richards, 'The Industrial Face of a Great Estate:
Trentham and Lilleshall, 1780-1860', *Economic History Review*, 2nd ser. xxvii
(1974), 414-16; T. J. Raybould, *The Economic Emergence of the Black Country.
A Study of the Dudley Estate* (Newton Abbot, 1973); Moir, *Local Government in
Gloucestershire*, pp. 25, 50, and 'Sir George Onesiphorus Paul', in *Gloucestershire
Studies*, ed. H. P. R. Finberg (1957), pp. 195-225.

century by his nephew and heir, the 4th Earl Fitzwilliam. Another West Midlands magnate, the Earl of Dartmouth, also had a considerable personal stake in the local iron industry; possibly this was the origin of his contacts with the Birmingham industrialist Matthew Boulton, but as often happens, one thing leads to another, and over a number of years their correspondence ranged over all sorts of political, social, and economic issues. At least a dozen major land-owners can be named who actively promoted mining, quarry-ing, ironworks, and associated transport systems in various parts of North and South Wales. Further north, Sir James Lowther, later Lord Lonsdale, and the family of Christian-Curwen, were actively engaged in coal-mining, ironstone working, harbour construction, and associated miscellaneous business ventures in Cumberland and Westmorland: in 1770 Arthur Young discovered Lowther in the throes of planning and erecting a new township of three hundred houses, to be named after himself. In addition, every region could produce examples of men who were moving from the business world into the landed class and strengthening the contacts which existed between the two: as, for example, the Ridleys of Heaton in Northumberland, the Milnes family and the Denisons in Yorkshire, and the Pauls of Gloucestershire. In all the industrializing districts the relationships of landlords and industrial tenants were as significant for both as were the relationships between landlords and agricultural tenants: upper and middling ranks were bound together in a web of mutually advantageous bargains. One reflection of this fact, perhaps, was the extraordinary responsiveness of Parliament to the representations of commercial and industrial pressure groups throughout the eighteenth century; and possibly in this responsiveness we may trace one more reason for the political and social stability of late eighteenth-century Britain.

III

An even more fundamental explanation is to be found in the state of the economy. How far the condition of the people may have deteriorated later, after the turn of the century, is perhaps an open question; but there is good ground for arguing that one of the chief factors making for stability in late eighteenth-century British society was the country's buoyant economy and growing prosperity. Important recent scholarship points towards this conclusion, and it has done so in revulsion against a previous tendency to write off the onset of industrialization as a period of gloom and doom for most of the population. One leading historian of North-East England, defending the newer approach, has recently observed that there is something very wrong with the emphasis in prevailing accounts, of English society in the decades of the Industrial Revolution reeling from one disaster to another, with little sign of the enormous successes which were also being achieved.[39] Perhaps this frequently adopted approach has reflected what seems an inborn human tendency to think that nothing is news unless it is bad news —a tendency which affected the people creating a good deal of the literary evidence two hundred years ago as much as it has affected some later historians. But a little reflection must show that on the whole economic success outweighed economic failure during the second half of the eighteenth century (and, indeed, later also), for a greater measure of prosperity was spread around among a far larger population by 1800 than had been the case about 1750. Certainly, there were numbers of people whose lives were disrupted and at times rendered miserable by economic change; but some historians have rarely stopped to reflect how much more misery there might have been had the changes not occurred, and how, in many ways, and for many people, the state of affairs was getting better.

The proposition that British society in general, and not just a small privileged part of it, was becoming wealthier during the second half of the eighteenth century can, I submit, be sustained by a number of different converging arguments. It would, of course, be incorrect to suggest that there were no losers, that greater prosperity was so evenly spread that all benefited. The literary evidence left by English travellers and social investigators of the time makes clear the

[39] Norman McCord, *North East England: An Economic and Social History* (1979), pp. 18–19.

ineligibility of any such conclusion. But there is a strong case on various grounds for arguing that between 1750 and 1800 more people were faring better than before, and that the general outlook was one of optimism and of reasonable hope for material gain. This was not merely because an increasing proportion of the population was rising into what were economically as well as socially the 'middling ranks' of society—though this indeed was happening—but because a significant element also of the lower ranks was feeling the beneficial effects of economic growth.[40] In dealing with this question it is possible to call up in evidence, firstly the information of contemporary travellers, secondly available elements of modern economometric analysis, thirdly scattered information on actual wages and family earnings, and lastly the work of contemporary social investigators. All these lines of approach appear to lead towards the same conclusion.

By no means all of the contemporary accounts were pessimistic. Foreign visitors, especially those traversing the Home Counties, were almost invariably impressed with the relative absence of signs of poverty.[41] One British observer whose constant peregrinations through a broad swath of semi-rural and industrial England gave him unrivalled opportunities to form judgements on the question was the founder of the Methodist movement, John Wesley. Parts of Wesley's pamphlet published in 1778, *Serious Address to the people of England*, revealed an astonishingly shrewd perception of

[40] Emphasis on the 'middling ranks' is the theme of D. E. C. Eversley's paper, 'The Home Market and Economic Growth in England, 1750–1780', in *Land, Labour and Population in the Industrial Revolution*, ed. E. L. Jones and G. E. Mingay (1967). Neil McKendrick argues (I believe correctly) that the improvement of earnings reached down to a considerable proportion of the class of skilled workers ('Home Demand and Economic Growth: A New View of the Role of Women and Children in the Industrial Revolution', in *Historical Perspectives. Studies in English Thought and Society in honour of J. H. Plumb*, ed. Neil McKendrick, 1974). Directories for the rapidly growing big cities convey something of the dynamic growth of the well-to-do, middling class elements of society. For example, the series of directories for late eighteenth-century Manchester produces lengthening lists of names of 'principal inhabitants': in 1773, 1,530; in 1781, 1,920; in 1788, 2,580; in 1794, 5,544—an increase of 3½ times in just over twenty years (Witt Bowden, *Industrial Society in England towards the end of the eighteenth century*, New York, 1925, p. 106).

[41] *Historical Perspectives*, ed. McKendrick, p. 168. His examples could be matched with others.

secular trends. With remarkable discernment he estimated that England's population had probably risen by a million in the past twenty years, and he noted the improvements which had been made in agriculture, in manufactures, and transport. One authority on Wesley has described this tract as 'one long contradiction of those who claimed that England was being ruined or destroyed'.[42] A few years later, in 1789, the politician William Eden, Lord Auckland, who had accumulated an unrivalled knowledge in this field while negotiating a commercial treaty with France, declared that the state of British prosperity was 'certainly at this hour far beyond what the nation has ever experienced'.[43] Shortly after the turn of the century the government statistician John Rickman deplored the propensity to believe common assertion, 'that everything in grumbling England grows worse and worse', and he pointed out that overall life expectancy had been increased by about a fifth; and since the well-to-do portion of the community had enjoyed the advantages of 'food and cleanliness abundantly before', the poor must in fact have benefited to a greater extent than this figure suggested.[44]

It is impossible to read very far in either contemporary descriptions or later studies of particular localities without accumulating detail which supports these views. Here again is Wesley, recording his impression of the Staffordshire Potteries district in 1781:

How the whole face of the country has changed in about 20 years, since which inhabitants have continually flowed in from every side— the wilderness is literally become a fruitful field. Houses, villages, towns have sprung up; and the country is not more improved than the people.

Josiah Wedgwood late in life, recounting the transformations in this region, recalled a previous generation's memory of 'miserable huts', infertile soil, and almost total isolation

[42] Maldwyn Edwards, *John Wesley and the eighteenth century* (1933), p. 185.

[43] Quoted in *The Cambridge History of British Foreign Policy*, vol. i: *1783-1815*, ed. by Sir A. W. Ward and G. P. Gooch (Cambridge, 1922), p. 190. The investigations of Sir Frederick Eden in 1796 convinced him that the lot of the poor had been improving steadily for the past fifty years and especially over the last ten (*The State of the Poor*, 3 vols., 1797, i. 404, 560, 574-5).

[44] Quoted in M. Dorothy George, *England in Transition* (1931), pp. 154-5.

for lack of roads, contrasting sharply with the present scene of good communications, new and comfortable houses, and 'workmen earning near double their former wages'.[45]

Arthur Young painted a similar word-picture of the favourable transformation by industry of the Tamworth district in the East Midlands, which he visited in 1791. The man primarily responsible was the Leicestershire entrepreneur Joseph Wilkes, who combined interests in industry and sheep-farming. Having bought the manor of Measham and its hamlet of tumbledown thatched cottages, he was busy transforming the place.

The buildings erected and erecting [wrote Young] will speedily change the face of it. Here are two cotton and a corn mill, two steam engines; many weaving shops and a number of cottages built; a large and handsome inn. . . . what is done here in ten or a dozen years by one man, who has been at the same time engaged in many other great undertakings, who in union with Mr Peel is giving a new face to Faseley and Tamworth, cannot but make anyone from the Continent admire at the wonderful exertions active in this kingdom.

Wilkes, he wrote, was 'filling this country with industry and population', and he contrasted the lot of people in this prosperous manufacturing centre with backward rural areas he knew elsewhere: 'A comfortable well-built brick cottage for 30s. which is fifty per cent less than in Suffolk etc. for a clay hovel, coals for almost nothing instead of roaming to break hedges; and constant employment at high wages by cotton, instead of starving by spinning wool.'[46] Nor was this an isolated example. Wilkes and Peel were but two of a number of leading cotton spinners and manufacturers who, in order to attract workmen, were building superior cottage accommodation in various parts of the East Midlands and often providing also substantial garden plots.[47]

Young was impressed with the country's economic progress

[45] Quoted in Roy Porter, *English Society in the eighteenth century* (1982), p. 355.

[46] *Tours in England and Wales by Arthur Young selected from the Annals of Agriculture* (1932), pp. 274–5, 286 and n. 'Mr Peel' was the father of the future Prime Minister. For other instances of the Peel family being involved in the erection of cottages for their work-people, see S. D. Chapman, 'The Peels in the Early English Cotton Industry', *Business History*, xi, no. 2 (1969), p. 69.

[47] S. D. Chapman, *The Early Factory Masters. The Transition to the Factory System in the Midlands Textile Industry* (Newton Abbot, 1967), pp. 157–60.

in a more general way when, about 1797, he revisited Hull after an interval of thirty years, saw its new ten-acre dock capable of accommodating 120 ships, and gleaned the statistics of its trade, by now estimated at twenty millions sterling per annum. 'This vast increase of commerce at Hull', he wrote, 'deserves particular attention; for it marks the rising prosperity of the kingdom in the last thirty years, much more clearly than the progress of London or Liverpool.' Indeed, though not rivalling the west-coast outports of Bristol, Liverpool, or the Clyde estuary in terms of population or range of enterprise, Hull furnished a remarkable example of the general boom of the late eighteenth century. In the thirty years after 1770 its population more than doubled. The construction of the fine new dock and quay, completed in 1778, provided the facilities for a phenomenal expansion of seaborne commerce: between 1760 and 1800, the inward and outward tonnage in foreign trade increased some three times, and coastal traffic expanded in much the same proportion. Shipbuilding and connected trades, processing industries of various sorts, and an increasing production of various consumer and luxury goods, created a steady demand for labour and a comfortable livelihood for numbers of entrepreneurs. As the transport centre linking northern Europe with the industrial North of England and the Midlands, as a centre of banking and solid commercial achievement, Hull stood out as a conspicuous example of economic success; and the apparent lack of labour troubles in the port and town suggests a fair degree of stable, widespread prosperity.[48]

In various districts the growth of the metallurgical industries brought not only employment and better wages, but also new housing, which, if poor by twentieth-century standards, nevertheless was often superior to the wattle-and-daub cabins which had housed so much of the country's pre-industrial population. The Swedish traveller Svedenstierna

[48] *Tours in England and Wales*, pp. 174–5; Gordon Jackson, *Hull in the eighteenth century. A study in economic and social history* (Oxford, 1972), *passim*, esp. pp. 2, 40–5, 60, 65, 72–3, 179–208, 243–8. For another, though less dramatic example of seaport growth, see M. M. Schofield, *Outline of an Economic History of Lancaster, 1680–1860*, Part I (trans. of the Lancaster Branch of the Historical Association, no. 1, 1946).

was astonished at the way in which, over some twenty years, the development of the iron industry on the South Wales coalfield had brought a prosperous population of thousands into an area of barren hills. At Merthyr Tydfil, where the provision of houses for a labour force was a particularly urgent problem, about a quarter of the cottage accommodation available in 1800 had been supplied by the leading iron-master.[49] An enormous demand for housing developed in Birmingham: according to one estimate about 8,000 houses, mostly occupied by working people, were put up during the first thirty years of George III's reign. The great Midlands industrialist Matthew Boulton recalled in later life how, thirty years before, he had transformed the barrenest of commons on the outskirts of the town into workplace and home town for many hundreds of people, a thousand of whom were employed in his Soho works alone.[50] William Champion, with 2,000 people on the payroll of his brass and copper works at Warmley near Bristol in 1787, spent part of his fortune of £200,000 on the creation of a model village, with cottages for all the work-people, and a village centre with a group of shops and a clock tower, and an ornamental pool with a figure of Neptune.[51] On the Shropshire coalfield north of Ironbridge, the building of houses was absolutely necessary in order to bring in workmen, and the great partnerships which dominated the area in the late eighteenth century created whole new communities in order to secure the labour for their enterprises. The seventeen parishes of this coalfield and its periphery had an estimated population of over 20,000 at the end of 1760: the enumerated population of 1801 was over 34,000. Associated with this expansion, housing and industrial construction called into being a whole new industry of brick-making and building in the district: in 1784 three leading entrepreneurs, John Wilkinson, William

[49] *Svedenstierna's Tour of Great Britain, 1802–3*, ed. M. W. Flinn (1973), p. 42; C. W. Chalklin, *The Provincial Towns of Georgian England. A Study of the Building Process, 1740–1820* (1974), p. 186—where similar developments in Lancashire are also noted.

[50] Witt Bowden, *Industrial Society in England towards the end of the eighteenth century* (New York, 1925), p. 99; A. Parreaux, *Daily Life in England in the reign of George III*, trans. Carola Congreve (1969), p. 64.

[51] Esther Moir, *Local Government in Gloucestershire* (1969), p. 9.

Reynolds, and the Earl of Dudley, protesting against one of William Pitt's proposed taxes, pointed out to the treasury that they used a million bricks a year.[52]

Not all new house-building catered for working people, though much of it did. That which did not also signalled the growing prosperity of the land. Arthur Young, approaching Birmingham from the south in 1791, noted that 'for the last three miles the country full of new villas, in every direction, and many brick houses and cottages', all dating, it seemed, from the last twenty or so years.[53] And every villa created new demands for half a dozen or so servants, for transportation, and for supplies of food from local sources, thereby quickening the economic life of the district and bringing work and livelihood to others.

Even areas remote from the great manufacturing centres and little touched by the Industrial Revolution felt the effects of economic development, which was reflected in a gradual enlargement of sectors of the populace ranging up from the skilled craftsmen to the professional classes in the towns. For instance, urban centres in Essex were small and expanding only slowly in the late eighteenth century, but they were floated along on the agricultural prosperity around them, which in its turn throve on the growing London market for foodstuffs. Such sources as directories and newspaper advertisements give some indication of the way in which, for example, Colchester and Chelmsford supplied the growing needs of their thriving neighbourhoods for clothes, shoes, houses, furniture, coaches, saddlery, wigs, clocks, cutlery, and books, all this entailing the activity of more and more wholesalers, retailers, and craftsmen. Innkeepers multiplied; lawyers prospered as estate and conveyancing business increased; more doctors set up in practice to look after larger numbers of patients. Well-to-do millers and tanners moved into substantial houses, enterprising schoolmasters offered to educate the young, other miscellaneous members of the middling classes like druggists, surveyors, auctioneers, revenue officers, Nonconformist ministers increased in numbers. The multiplication and diversification of employments reflected

[52] Barry Trinder, *The Industrial Revolution in Shropshire* (1973), pp. 58-60, 76, 214-23, 323, 325, 311-12.   [53] *Tours in England and Wales*, p. 253.

a steady growth in such parts of the non-agricultural sector and in the numbers of the modestly well-to-do, whose wants and whose purchasing power helped to sustain the onward course of industrialization. This kind of creeping urban growth provided opportunities for younger sons of crafts-men and farmers, who might gain entry to a craft by apprenticeship, while a little higher up the scale, the sons of small freeholders moved into the openings which were avail-able in the expanding professions for attorneys, surveyors, engineers, doctors, Nonconformist ministers of religion, schoolmasters, and others.[54] And even Essex could furnish at least one example of planned development. In the north-east of the county, responding to the quickening pulse of economic activity, Richard Rigby, the immensely wealthy owner of the estate of Mistley, created a new port village near the head of the Stour estuary. By 1784 it contained some fifty households, an inn, a kiln for limeburning, an extensive quay faced with brick and stone, a large warehouse, with a wet dock beside it capable of holding two or three ships, a ship-carpenter's yard (with a 32-gun frigate under construction), and a small fleet of four or five coastal vessels which were employed mainly for shipping in coal and corn. Himself profiting by the added rental of his estate, he created livelihoods for a whole new small community.[55]

IV

While much descriptive material of this kind points to a steady improvement in the general social and economic con-ditions of the British people during the late eighteenth century, this hypothesis also finds support in investigations of levels of earning and spending. This subject can be approached through three different sorts of evidence: infor-mation about actual wages, macro-economic analysis, and

[54] A. F. J. Brown, *Essex at Work, 1700–1815* (Chelmsford, 1969), pp. 51–62, 111–12, 115–27, 159–60.

[55] Rochefoucauld, *A Frenchman in England, 1784*, pp. 163–4; *Tours in England and Wales by Arthur Young*, pp. 64, 274–5. The spirit of English inde-pendence is typified in Rochefoucauld's anecdote about the one house owned independently of the Mistley estate, whose proprietor refused to sell it to Rigby and painted it red in glaring contrast with the white house-decoration of Rigby's properties.

contemporary enquiries into the socio-economic structure of the population.

There is a fair amount of information about wage-rates, though this sort of evidence is particularly difficult to interpret. Travellers like Arthur Young and the Hon. John Byng, later Viscount Torrington, made a habit of noting down rates of wages during their peregrinations, employers sometimes mentioned their offers when advertising for labour, local clergymen and also social investigators like Sir Frederick Morton Eden gathered details on earnings, and at least some surviving records of industrial undertakings have been used for this purpose. But given this information, numbers of variables have to be taken into account. An average going rate does not help a great deal by itself, although it may provide some sort of yardstick for comparison. But both the average and the actual rates varied from one part of the country to another—like the cost of living they were higher in London than elsewhere—were dependent to some extent on the relationship of supply and demand, and meant little in the event of a trade depression. Premiums on skill meant that some workers might be capable of much higher earnings than others in the same craft; however, these men might trade earnings for leisure, and be content with less money than a full week's work would have brought them. The problem of by-employments also adds greatly to the difficulty of assessing how well or how poorly people lived.

Some recent examinations of wage-rates seem to indicate that if the general level of real wages was not rising during the years 1760–1800, at any rate it was not falling either. Broadly, wages advanced with prices. These enquiries do not exclude the likelihood that, measured in these terms, some categories of workers were losing ground while others were gaining: assuming that an increase by two in the normal pay rate was necessary to keep up with the rising cost of living, of eighteen categories examined, over the period 1755 to 1805 only three fell seriously below this level, two were marginally below it, and four were well in excess of it, while the remainder maintained parity.[56]

[56] M. W. Flinn, 'Trends in Real Wages, 1750–1850', *Economic History Review*, 2nd ser. xxvii (1974), 408; a judgement which, so far as the period up

Agricultural labourers and day labourers in the towns undoubtedly formed a depressed class of wage earners, whose
weekly takings were often below subsistence level, and might
stand at anything between 6s. and 12s. a week in the 1780s
and early 1790s.[57] But what this meant in practice is difficult
to establish, because a large, though decreasing number of
farm labourers still lived in and were fed by their employers,
while others, hired for harvest only, received considerable
allowances in food and beer during the period they were at
work. The contribution to the family income of supplemen-
tary earnings by wives and children further complicates the
problem of assessing the incomes of people in this class.
Clergymen interested in social questions occasionally
published sample budgets indicating that such families could
not get through the year without an element of help from
charity or the Poor Law, and no doubt numbers of such cases
occurred. On the other hand the amount that women might
add to their husbands' earnings could sometimes be significant. For instance, lace-making and straw-plaiting were two
occupations employing large numbers in parts of Bedfordshire and Buckinghamshire, and the earnings could make all
the difference for a family between real poverty and ability
to keep financially afloat.[58] The evidence confirms the
pattern of labourers' wage-rates being higher in the North and
East, largely due to the upward pull of competing industrial
rates. In the Skipton area of Yorkshire industry at one stage

to 1810 is concerned, is not materially challenged by G. N. von Tunzelmann,
'Trends in Real Wages, 1750-1850, Revisited', ibid. xxxii (1979), 33-47; Peter
Lindert and Jeffrey G. Williamson, 'English Workers' Living Standards during the
Industrial Revolution: a New Look', ibid. xxxvi (1983), 1-25, especially table 2,
p. 4.

[57] For a selection of information supporting this generalization, see *Tours in
England and Wales by Arthur Young*, pp. 25 (Forest of Dean), 184 (Hull): Roche-
foucauld, *A Frenchman in England, 1784*, pp. 217, 119-30; Alasdair Geddes,
Portsmouth during the Great French Wars, 1770-1800 (Portsmouth, 1970), p. 18;
Sir Francis Hill, *Georgian Lincoln* (Cambridge, 1966), p. 156; J. D. Chambers,
Nottinghamshire in the Eighteenth Century (1932), pp. 287-9; Alan Armstrong,
*Stability and Change in an English Country Town. A Social Study of York,
1801-51* (Cambridge, 1974), p. 102; Frances Collier, *The Family Economy of the
Working Classes in the Cotton Industry, 1784-1833* (Manchester, 1964), p. 41;
Barry Trinder, *The Industrial Revolution in Shropshire*, pp. 335-7.

[58] Ivy Pinchbeck, *Women Workers and the Industrial Revolution, 1750-
1850* (1930), pp. 207, 215-21.

threatened to price agriculture out of existence, and Colonel Byng found one district reduced to 'large wild pasture grounds'. In remote Elgin, in the north of Scotland, industrial competition for labour contributed to a near doubling of agricultural wages between 1780 and 1796. Even in the non-industrializing South-East exceptional circumstances could force up rates. The shortage of labour caused in parts of Essex by the outbreak of war in 1793 enabled farm workers to stand out for piece rates yielding weekly earnings of between 14s. and 21s.——about twice the normal rates—— and a similar situation developed in parts of Bedfordshire and Nottinghamshire in 1796-7.[59]

There was much variation in industrial wages from one part of the country to another, but in general these tended to be substantially higher than the earnings of common labourers. Data given by such investigators as Arthur Young, Sir Frederick Morton Eden, and Colonel John Byng confirm the impression 'that a craftsman in a skilled or a dangerous occupation might earn up to two or three times more per week than an unskilled artisan', whose income might differ little from that of a common labourer.[60] The number of these higher wage earners was increasing steadily during the last twenty years of the century: this was quite apart from the emergence also of the smaller but significant groups of supervisors and managers in industry, with wages in the range of £100 to £200 a year, to which the Industrial Revolution was giving birth. Here are a few of the possible earnings of skilled men during the 1770s and 1780s, which may be set against a mean level of from 8s. to 10s. a week for the common labourer: Sheffield razor polishers (in 1770), 10s. a day;

[59] *Torrington Diaries*, iii. 108; Witt Bowden, *Industrial Society in England*, pp. 256-7; A. F. J. Brown, *Essex at Work, 1700-1815*, pp. 131-2; Clive Emsley, *British Society and the French Wars, 1793-1815* (1979), pp. 74-5. Some qualifications thus have to be made to the suggestion of a general fall in the level of real earnings in agriculture in the 1790s (K. D. M. Snell, 'Agricultural Seasonal Unemployment, the Standard of Living, and Women's Work in the South and East, 1690-1860', *Economic History Review*, 2nd ser. xxxiv (1981), 407-37). See also E. L. Jones, *Agriculture and the Industrial Revolution* (Oxford, 1974), pp. 212-14.

[60] Penelope J. Corfield, *The Impact of English Towns, 1700-1800* (Oxford, 1982), p. 135. However, there were exceptions, such as Exeter (W. G. Hoskins, *Industry, Trade and People in Exeter, 1688-1800, with special reference to the Serge Industry*, Manchester, 1935, pp. 129-31).

skilled Norwich weavers 21s. a week (this in 1794 at a time when 12s. a week was reckoned sufficient for a local family to live on 'comfortably'); Birmingham craftsmen up to 25s. a week; wool-combers and silk-weavers in Essex, 14s. to 16s. a week (but the London rate was 21s. to 30s.); skilled men in Portsmouth dockyard between 2s. and 2s. 8d. a day, but with perquisites such as 'chips' which added considerably to weekly earnings, and extra for overtime in periods of war.[61]

Copper-workers near Macclesfield were paid a wage of 14s. a week but may have received more, for at Ravenshead in South Lancashire the wage of 15s. was supplemented by perquisites worth 4s. or 5s. Iron-workers were earning 18s. to 20s. a week at Tintern Abbey in 1787; a few years later those in Shropshire were getting between 30s. and 40s. During the 1790s the combination of wartime labour shortage and rates for danger pushed the wages of coal-miners in the Black Country up to a level which made it impossible to get more than three or four days' work out of them. In the transport industry some employees gained enormous advantages out of the wartime shortage of labour. The seamen on the colliers plying between the Tyne and the Thames provide a conspicuous example. In 1792, the last year of peace and a good season for the trade, they were being paid £2 10s. a voyage. The outbreak of war in 1793 soon forced the rate up to six guineas or more, and it briefly reached a peak of eleven guineas at the turn of the century, an escalation far in advance of any increase in the cost of living. Earnings in land transport seem difficult to find; but what is certain is that very large numbers of people found work in the coaching inns and on the roads: the little town of Dunstable (population about 1,300 in 1801) was largely kept going by 'the great passage of travellers'.[62]

[61] Corfield, *English Towns*, loc. cit.; C. B. Jewson, *Jacobin City, A Portrait of Norwich in its Reaction to the French Revolution, 1788-1802* (1975), pp. 4-5; *Tours in England and Wales by Arthur Young*, pp. 257, 59; Geddes, *Portsmouth*, pp. 18-19.

[62] *Torrington Diaries*, iii. 24, 122; T. C. Barker and J. R. Harris, *A Merseyside Town in the Industrial Revolution. St. Helens, 1750-1900* (Liverpool, 1954), p. 86; Trinder, *Industrial Revolution in Shropshire*, p. 336; Raybould, *The Economic Emergence of the Black Country*, p. 187; Emsley, *British Society and the French Wars*, pp. 32-83; Simon Ville, 'Wages, prices and profitability in the shipping industry during the Napoleonic Wars. A Case Study', *Journal of Transport*

In Lancashire weavers of fancy muslins could get over
17s. a week in the 1780s; and a decade later cotton-weavers
could earn up to 30s., and there was more work to be done
than men to do it. Mule cotton-spinners might earn between
30s. and 38s. a week during the 1790s. Analysis of the wage
books of fourteen leading firms of textile printers towards
the close of the century indicates that the highest-paid
journeymen were receiving £103 per annum and the lowest
over £51. Average weekly wages over a three year period
were 28s. Numbers of jobs were available for women at wages
of upwards of 12s. to 14s. a week. Furthermore, this
industry, like pottery, generated a number of still more
highly paid appointments for people with artistic flair and
skill. Around 1800 the elder Sir Robert Peel's print designers
at Bury were earning between 40s. and 60s. weekly. Millwrights, who were among the best-paid craftsmen in the
eighteenth century, could command 40s. a week plus board
in Essex in 1770. A collection of information on wage-rates
in Manchester is much in line with these figures and indicates
that, given normal employment, about the turn of the
century craftsmen were improving their position in relation
to the cost of living.[63]

London rates were untypically high, but they related to
a very large minority, perhaps an eleventh of the population. According to the recollections of Francis Place, his
brother-in-law, a skilled cabinet-maker, had unlimited opportunities before him in the early 1790s and could easily have
earned £4 a week, had he not been addicted to the bottle.
Place himself was earning a guinea and a half as a foreman
leather-breeches-maker at the age of nineteen, and 26s.

History, 3rd ser. ii, no. 1 (1981), 39–52; Chalklin, *The Provincial Towns of Georgian England*, pp. 30, 321.

[63] Duncan Bythell, *The Handloom Weavers. A Study in the English Cotton Industry during the Industrial Revolution* (Cambridge, 1969), pp. 98–100, 50–1, 132; Frances Collier, *The Family Economy of the Working Classes in the Cotton Industry, 1784–1833*, ed. R. S. Fitton (Manchester, 1964), pp. 17, 41; S. D. Chapman and S. Chassagne, *European Textile Printers in the eighteenth century. A Study of Peel and Oberkampf* (1981), pp. 95–7; Brown, *Essex at Work*, p. 137; L. S. Marshall, *The Development of Public Opinion in Manchester, 1780–1820* (Syracuse, 1946), pp. 26–7. Norman Murray, *The Scottish Handloom Weavers, 1790–1850. A Social History* (Edinburgh, 1978), notes the relatively high level of wages up to about 1812 (pp. 40–1, 51, 62–3).

a week a little later as a journeyman stuff-breeches-maker. By 1801, when he had become head of his own business, he was able to pay his foreman three guineas a week and a wage of 36s. to an expert leather-breeches-maker. By and large the members of the London crafts all held their standard of living steady against inflation until well into the 1800s, and their weekly rates in 1812 were reported to be from 30s. upwards to five guineas.[64]

Still other factors—women's and joint family earnings—need to be taken into account in assessing working-class incomes during this period. As wives women made their contributions in a number of ways. In some districts colliers and miners combined a smallholding with their pursuits in the pits, and the care of this was often left to the wife, who in some instances could even bring in by cash sales of produce almost as much as her husband earned.[65] From the 1770s onwards industrial development opened new doors to women and greatly increased their earning capacity. The adoption of the multiple-spindle jenny in place of the spinning-wheel permitted them to increase their takings two or three times, and in Essex, where mechanization had not arrived, a case could still be cited in 1790 of a woman and her two daughters being able to bring in the equivalent of her husband's wage and so double the family income.[66] Where the machines were advancing, the opportunities were sometimes even greater. Women working as 'stretchers' in a cotton-spinning firm might earn 17s. 6d. to 21s. a week, and there was plenty of other employment available at lower rates.[67] To a significant degree women's liberation started in the eighteenth century, not in the twentieth, and was a consequence of the Industrial Revolution. Far from

[64] *The Autobiography of Francis Place*, ed. Mary Thale (Cambridge, 1972), pp. 92-101, 210-11; E. P. Thompson, *The Making of the English Working Class*, p. 238.

[65] Ivy Pinchbeck, *Women Workers and the Industrial Revolution*, p. 21. In some areas landlords offered smallholdings to attract workmen into their districts (Bythell, *Handloom Weavers*, p. 45).

[66] Brown, *Essex at Work*, pp. 132-3. This ceased to be possible in this district during the following decade. Kenneth E. Carpenter, ed., *Labour Disputes in the early days of the Industrial Revolution* (New York, 1972), pp. 31-3.

[67] Frances Collier, *Working Classes in the Cotton Industry*, p. 18; *Torrington Diaries*, iii. 106.

being impoverished by technological redundancy as the hand-jenny was replaced by power-driven spinning machinery, women exploited the new opportunities this afforded in the factories, and also moved into the wide-open field of hand-loom weaving. Their lighter physique did not disable them from the finer types of cloth-production; they became manu-facturers of calicoes, coarse muslins, and cambrics; and they often replaced men during the period of wartime military enlistment after 1793. Women weavers at Wigan who had followed this course declared in 1799 that they were better off than they had been when their men were at home. By 1808 half the country's weavers were said to be women and child-ren.[68] Joint earnings in the cotton-spinning industry could be considerable: instances have been culled from the records of two or three firms which have been investigated of families taking home sums ranging between 25s. and 40s. a week.[69]

Other sectors of industry yield similar findings. In 1791 women in industrial employment in the Birmingham region averaged only 6s. a week—a modest sum though a useful addition to the rather larger wage of a husband—but some of them could earn up to 20s. When such family incomes were aggregated, these were, so Arthur Young remarked, 'immense wages, when it is considered that the whole family is sure of constant employment'.[70] The Staffordshire pottery industry presented similar opportunities: here a woman with a highly developed artistic gift might even outshine her husband and contribute more than he did to the family budget. Before 1760 female employment in the Potteries had been unknown. Thirty or forty years later wives were helping to win family incomes which could sometimes amount to between 40s. and 60s. a week, or £100 to £150 a year: by working people's standards this was affluence.[71] All this evidence corroborates the view that by the end of the eighteenth century a considerably increased number of

[68] Collier, op. cit., pp. 3, 15–17; Ivy Pinchbeck, *Women Workers and the Industrial Revolution*, pp. 157, 160, 163–4; Bythell, *Handloom Weavers*, pp. 50–1, 60–1.   [69] Collier, op. cit., pp. 28–33, 54–5, 74–89.
[70] *Tours in England and Wales by Arthur Young*, p. 257.
[71] Neil McKendrick, 'Home Demand and Economic Growth', in *Historical Perspectives*, pp. 186–8. Cf. the general thrust of his papers in Neil McKendrick, John Brewer, and J. H. Plumb, *The Birth of a Consumer Society. The Com-mercialization of Eighteenth Century England* (1982).

families, including many working folk, had carried the level of their earnings well above the margin of bare subsistence and had a sufficient income to permit a modest degree of consumer expenditure on comforts and the accumulation of household possessions.[72]

Servants, indoor and outdoor, constituted a large section of the working population, perhaps as much as 8 per cent.[73] It is no more easy to evaluate evidence about the levels and trends of wages paid to servants than it is in respect of other sectors—there were wide variations linked with different conditions of age, experience, degree of responsibility, and so forth—but there is good ground for believing that, at least up to 1800, emoluments were reasonably good and were more than keeping pace with price rises. Moreover, since most servants lived in and had their board, increases in food prices passed them by and fell upon their employers.

It is possible to compare household accounts and wage bills for domestic service in the household of Sir John Griffin Griffin, later Baron Braybrooke, at Audley End, Essex, for two well-separated years near the beginning and the end of the period under review, 1763 and 1791.[74] Judging by the growth of his household Griffin's affairs were in a flourishing state. By the second date the domestic staff had increased from sixteen to twenty-eight and a much more elaborate organization was evident. In 1763 the total annual wages bill had been £168 16s. By 1791 it was £578 5s., more than three times as much: the family's living standard had risen considerably. Part of this increase was due to the addition to the household of several highly paid domestic appointments. The butler of 1763 at £20 per annum had been replaced by a house steward and butler at £63; a cook at £12 by one presumably much more skilled at £50; and the 1791 establishment also included

---

[72] McKendrick, opera cit., passim.

[73] J. Jean Hecht, *The Domestic Servant Class in eighteenth-century England* (1956), pp. 33–4.

[74] For biographical details on Griffin, see Namier and Brooke, *The History of Parliament. The House of Commons, 1754–1790*, ii. 553. For the two lists of domestic wages, and household bills for 1765, see A. F. J. Brown, *English History from Essex Sources, 1750–1900* (Chelmsford, 1952), pp. 42, 155–6. Household expenses for 1791 are estimated at one-third higher per head than in 1763.

a gamekeeper (£59), a bailiff (£50), a valet (£30), and a groom of chambers (£30).

Wage levels increased substantially for Griffin's servants in continuing categories between 1763 and 1791. In the case of twelve lower servants, ranging from second coachman and footman to housemaid, the scales of payment in all but two cases had individually risen by from 25 to 100 per cent, and over the group of appointments as a whole by nearly half.[75] At the bottom of the scale, the rise in the wages of the housemaid (£3) and the stillroom maid (£3 16s.) both to £7 looks like a clear indication of the scarcity of this kind of labour. The wages of the housekeeper (£16 to £25), the lady's woman (£8 to £12), and the upper housemaid (£7 to £9 9s.) had also advanced considerably. All these servants were also consuming their shares of an inflow of food supplies which for one week in 1765 cost Griffin over £16 and which would have cost at least a third more per head in 1791. Assuming half the £16 worth was consumed by Griffin and his family and guests and the other half by the sixteen members of his staff, each of these servants was receiving about 10s. a week or £26 a year in food in 1765. In 1791 this supplement would be costed at about £35. In most, if not all cases they also had their accommodation found. In all probability, since this was a usual custom, working outfits or livery were provided. And there would also be perquisites in the form of cast-off clothes and other items. Translating the various kinds into cash terms the four most highly paid servants were receiving around £100 per annum or more in 1791, and the lowest paid were getting over £50. In such a household the diet was better than that of many working folk, so were the general conditions, the work was relatively light, on condition of good behaviour employment was exceptionally secure, and there were opportunities for self-improvement and self-advancement.[76] Furthermore, many employers accepted the obligation to provide retirement pensions after long service. Generalizing on the basis of one example is of

[75] This detail matches Parson Woodforde's experience with the wages of footmen in the 1780s (Hecht, op. cit., pp. 152–3).

[76] Hecht, op. cit., pp. 20–2, 60–2, 106–15, 208–14. In the early 1800s servants in London offering themselves on short-term engagements demanded 31s. 6d. a week (*Svedenstierna's Tour of Great Britain*, ed. Flinn, p. 7).

course unwise, but at least some other scattered information suggests that Audley End was not untypical, and that if there were many servants at the bottom of the pile, low paid and working in poor conditions, nevertheless opportunities to rise were open to them, and a good number of their group lived in reasonably comfortable circumstances.

There is, then, a sufficient amount of information about working people's incomes to suggest that a significant proportion of the individuals in this social group were raising total family earnings to a point at which living standards were comfortable and rising. There were numbers of them—they would appear to be numerous—who were doing likewise by rising to entrepreneurial independence, some of them directly involved in industrial undertakings, others in the service industries required by the growing towns. To take one instance: the boom in the East Midlands textile trade caused the number of hosiers, the merchant employers, at Nottingham to increase from 70 in 1771 to 199 about 1800, an increase quite disproportionate to the growth of population either nationally or locally. The expansion in production created other demands also, and by 1807 the town had 47 master framesmiths to deal with the supply and repair of machines. In every growing town there was a proliferation of merchants, victuallers, grocers, and other tradesmen, numbers of whom accumulated enough surplus trading capital to invest and make profit out of the building boom of the late eighteenth century.[77]

These impressions of a significant improvement in living standards among sections of the lower and middling classes are supported both by statistical enquiries into the state of the economy and by the evidence about levels of income culled by social investigators at the time.

There is an acknowledged dearth of good statistics for British economic history in the eighteenth century. Nevertheless various historians have made attempts to quantify British economic advance; and while there may reasonably be doubts about the precision of their figures, at least the trends they reveal seem unmistakable.

[77] Chalklin, *The Provincial Towns of Georgian England*, pp. 41, 170–4, 182; and for the expansion of these classes in Essex see pp. 76–7 above.

It has been suggested, that while the percentage increase
per annum of the population was 0.7 between 1740 and
1780, and 1.0 between 1780 and 1800, the percentage
increases for 'real output' for these two periods were respec-
tively 1.0 and 2.0 and for 'real output' per head 0.3 and 1.0.
Between 1780 and 1800 output was expanding twice as fast
as population, and industrial output was expanding nearly
three times as fast as population.[78] In the textile industries,
particularly cotton, the scale of expansion was greater still.
The general effect, after 1780, as compared with previous
decades, was of a growing flood of consumer goods, coming
from the makers at progressively lower prices, while increasing amounts of earnings were generated for the men and
women who provided them. Although there is not full agreement over the question whether the diversion of part of the
national income into domestic investment damped down
consumer expenditure, the balance of the argument seems to
be in favour of the view that so small a proportion was
diverted in this way that, in substance, 'the rate of increase
of per capita consumption was nearly the same as that of
per capita income'.[79]

Had foreign markets taken the greater part of increased
British industrial production, less of this flood of goods
would have been available to raise the British standard of
living. Some past analyses of the British Industrial Revolution
have assumed that foreign demand was paramount in sustaining industrialization, and that home demand, and therefore
domestic spending power, was limited. More recent scholarship has tipped the balance the other way. One suggestion
now is that during the eighteenth century British exports
were not, by themselves, sufficient to account for more than
one-fifth of the increase in the economy as a whole, although
overseas markets were much more important for some sectors

[78] Phyllis Deane and W. A. Cole, *British Economic Growth, 1688–1959*
(Cambridge, 1964), p. 78, table 19; *The Economic History of Britain since 1700.*
Vol. i: *1700–1860*, ed. Roderick Floud and Donald McCloskey (Cambridge,
1981), p. 2, table 1.1. For a differently based calculation yielding similar results,
see ibid., p. 64, table 3.2, under the column 'total' at 1700 prices. 'Pessimistic'
estimates of consumer expenditure given by C. H. Feinstein (ibid., p. 136), do
not seem to square with these figures or with other evidence from various sources.
[79] Ibid., p. 172.

of the economy than for others. In particular, during the 1760s and 1770s, home consumption seems to have increased at a more rapid rate than exports. Once established the trend towards greater home consumption continued. Revenue records indicate that between 1785 and 1800 the rate of consumption of a range of excised commodities in mass demand, such as tobacco, soap, candles, printed fabrics, spirits, and beer, was increasing more than twice as fast as the population: far more people were enjoying more basic amenities.[80] Both gross home consumption and per capita home consumption were on the increase throughout the later eighteenth century, and by its very nature a great deal of this home consumption was widely spread, not simply confined to a small, increasingly wealthy minority located in the upper or the upper and middle classes. Such a conclusion is also buttressed by evidence both of the very considerable output of cheap cotton textiles which is not recorded in the export figures and therefore can only have been absorbed by the home market, and of the holdings of household goods by working people, disclosed in inventories made when they died or passed into the care of the parish authorities.[81]

Study of the macroscopic aspects of the early British Industrial Revolution also emphasizes another point relevant to this standard-of-living debate. By the third quarter of the eighteenth century the country was moving with increasing rapidity into a situation in which there was widespread investment in a series of interrelated fields essential to the underpinning of large-scale industrial growth. These sectors included a transport network, factory construction, machinery, and sources of power, leading in turn to an

[80] Ralph Davis, *The Industrial Revolution and British Overseas Trade* (Leicester, 1979), pp. 9–10, 63–5; *Economic History of Britain since 1700*, ed. Floud and McCloskey, i. 39–40; D. E. C. Eversley, 'The Home Market and Economic Growth', in E. L. Jones and G. E. Mingay, ed., *Land, Labour and Population in the Industrial Revolution. Essays presented to J. D. Chambers* (1967), p. 221; M. W. Flinn, *Origins of the Industrial Revolution* (1969), chapter IV; P. Mathias, 'Leisure and Wages in theory and practice', in his *The Transformation of England* (1979), p. 162.

[81] Eversley, 'The Home Market and Economic Growth', p. 224; McKendrick, in *Historical Perspectives*, pp. 190–2, and in *The Birth of a Consumer Society*, p. 26. For the suggestion that falling transport costs helped to put more purchasing power in the pockets of farmers as well as consumers see E. L. Jones, *Agriculture and the Industrial Revolution* (Oxford, 1974), p. 113.

engineering industry to supply the machines, extraction of sources of energy to supply the power, and a considerable construction industry to build the factories in which people would work, the houses in which they would m ke their homes, and such elements as locks, weirs, viaducts, and bridges of the transport system which carried their materials and their products. Each of these developments required a critical minimum level of investment to be economically viable and was also dependent on the others for success.[82] All of these sectors involved skilled labour forces for which there was a strong and expanding demand, and this last condition made for high wage levels. Later on, in the nineteenth century, engineers and construction workers were among the working class élites, relatively successful both in the development of trade-union organization and in the maintenance of their living standards. There is no reason to doubt—and at least some scattered evidence to confirm— that they also enjoyed an élitist position in the eighteenth century, that in these sectors of the economy, in the years before 1800, were to be found numbers of increasingly prosperous craftsmen, who found the existing world a place of promise and felt no urge to mould it nearer to the heart's desire.[83]

Finally, there is the evidence concerning the general pattern of incomes. About 1760 the pamphleteer Joseph Massie produced a polemic against the monopoly of the West India sugar planters, in which he gave figures for income and taxation over the whole spectrum of the population for the year 1759–60, which were based on categories similar to though somewhat more elaborate than those used by Gregory King for the 1680s. These figures can be recalculated to give data of numbers of families and levels of average income in a series of socio-economic brackets similar

[82] W. A. Cole, 'Factors in Demand, 1700–80', in *Economic History of Britain since 1700*, ed. Floud and McCloskey, i. 37.

[83] C. W. Chalkin, for instance, quotes rates for carpenters and bricklayers in the north-west industrial area in the 1790s which were well over the rates for general labourers, though in other regions rates were less favourable (*The Provincial Towns of Georgian England*, p. 221). On the London carpenters see E. P. Thompson, *The Making of the English Working Class*, p. 238, and on Essex millwrights p. 82 above.

in style though not precisely corresponding with those of King and with those produced by Patrick Colquhoun for about 1803.[84]

None of these figures in Massie's or Colquhoun's writings can be treated as precise. They are merely rough estimates and approximations. But taken together they are amply sufficient to support the general view that a very significant proportion of the population was gaining in financial status between 1760 and 1800.

In 1760 a family which had only £50 a year or less to live on was not far above the borderline of poverty. If Massie's families are divided into two categories, those with incomes of over £50 per annum and those with incomes of £50 or less, the totals in very round figures are 200,000 and 1,200,000, a ratio of 1:6.[85] Analysis of Colquhoun's data for families on the same basis (again in round figures) produces a remarkably different pattern: 1,200,000 families with incomes in groups in the range over £50 p.a., 800,000 families with incomes of £50 or less—a ratio of 3:2.[86] Now admittedly, a straight comparison on this basis cannot be made. By 1803 the purchasing power of the pound sterling was no longer what it had been forty years before. There had since been a degree of inflation. Also grain prices (ignoring the excessive effects of occasional bad harvests) were running at about 30 per cent higher than in the early 1760s. But if we make what is almost certainly an over-generous allowance for this, and redistribute Colquhoun's categories of families on either side of the

[84] Peter Mathias, *The Transformation of England: Essays in the Economic and Social History of England in the eighteenth century* (1979), pp. 171–89. Mathias's arrangement of Massie's data is at pp. 186–7. His method of deriving them is explained at pp. 175–6.

[85] The German pastor Frederick Augustus Wendeborn, who lived and worked in London during the 1770s and 1780s, put on record an estimate, based on different economic borderlines, of the situation in the 1780s. He considered that only two million people out of seven millions were above the 'poverty line' (a line probably represented by an income rather below £50 a year). Such an estimate fits fairly plausibly between Massie's and that derived from Colquhoun's figures (below). Francesca M. Wilson, *Strange Island. Britain through Foreign Eyes, 1395–1940* (1955), p. 68.

[86] Patrick Colquhoun's figures, published in his *Treatise on Indigence* (1806), have often been reproduced. They are conveniently presented in M. Dorothy George, *England in Transition: Life and Work in the eighteenth century* (1931), pp. 218–21.

annual income figure of £100, then the same trend is still clearly demonstrated. Approximately 550,000 families emerge with incomes of over £100. The number with incomes of £100 and downwards is 1,500,000. This gives a ratio of 1:3. In other words, if we regard £50 as the borderline of modest prosperity in 1760 and £100 as the similar borderline in 1803, then six families out of seven fell below it in 1760 but only three families out of four in 1803. The number of families of at least modest affluence and spending power had nearly trebled, and in just over forty years had grown from one in seven of the total number of families to one in four. If, as I suspect, the borderline figure of £100 is pitched too high—possibly the intermediate figure of £75 would be nearer the mark—then the number of families and the proportion of families on the favourable side of the line was even higher than these calculations suggest.

Such a change in the national income pattern over these forty years is significant in the first place insofar as economic demand is seen as a key factor in the development of the Industrial Revolution. It is a manifestation of the growth of a consumer society, a reflection of the capacity to buy, and by that same token an explanation of the ready availability of employment for working people and small entrepreneurs. It also has significance as a stabilizing circumstance in society, because quite clearly the opportunities for betterment were considerable, and men who can see this plainly are less likely to be successfully wooed by visionaries offering the panaceas of revolutionary Utopias. Moreover, the opportunities for betterment were even greater than the bare figures noted above would suggest. Blocks of statistical data conceal the dynamics of change in individual cases; we may confidently assume, on the basis of common experience, that at any one time in the last decade of the eighteenth century, a proportion of people who were at the early stages of the family life-cycle would be below the borderline but within a reasonable time would rise above it, and could from the outset look forward to making this progress with a fair degree of confidence. Such upward movement was noticeable in the higher as well as the lower echelons of industry. Men who began as supervisors and mill managers moved on to become partners or owners of their own businesses in due course, sometimes with the active help of their former employers.[87] Finding a satisfactory and rewarding fulfilment in their lives, they were not racked by the frustrations and disappointments which might fuse into a dangerous movement of social or political unrest. Undoubtedly the lower ranks of eighteenth-century society contained numbers of people who were unfortunate and economically depressed throughout their lives, but for a great many, and those the most restless and enterprising, such a fate was not seen as inevitable and did not therefore provide a driving force for revolutionary discontent.

Economic conditions thus provide a cogent explanation why, despite occasional fears and alarms, there was no danger of revolution in Britain in the 1790s. Men were too concerned with the fascinating business of getting and spending, and for every one who at any one time was enjoying the fruits of modest success, there were several more who had good if not always realized grounds to believe that a share of prosperity would be coming their way. Leaders of the French Revolutionary government, who anticipated a conflict, and who believed that a fifth column existed in Britain which could destroy a hostile British government and swing the country into the position of a revolutionary satellite, were to be rudely undeceived. They should have known better, for they were not without the best advice. In 1792 the French diplomat Talleyrand warned his principals at Paris not to misunderstand the country's mood and preoccupations:[88]

The mass of the nation . . . attached to its constitution by ancient prejudices, habit, comparison of its lot with other states, and prosperity, does not imagine anything would be gained from a revolution of which the history of England makes it fear the dangers. The country is solely occupied with questions of material prosperity.

[87] For one set of examples see S. D. Chapman, 'The Peels in the Early English Cotton Industry', *Business History*, xi. no. 2 (1969), p. 81. Cf. George Unwin, *Samuel Oldknow and the Arkwrights. The Industrial Revolution at Stockport and Marple* (Manchester, 1924), p. 126.

[88] *La Mission de Talleyrand à Londres en 1792*, ed. G. Pallain (Paris, 1889), p. 289, quoted in Christine Bewley, *Muir of Huntershill* (Oxford 1981), p. 27.

IV

Social Support: The Poor Law

I

From time to time historians have remarked on the probability that the poor-law institutions developed in Great
Britain played a significant part in preserving the country
from revolution, not least during the intense economic stress
of the Revolutionary and Napoleonic Wars.[1] That there is an
element of truth in this view can hardly be doubted. The
English Poor Law was part of a web of institutions that knit
together people of different degrees. The obligations it
affirmed gave at least some sense of security to the poorer
elements in the community and in most, though not all,
cases recognized their human dignity. Lesser clergy and rate-
paying parishioners of modest fortune were brought constantly into contact with the problems of those less fortunate
than themselves in the work of their parish meetings and
vestries. As justices of the peace members of the landed
class had statutory responsibilities for the running of the
Poor Law. These could and at times did merge with their
preoccupation with the more general question of law and
order; and especially from the 1780s it was a business which
consumed much time at quarter sessions and at other
meetings of justices. The almost automatic positive response
given within the Poor Law to problems of maintenance for
such relatively helpless groups as the widows and the very
elderly cannot but have averted tensions arising out of worry
and discontent about one's personal future, which might
otherwise have been generated, had such a safety-net not
existed.

The belief that the deprived and unfortunate deserve
support from the rest of the community to which they
belong has roots that go far back to the origins of civilized
society. In the Europe of the Middle Ages this social function

---

[1] For example, E. M. Hampson, *The Treatment of Poverty in Cambridgeshire,
1597–1834* (Cambridge, 1934), p. 272.

had become inextricably linked with the role of the Church, and in most western countries it still so remained at the end of the eighteenth century. The prevailing assumption was that the poor should rely on Christian charity, and the mobilization of this support was the responsibility of the clergy. In the Christian West the British people were almost unique in having evolved, during the generations after the Protestant Reformation, a Poor Law which, although bearing many traces of its ecclesiastical origins, rested firmly on secular authority.[2]

In England, where this development had proceeded furthest, these origins were still plainly visible in the survival of the parish as the typical unit of poor-law administration, and in the formal responsibilities borne by parish officers, the churchwardens and the poor-law overseers. In the local accounts poor-law moneys were not always clearly separated from other parish funds. Even in the more secularly minded eighteenth century, this interpenetration of the ecclesiastical and lay personnel in the handling of a crucial social question could be significant. An active, conscientious, and respected resident clergyman in a small country parish, chairing monthly parish or vestry meetings at which claims for relief were considered, could be influential and, it may be presumed, likely to oppose in the interests of the deprived rigorous economies which appealed to ratepayers.[3] But the interventions of the secular power were decisive. The obligations of the poor-law authorities were prescribed by statutes made by the legislature. Their conduct was subject to the jurisdiction of the courts, normally at the level of the justices of the peace, but with higher authority participating at need. The relief of the poor had become a legal duty required by the state, not simply a Christian obligation adjured by the Church.

At the core of the English Poor Law in operation in the late eighteenth century lay principles formulated in a series of Elizabethan statutes of 1563, 1572, and 1576, culminating

---

[2] G. W. Oxley, *Poor Relief in England and Wales, 1601–1834* (1974), is a valuable survey of the scholarship up to the early 1970s, with an excellent bibliography.

[3] This pattern seems to have been common in Devon at least (Arthur Warne, *Church and Society in eighteenth-century Devon*, Newton Abbot, 1969, pp. 154–5).

in the codifying measures of 1598 and 1601. These Acts stated unequivocally that the parish had three essential obligations: to provide adequate maintenance for the lame, blind, and aged and impotent, who were unable to work; to put to labour children whose parents were unable to maintain them; and to provide employment for the able-bodied who were unable to find work to maintain themselves. The expense was to fall on the whole local community in the form of a rate. Sixty years later, the problem of strangers entering a parish and demanding relief was met in 1662 by the Act of Settlement, tightened up by subsequent legislation, which permitted a parish to expel within forty days an immigrant who might be regarded as a future poor-law liability. Only those with a sufficient financial standing revealed by their renting a tenement at £10 a year or over were exempted from this provision. Men or women migrating to secure temporary or seasonal employment were to carry a certification of residence from their parish officers, which was, in effect, an undertaking to receive them back if they became dependent on public support.

The certificate of settlement became a widely used device, permitting a degree of mobility of labour which might otherwise have been cripplingly obstructed by apprehensive poor-law overseers.[4] However, by the late eighteenth century the system was breaking down. Considerable freedom of movement was being exercised with impunity.

While surviving concern about the law of settlement reflected a reluctance on the part of ratepayers and parish officers to tolerate any expense that could possibly be avoided, the spirit of the Poor Law was by no means negative. The positive sense of social responsibility which infused it rings out (as it does also in the preambles to items of legislation) in the legend inscribed over the door of the Rollesby House of Industry built in 1777:[5]

---

[4] For instance, the local historian of Cowden in Kent reported a 'large bundle' in his possession of churchwardens' acknowlegements of settlement from various parishes in respect of immigrants to Cowden, extending in date from 1692 to 1794 (Guy Ewing, *A History of Cowden, compiled from the records of the manors and the parish*, Tunbridge Wells, 1926, p. 172).

[5] Pamela Horn, *The Rural World, 1780–1850: Social Change in the English Countryside* (1980), p. 101.

For the Instruction of Youth
The Encouragement of Industry
The Relief of Want
The Support of Old Age
And the Comfort of Infirmity and Pain

Numbers of magisterial pronouncements show that those in authority took these commitments seriously. Thomas Butterworth Bailey, Chairman of Lancashire Quarter Sessions, declared in an address given in July 1793:

> There is no country in the world where the poor are so amply provided for as in this. An immense sum of money is annually raised for their support, and they are the peculiar objects of a very extensive and important branch of the law. So far are they from being left to the charity and benevolence of individuals, that the law is compulsory, upon all persons who are rated, to contribute to the relief of the poor, and the officers who distribute the poor rates are obliged upon application to afford every pauper such relief as his circumstances require.

In this same spirit his colleague on the bench, Michael Hughes, a leading copper manufacturer in the St. Helens district, went about his supervision of poor-law activities in his bailiwick. 'These are not times for trifling with the distresses of the poor', he wrote reprovingly to one overseer during a period of scarcity and high food prices. Finding one parish officer had awarded an old man 7*s.* to work on the highways, he issued an order for 9*s.* a week, describing the former wage as 'considerably less than his work deserves'. During the crisis of 1801 the overseers of the parish of Parr were ordered on more than one occasion to attend him at home at breakfast time in order to receive reproofs for not giving sufficient relief. In a letter to overseers of Overton in Cheshire, about relief for a certified resident out of work in the parish of Sutton, he wrote that, in sending to represent the man's case for relief, he felt he was 'performing one of the most important and essential duties of his office'; and in appealing to the feelings of men of humanity and consideration he stressed the need for liberality in the strongest terms: 'Humanity and good policy require it.' Apart from his public concern as a magistrate, his account books yield dozens of examples of small acts of private charity involving a few pounds or shillings to all sorts of people. The Cambridgeshire bench of justices likewise echoed this sense of responsibility in 1814, when they declared 'instruction for youth, employment for the healthy, comfort for the aged and infirm, reformation for the profligate' to be the guiding principles of the statutes of 1598 and 1601. The outstanding aims of the Elizabethan statutes, still seen as the main objects of the law at the end of the eighteenth century, were the prevention of poverty and the amelioration of its effects.[6] Of a piece with this general conception of the Poor Law was the fact that receipt of public relief was an accepted part of life for a large minority of the population, was regarded as a right, and carried little of the stigma later fixed upon it as a deliberate policy by the poor-law reformers of the nineteenth century.

In the approach to these social objectives, a change of emphasis seems to have occurred about the middle of the century—a change of significance for the period with which we are concerned. It has been traced in part to developments in thought about economic behaviour and human psychology, and the effect described as 'an increasing reliance . . . on the efficiency of incentives to labour, as opposed to deterrents to idleness'. In part it was fostered by the growth of humanitarian feeling. Thus, for example, the philanthropist Jonas Hanway campaigned successfully for a statute, passed in 1769, compelling parish authorities in the London area to send pauper infants in their care out into the country to be nursed, with greatly increased chances of survival as a result. The legislature, usually in favour of economies on behalf of the tax- or ratepayer, here supported the principle of greater generosity at public expense. Growing public concern appeared in the decisions of the House of Commons to set up committees of enquiry into the state of the poor in 1775–8 and again in 1783–5. Private concern is evident from the number of books and pamphlets dealing with the

---

[6] G. B. Hindle, *Provision for the Relief of the Poor in Manchester, 1754–1826* (Chetham Society: Manchester, 1975), p. 112; T. C. Barker and J. R. Harris, *A Merseyside Town in the Industrial Revolution. St. Helens, 1750–1900* (Liverpool, 1954), pp. 158, 165–6 (like so many of the new capitalists Hughes hardly fitted the stereotype projected by doctrinaire critics of modern capitalism); Hampson, *Poverty in Cambridgeshire*, pp. 261, 272.

subject: Sir Frederick Eden noted over a hundred published between 1775 and 1796.[7]

These shifts of opinion helped to mould the Poor Act of 1782, commonly known as Gilbert's Act. Its general purpose was to confer upon parish authorities by grant of permissive powers the option of pursuing humane practices which to some extent had already been adopted by local initiative under the more costly procedure of promoting local Acts. Parishes adopting the Gilbert Act might obtain greater facilities for making use of poorhouses which were clearly designated as refuges for those classes of paupers who could not look after themselves in their own homes. 'Deterrence' of able-bodied paupers by the 'workhouse test', common earlier in the century, was in effect abandoned. People who were in difficulties for lack of employment were to be guaranteed subsistence, with no limit to the period concerned, though the obligation to find work for them remained imperative. To some extent this new policy was a response to the hard fact well understood by commentators and by the authorities, that the workhouse was not a practicable institution for dealing with temporary large-scale unemployment caused by slumps or war.[8] The humanitarian concern of Thomas Gilbert, MP, the framer of the Act, was also apparent in two other of its provisions. One clause placed upon parishes adopting the Act the obligation to nurse non-settled sick paupers back to health before sending them back to their native parishes under the law of settlement, and they could not be moved until a JP had given his sanction. Another clause provided that non-settled pregnant women were not to be moved without an order by two JPs. Humanitarianism and economic theory seem equally to have entered into the shaping of two further Poor Acts of 1793 and 1795. Both gave additional protection against the untoward consequences of neglect (which was increasingly prevalent) to meet the requirements of the Settlement Acts by securing certificates of settlement. By the first of these Acts

[7] A. W. Coats, 'Economic Thought and Poor Law Policy in the eighteenth century', *Economic History Review*, 2nd ser. 13 (1961), 39–45; M. Dorothy George, *England in Transition* (1931), pp. 96–7; Sir Frederick Morton Eden, *The State of the Poor* (3 vols., 1797), iii. pp. ccclxxx–ccclxxxvi.

[8] Coats, 'Economic Thought and Poor Law Policy', pp. 48, 50.

unemployed men without certificates who were members of
friendly societies and had thus taken steps to guarantee themselves maintenance by some other method in time of need,
gained the right to remain undisturbed in districts other than
their parish of settlement, provided they did not actually
apply for relief.[9] This provision was made generally applicable
irrespective of membership of a friendly society by the Act
of 1795. This statute also contained a mandatory extension
of the principle regarding sickness in the permissive Act of
1782, by giving JPs powers to control and prevent the
execution of orders of removal in respect of sick persons.

Throughout the eighteenth century the framework of
English parish poor-law administration was subject to modi-
fication on a local *ad hoc* basis. The absurdities of parochial
handling of the matter in large towns had become apparent
before the end of the seventeenth century. The pioneering
move of the people of Bristol to secure a local Act in 1696
setting up a unified Corporation of the Poor for the whole
city soon found emulators elsewhere. Tiverton, Exeter,
Hereford, Colchester, Kingston, and Shaftesbury obtained
similar Acts during the next two years, and King's Lynn,
Sudbury, Plymouth, Gloucester, Worcester, and Norwich
soon followed their example. In such towns the resources of
rich parishes were thus pooled together with those of poor
parishes which otherwise would have faced an impossibly
crippling burden.[10] Such a pooling of resources was rarely
seen as desirable in rural areas, but sharing workhouse facilities was possible under a statute of 1722, or could be set up
by private inter-parochial arrangement, or by means of a
local Act. One object of the Poor Act of 1782 was to facilitate
the establishment of such unions, to permit co-operative and
more economical use of poorhouse accommodation; but
outside East Anglia and parts of the northern industrial
belt the formation of unions had made little progress up to
the end of the eighteenth century.

[9] In particular this measure sanctioned the informal practice which had
developed wherever factory owners had promoted benefit clubs for their employees or otherwise undertaken to support them in times of adversity, thus in
practice absolving the parish of responsibility. See pp. 122, n. 55, and 126.

[10] *Bristol Corporation of the Poor: Selected Records, 1696–1834*, ed. E. E.
Butcher (Bristol Record Society, 1932), p. 2.

Poor-law authorities engaged in the administration of relief in one or other of two ways—by grants of assistance to families remaining in their homes ('outdoor relief') or by provision of board and accommodation, linked or not, as might be appropriate, with an obligation to work: such provision might be directly administered by the authority or else placed in the hands of a contractor.

The name 'workhouse' implies that this was a place in which work was to be performed, but this idea was honoured as much in the breach as the observance. The belief that craftsmen who could not find work in the open market could be provided with it in a local institution was fatally flawed by the circumstance that often no market for goods so made would be found. Apart from this, the provision of raw materials and the arrangements for marketing often involved a degree of organization and expense which proved to be simply not worth while. A return might indeed be obtained from some of the inmates. Cultivation of the workhouse garden helped to provide food. The deserted or unmarried mother might be admitted with her children on the condition that she acted as unpaid nurse and domestic servant to the sick and elderly who were beyond such chores. Where there was an industrial outlet, as for instance at Norwich, the woman and her offspring might be employed in the spinning of wool or flax, the price obtained for the yarn making some contribution to their upkeep. The demands of the navy made it possible to keep inmates busy picking oakum in the poorhouses in the Hampshire port towns. Pauper children at Bristol were employed by local pinmakers. One Suffolk union found a market for ropes and sacking made by men and boys in a house of industry: overall, in this establishment, industrial earnings met about one-third of total expenditure, the rest coming from the various parishes' poor-rate contributions. But it was the general experience that such expedients merely made a partial contribution to the upkeep of what were in the main houses of refuge rather than houses of industry.[11] Usually

[11] For some examples of the earning of partial maintenance in these various ways, see Eden, *The State of the Poor*, ii. 219, 225, 227 (on the Hampshire towns); Hugh Fearn, 'The Financing of the Poor Law Incorporation for the

the greater proportion of the inmates were incapable of making much contribution by their labour, being aged, or sick, or otherwise incapacitated, or children from whom relatively little could be expected. In other words the poorhouse had taken on something of the role of a geriatric hospital, something of that of an orphan asylum, a development that was encouraged by Gilbert's Act.[12]

Partly perhaps because a significant proportion of the inmates of poorhouses were short-term residents near the end of their lives, the scale of support for paupers in this way was surprisingly small. One cannot claim, on the basis of such figures as are available, that these establishments made any massive contribution to the relief of pauperism. The residents in the Corporation House of Bristol, a city of over 60,000 inhabitants, seem to have fluctuated between three and four hundred during the 1780s and 1790s. The house maintained by the Town Trustees of Sheffield (*c*.40,000 inhabitants) had 156 residents in 1786. Liverpool (*c*.95,000 population) was housing around 1,200 paupers in 1794, less than a third of whom were in the age-range 20–60. The new poorhouse opened at Manchester in 1792 to deal with the paupers in a population much the same as that of Liverpool seems to have accommodated between 300 and 400 during the 1790s. About the same time Exeter was housing about 250. At Hull, visited by Arthur Young just after the food crisis of 1795–6, only about 350 people were maintained in the 'Charity House', while some 2,600—a tenth of the population—were in receipt of outdoor relief.[13] From the

Hundreds of Colness and Carlford in the County of Suffolk, 1758-1820', *Proceedings of the Suffolk Institute of Archaeology*, vol. 27 (1950), 96-102; Barker and Harris, *A Merseyside Town . . . St. Helens*, pp. 135-6; G. W. Oxley, 'The Permanent Poor in South-West Lancashire under the Old Poor Law', in *Liverpool and Merseyside*, ed. J. R. Harris (1969), pp. 38-9; Sir J. W. F. Hill, *Georgian Lincoln* (Cambridge, 1966), p. 184; *Bristol Corporation of the Poor*, ed. Butcher, pp. 112-14, 119-20, 126-7, 127-8, 129-32; A. F. J. Brown, *Essex at Work*, pp. 2, 144, 146, 149. On the conception and downfall of the ambitious project of a House of Industry at Forden in Montgomeryshire, see A. H. Dodd, *The Industrial Revolution in North Wales*, pp. 389-91.

[12] In about half the accounts of workhouses or poorhouses in the parish reports gathered by Sir Frederick Eden, the inmates are described as being prinicipally or wholly in these categories, and it seems likely that the same point was simply omitted in other cases (*The State of the Poor*, vols. ii and iii, *passim*).

[13] *Bristol Corporation of the Poor*, ed. Butcher, p. 12; R. E. Leader, *Sheffield*

data unearthed by the parliamentary enquiry of 1802–3 it has been calculated that at the time about 83,000 paupers were being maintained in pauper premises in England and Wales; but only two counties had more than 2,000 indoor paupers, and seven had fewer than 500.[14]

It is difficult to generalize with certainty about conditions in these establishments. The reports put together by Sir Frederick Eden indicate a wide range, from the clean and well-run to the badly managed, squalid, and verminous. The Manchester poorhouse was the subject of an appalling scandal in the 1790s. Large-scale peculation of food supplies caused undernourishment and this together with general neglect of the inmates resulted in an excessive death-rate. In this case at least the mismanagement was uncovered after a year or two, but the exercise of control by the Manchester authorities was evidently defective for such fearful conditions to be inflicted on the residents for even that length of time. Experience in other towns showed that supervision could be effective. For instance, the Bristol Corporation of the Poor seems to have had a systematic and efficient system. The Guardians of the Poor established a committee of visitors, who took it in turns to attend at the house. Inspection took place on five days a week (Fridays and Sundays being excepted). This appears to have guaranteed that inmates were not subjected to privation as a result of maladministration, though it did not wholly check peculation in the form of over-purchase of foodstuffs and disposal of the surplus for private gain.[15]

Historians from the Webbs onwards agree that in general food allowances in workhouses and poorhouses seem to have been generous. Manchester reformers compared their diets in the 1780s favourably with those of the house of industry

in the eighteenth century (Sheffield, 1901), pp. 3–4; G. Chandler, *Liverpool* (1957), p. 396; Hindle, *Poor in Manchester*, pp. 31, 44; W. G. Hoskins, *Industry, Trade and People in Exeter, 1688–1800* (Manchester, 1935), p. 146; *Travels in England and Wales by Arthur Young selected from the Annals of Agriculture* (1932), pp. 180–1, 190.

[14] J. R. Poynter, *Society and Pauperism: English ideas on poor relief, 1795–1834* (1969), pp. 187–9.

[15] Hindle, *Poor in Manchester*, pp. 47–9; *Bristol Corporation of the Poor*, ed. Butcher, p. 21.

at Shrewsbury, a place which had a reputation for being particularly well-run. The diet in the Bristol poorhouse was the object of repeated favourable comment throughout the century, and Guardians periodically declared that it was far better than the average labourer's family could afford. During the month of June 1765 the house of care in the Devon parish of West Alvington fed its twenty-one inmates with a total of 176 lb. of beef and mutton (about ¼lb. per head per diem), a 28lb. conger eel, a 60 gallon hogshead of cider, 2 quarts of wine, 2 quarts of brandy (whether smuggled or not is not stated), and one quart of gin, apart from the routine bread and vegetables. The workhouse diet prescribed at Lincoln under by-laws of 1797 provided for a meat meal every day (a scale more generous than that fixed after 1834).[16] Only a very extensive survey of poorhouse dietaries would permit reliable generalizations to be made, but it appears that it would be wrong to regard the inmates as usually badly treated in this respect.

From Eden's reports, and other information, there appears to be more ground for criticizing these institutions for over-crowding, dirtiness, and general discomfort. But conditions of overcrowding that seem horrific in the twentieth century were often not far removed from what the people of the eighteenth century were accustomed to in their own homes. Some authorities made deliberate efforts to cope with these problems as well as they could by contemporary standards. At Liverpool, for instance, in the 1790s, elderly women, a considerable and 'deserving' section of the pauper inmates, were accommodated in groups of eight to ten in apartments consisting each of three small rooms, in which were a fire-place and three or four beds, and they were able to retain in their possession beds and other personal items of furniture, which gave an element of homeliness to their lives.[17]

In 1802-3, according to the returns of information to Parliament, over 90 per cent of those dependent on the Poor Law were receiving help in the form of outdoor relief,

[16] Sidney and Beatrice Webb, *History of the English Poor Law*, Part I, p. 247; *Bristol Corporation of the Poor*, ed. Butcher, pp. 15-16; Hindle, *Poor in Man-chester*, p. 48; Warne, *Church and Society in eighteenth-century Devon*, pp. 158-9; Hill, *Georgian Lincoln*, p. 186; Brown, *Essex at Work*, pp. 150, 153.

[17] Oxley, 'The Permanent Poor in South-West Lancashire', p. 37.

and a limited amount of data on particular centres seems to indicate that this proportion was fairly typical for the 1790s.[18] The predominance of outdoor relief had a number of explanations, but undoubtedly the most compelling reason for it was its cheapness. Resident paupers seem to have cost anything between twice and four times as much to maintain. Spasmodically throughout the eighteenth century those responsible for poor relief showed an interest in setting up 'workhouses', either as a means to provide work and secure some financial return to set against their outlay, or else to fend off the importunities of those who sought relief because they preferred—or were thought to prefer—idleness to work. Increasingly as the century wore on, it became evident that when the able-bodied ran into problems of finding employment, the trouble was usually temporary, caused by a trade recession or the interruption of traffic by war. It was recognized that in these circumstances breaking up a home by taking its members into a workhouse was obviously not the way to keep the family of a wage-earner afloat. And for those who were elderly but not necessarily incapable of part-time work, assistance to maintain themselves at home was a more practical as well as more humane method of support, and was also cheaper.

Much of the outdoor relief provided was in payments which were pensions allotted for one reason or another. Almost every authority had its regular pension list, and elderly people and widows formed a significant proportion of the pensioners. In such cases there was a clear sense of entitlement on the part of recipients and officers alike. G. W. Oxley's examination of records in parishes of South-West Lancashire in the early nineteenth century indicates that the claims of widows, the elderly, and the infirm appear to have been readily recognized, and the authorities did not refuse relief until such time as people like these were falling into extremes of poverty. Judging by Cambridgeshire practice, in many instances pensions were merely intended to supplement insufficient wages received by widows, children, and the elderly and infirm who still did some part-time work. But provision was often more generous. A French visitor to

[18] Poynter, *Society and Pauperism*, p. 189.

Suffolk in 1784 was astonished at the extent of the assistance given to the aged, which, he commented rather intemperately, 'is so excessive that, once given, the recipients have no further need to work and from poverty they pass to ease and idleness'.[19]

Such pensions were usually given in small money payments, but there were some categories of the poor for whom support was given in other ways. A pauper at East Bridgford in Nottinghamshire received complete maintenance, including fuel, clothes, mending, and laundering, for a period of over ten years. At Cadleigh in Devon one individual who was a child at the time of his father's death in 1763 continued to be fed, clothed, and sustained by the parish until he died in 1795. These instances suggest cases of congenital physical or mental handicap.[20] Parish officers frequently made clothes available for children, and a boy or girl sent off to apprenticeship at parish expense was customarily kitted out with a new wardrobe. Then there was a range of subventions which may have been made either to the elderly or to able-bodied people temporarily in need of support. The parish would pay the rent, would supply fuel, or provide necessary household items.[21] At Cowden in Kent (and the practice was probably not singular to that place) the poor-law officers seem to have customarily provided a money allowance or meal to enable poor parishioners to fatten their pigs, the eventual sale of which would contribute to their own upkeep.[22] Considerable help was given with medical advice and treatment. Bills for medical attendance and physic appear frequently in poor-law overseers' accounts, and could sometimes amount to considerable sums. At Cowden in 1759 the overseers paid

[19] Oxley, 'The Permanent Poor in South-West Lancashire', p. 27; Brown, *Essex at Work*, p. 144; Hampson, *Poverty in Cambridgeshire*, pp. 269–70; Rochefoucauld, *A Frenchman in England, 1784*, p. 27.

[20] J. D. Chambers, *Nottinghamshire in the eighteenth century. A Study of Life and Labour under the Squirearchy* (1932), pp. 223–4; Warne, *Church and Society in eighteenth-century Devon*, p. 156.

[21] In Montgomeryshire, by the 1770s, a tenth of poor-law expenditure was on rents (Dodd, *Industrial Revolution in North Wales*, p. 391). At Oswestry, in West Shropshire, in 1788, a widow, Mary Francis, not only received a grant of three years' rent and a pension allowance, but was given 1s. to have her garden hedged, 3s. for seed potatoes to sow in it, and £1 for straw to thatch her cottage (Roy Porter, *English Society in the eighteenth century*, 1982, pp. 143–4).

[22] Ewing, *History of Cowden*, p. 189.

£1 0s. 6d. for attendance for the period of a month on a woman who had become insane, and who required two and sometimes three attendants to watch over her at night. During the terminal illness of one housewife in Butlers Marston, Warwickshire, in 1775, the family was subsidized over some weeks to the extent of over £18, disbursed on shoes, clothing, food, nursing, and invalid diet; and at the end £1 was paid for the funeral. The last days of an old man at Great Bentley, Essex, were eased with a generous diet of wine, veal, and 'ample' beer, and extra spending allowance, and attendance by a nurse and physician. When practicable, parish authorities sometimes joined in the lists of subscribers to local hospitals or dispensaries, and so secured the right to send their sick paupers for treatment.[23]

However careful of their finances, parish officers seem not to have stinted over the last rites for their charges, and the records usually show an appreciable lay-out of money in food and drink—especially drink—on the occasions of funerals for which they were responsible. The poor records of one Lancashire parish show that 'funerals were supplied with plenty of beer, mourners were summoned even from some distance, a seemingly expensive coffin was provided, the church bell was tolled, and indeed, apart from the sermon, the pauper was seen out of this world with as much ceremony as some of his wealthier fellows'. Poverty or not, human dignity was preserved, and the sense of human social status maintained.[24]

While the intimacies of life in small rural parishes gave the authorities a head start in dealing with bogus claims for relief, they could occasionally be caught napping. The following example, though it comes from slightly before the middle of the century, probably could be paralleled elsewhere during its close. Joan Wickenden, who died in the parish of Cowden in 1741, after having been relieved by the parish practically

[23] Ibid., p. 181; Ursula R. Q. Henriques, *Before the Welfare State. Social Administration in early industrial Britain* (1979), p. 12; Brown, *Essex at Work*, pp. 144–5. Liverpool Parish Vestry, for instance, made the substantial annual subscription of £105 to the Liverpool Dispensary (F. Vigier, *Change and Apathy: Liverpool and Manchester during the Industrial Revolution*, Cambridge, Mass., 1970, p. 59).

[24] Barker and Harris, *A Merseyside Town . . . St. Helens*, p. 141.

all her life, was saved the ignominy of a pauper burial by the discovery that she had somehow been possessed of a nest-egg of £250—no mean feat for one who had been receiving for years an allowance-in-aid of 4s. a month. At any rate, the parish had the last laugh in this case, for as a pauper her possessions became parish property; and a substantial restoration of the church took place in 1742.[25]

A particular thorn in the flesh of the poor-law officers was the female barque of frailty who periodically presented herself requiring assistance with the birth of an infant for whose maintenance, in the absence of an acknowledged father, the parish would have to assume responsibility. If a father was known and living in another parish, the officials of the parish where the child was born still had no hope of freeing their ratepayers from financial liability unless, by threats of punishment in the local House of Correction, the parents could be coerced into marrying. The overseer of Royston in Hertfordshire learned this lesson the hard way in the 1790s, when he persuaded a happy-go-lucky parishioner named Sarah Gear to join her lover at Waltham when her *second* child by him was arriving, the parish undertaking to re-clothe her and pay her travel expenses. No marriage took place and two years later, deserted at Waltham by the father, Sarah was sent back to her parish of settlement with her second unwanted offspring. For four or five years she continued to be a charge on Royston poor funds, until at last a young man from outside the parish became entrapped by her charms and then pressured into becoming lawful father of her third. Although he subsequently deserted her—we may imagine, probably not without cause—his home parish now had responsibility, and Royston was able at last to wash its hands of Sarah Gear.[26]

Overseers found themselves involved in much tedious labour and the parish in much expense with cases of this kind, and the atmosphere of such shot-gun weddings must have left much to be desired. Parson Woodforde recorded one occasion in his diary when the officers of the parish, having got their man, and determined he should not escape them,

[25] Ewing, *History of Cowden*, p. 183.
[26] Hampson, *Poverty in Cambridgeshire*, pp. 173-4.

delivered him at the church in handcuffs.[27] The parish officers of Bradford in Devon were not so fortunate in the affair of the local *femme fatale*, Ardilla Bassett. They never caught up with the young men who, through Miss Dilly, presented their ratepayers with three additional young charges between 1746 and 1750. They were sufficiently annoyed at the third lying-in to commit her to the local Bridewell for a lengthy spell of correction, but they fitted her up first with a new cap and gown; and when she returned from durance in 1752, they gave her a new start with clothes and bedclothes and thereafter periodically supported her with food, fuel, and items of raiment, up till the overseer's final entry of payment for a pint of gin for her funeral.[28] Aggravating as these cases might be to ratepayers, the point is that they were treated with a considerable degree of tolerance and forbearance, the illegitimate children deserted by their parents were taken into care by the parish, and patience was often shown towards the feckless over a period of many years.

The care of pauper children entailed its own peculiar range of responsibilities. These included boys and girls whose fathers, though in employment, could not earn enough to maintain them, as well as orphans who ended up in the workhouse. The parish authorities had three main duties, which were not always well performed: to educate the children; to get employment for them; and to have them apprenticed. The general impression is that education was largely neglected, though some exceptional parish authorities did give serious attention to it. Attempts were made to find work children might do, either in their homes or in the workhouse. Bristol Corporation of the Poor, for instance, was periodically in touch with pin manufacturers in the town, who were willing to use child labour, although this was a hazardous employment in which injuries were common. The arrangement of apprenticeships in the locality tended to be unsatisfactory, since parish or corporation authorities were unwilling to pay the higher premiums demanded by more skilled

[27] Entry for 22 Nov. 1769, cited in M. Dorothy George, *England in Transition*, p. 139.

[28] Warne, *Church and Society in eighteenth-century Devon*, pp. 157–8.

and respectable craftsmen; but some of them—and again the Bristol Poor Corporation is an example—were conscientious about the welfare of their pauper apprentices and were prepared to invoke the law in order to protect them against cruel and unscrupulous employers.[29]

With the multiplication of spinning-mills towards the end of the century, a new problem was posed by the demands from Northern and Midlands industrialists for large amounts of child labour in 'apprentice' form. Distance made protection of such apprentices by the guardian body virtually impossible, and thus placed a responsibility on employers and local authorities at the receiving end, which was often dishonoured. The pauper industrial apprentices of the 1790s and afterwards are generally regarded as among the worst victims of the Industrial Revolution. There is no doubt that sometimes this was the case; but there is also some evidence at least that some of the employers who entered into arrangements with poor-law officers for the supply of child apprentices often accepted and honoured obligations towards the young people concerned. Some of the charges against mill owners seem to have been scurrilous. Samuel Oldknow at Mellor, the Gregs at Styal, for instance, both had a reputation for housing and feeding their apprentices well, seeing that they got some education, and generally treating them with kindness, and other cases can be adduced. One former Lancashire mill girl apprentice later declared that, 'if ever there was a heaven upon earth, it was that Apprentice House where we were brought up in such ignorance of evil'.[30] Manchester magistrates in the 1780s agreed that they would not sanction the indentures of parish apprentices to cotton-mills where they were to be worked over ten hours a day, and their example was followed by numbers of other North-Country JPs. There is evidence also, that some authorities at the supplying end took their responsibilities for the welfare

[29] *Bristol Corporation of the Poor*, ed. Butcher, pp. 7, 21, 112, 119-20, 133; cf. Chandler, *Liverpool*, p. 396, for action there in defence of apprentices.

[30] S. D. Chapman, *The Early Factory Masters. The Transition to the Factory System in the Midlands Textile Industry* (Newton Abbot, 1967), pp. 174-8, 195-209; M. Dorothy George, *England in Transition*, pp. 188-9; George Unwin, *Samuel Oldknow and the Arkwrights. The Industrial Revolution at Stockport and Mellor* (Manchester, 1924) pp. 173-5.

of such industrial apprentices seriously. The vestry at Chelmsford, Essex, having heard disturbing reports about some local children sent into apprenticeship near Manchester, spent the substantial sum of £14 on an investigation and was satisfied only when it had received a favourable first-hand account of their situation. When the Essex parish of Bocking sought industrial apprenticeships in the North for ten of its juveniles, it required detailed testimonials from prospective masters.[31]

What help was the Poor Law to the able-bodied men, to the family bread-winners?

Relief of the able-bodied tended to be a local rather than an overall national problem, one more acute in rural than in industrial and urban areas. For instance, in the coal-mining and iron-working region of eastern Shropshire, the good wages and high level of employment meant that the able-bodied rarely sought any help from the parish, and the overseers found themselves concerned almost exclusively with the sick and injured, the orphans, and the aged. In Broseley, the poor-rate was actually reduced by half between 1770 and 1793, contrary to the national trend. Generally speaking some such pattern held good during the late eighteenth century throughout the industrial areas of the North and Midlands. Travellers in these parts were struck by the absence of beggars, an agreeable contrast with the London area and other parts of the South. Sometimes a local socio-economic pattern caused the problem of poverty to be little felt: the chronicler of Sheffield has suggested that indigence there was kept to a minimum owing to the very tight control of admission into the cutlery trade imposed by the Cutler's Company. Often in such areas the help the able-bodied required was temporary and due to aberrant circumstances: for instance, according to one estimate, stoppage of trade caused by the American War had by 1781 reduced 'not less than 10,000 of the poorer classes' of Liverpool to dependence on the parish or on charitable donations.[32]

A good deal of the help given in areas where some industrial

[31] Vigier, *Change and Apathy*, p. 32; Brown, *Essex at Work*, p. 146.

[32] B. Trinder, *The Industrial Revolution in Shropshire* (1973), p. 343 (relief of the unemployed did not become a serious problem here until the post-war slump after 1815); *The Torrington Diaries*, ii. 42; Leader, *Sheffield in the eighteenth century*, pp. 3–4; Barker and Harris, *Merseyside Town*, p. 50.

employment existed was intermittent, or of the 'one-off' variety intended to re-establish a man or woman as an independent earner. In the case of women the supply of a spinning-wheel was a typical expedient. Records for the North-East provide an example of a payment to a man to replace a dead cart pony. On occasion poor-law authorities seem to have branched out into the annuity business. The Bristol Corporation of the poor entered into such arrangements, though at least once it unwarily undertook what it deemed afterwards an unwisely generous bargain. More normal forms of help given at Bristol included the settling of a prisoner's debts, the establishment of a young man in business, the recovery of property sequestered from poor owners—all measures intended to prevent pauperism by setting the individual concerned back on his feet. Help was sometimes given with the payment of rents or of lodgers' bed and board. Ratepayers thus sometimes found themselves in the position of subsidizing the employers in the district: the rents went into the pockets of industrialists who owned the cottages concerned, which they had built in the first place in order to attract and house their labour force.[33]

The situation of the able-bodied worker was different in the southern agricultural counties, where the rates of labourers' wages tended to be closer to bare subsistence level, where alternative jobs were fewer, and where increasing numbers of men were being squeezed out of the ranks of small cultivators and squatters on the commons by the sweeping tide of enclosures.[34] In Cambridgeshire, even before the middle of the century, poor-law authorities were beginning to act on the assumption that customary wage-rates would never meet the living costs of very large families and, in such cases, were making grants in supplementation of earnings. In 1783 the magistrates of the county took

---

[33] N. McCord, *North East England*, p. 90; *Bristol Corporation of the Poor*, ed. Butcher, pp. 24–5; Barker and Harris, *Merseyside Town*, pp. 138, 144.

[34] This trend was the subject of a good deal of criticial comment by people concerned more with the social repercussions than with the urgency to improve agricultural production. John Byng, the later Viscount Torrington, animadverted against enclosures on a number of occasions in his travel journals, and the issue was forcibly stated by the Rev. David Davies, in his *The State of the Poor in Husbandry*, published in 1797.

steps to standardize the relief given to the unemployed throughout their divisions, and in 1785, in face of a deficient harvest, they took a step of an essentially similar nature with respect to the underpaid, by ruling that all wages in the county should be made up to a level of 6 shillings a week.[35] Even districts which did not adopt the permissive Gilbert Act of 1782 could deduce from its provisions that the legislature regarded this practice as entirely consonant with poorlaw principles.[36] From 1783 poor-law officials in Nottinghamshire were adopting the practice of letting out their ablebodied paupers to work by 'house-row' to the chief farmers, who paid only a sub-maintenance wage, the balance being made up out of the parish poor fund. In Sussex and the South-West, the rates were used to subsidize grain and potato purchases for the poor. During the early 1790s two or three other counties at least extended the practice of subsidizing wages to a subsistence level in accordance with various scales and criteria of need, which subsequently became known as the 'Speenhamland system'.[37] Whatever the drawbacks of this expedient, it had the virtue of cushioning a particularly vulnerable section of the community from the effects of sudden bread-price rises in times of dearth.

In one way wars may have reduced the charges on the Poor Law by creaming off some surplus manpower from the countryside (though men who enlisted as a way of escaping their extramarital entanglements often left their bastards on a parish not their own); but in others it brought additional burdens. The Bristol Corporation of the Poor found itself heavily committed in 1783 to shipping back to Ireland poverty-stricken men who had been discharged from returning regiments at the end of the American War of Independence. In the 1790s it faced another difficulty, with wives and camp-followers attached to regiments moved from Ireland coming over to England in the wake of the men. This was a problem fairly local to Bristol and of a temporary nature. More general was the responsibility that fell upon the

---

[35] Hampson, *Poverty in Cambridgeshire*, pp. 269–70.
[36] See p. 99 above.
[37] Chambers, *Nottinghamshire in the eighteenth century*, p. 243; Pamela Horn, *The Rural World*, p. 49.

Poor Law to support the wives and families of men called away from their employments on militia service, perhaps for months on end, and those of men pressed for the navy. In the 1790s especially, when the calls on manpower were heavy, it is not easy to conceive what would have been the lot of thousands of women and children if the safety-net of the parish poor-law organization had not been extended throughout the country; and any consideration of the mounting cost of the Poor Law during that decade needs to take into account this sometimes neglected aspect of its functions, which must have added considerably to its financial liabilities. Without it the grievances of husbands on behalf of their families would surely have been much greater than in fact they were.[38]

One of the aspects of the eighteenth-century Poor Law which has often given it a bad name was the enforcement of the law of settlement. Any textbook will produce the horror-story of the young woman heavy with child being hastily carted out of the parish, often with dire results to both.

While these cases did occur, at least before 1782, it has to be said that during the latter part of the century public opinion was steadily turning against such callous behaviour and the legislature began to place at least some limited curbs upon it. For the rest, after 1750 the law of settlement caused little difficulty to people who migrated in search of work and were then able to maintain themselves. Towns and industrial districts especially, where employment opportunities were good, made little fuss about the arrival of immigrants provided they presented certificates of settlement from their home parishes. At the worst they could then be sent home without question if they came on the parish, but this last resort was rarely adopted. In industrial areas the urgent need of employers for workmen made the overcoming of restrictions on migration by any means an urgent matter. Ratepayers in such areas were often entrepreneurs who knew they stood to gain far more than they were likely to lose, even if they

[38] *Bristol Corporation of the Poor*, ed. Butcher, pp. 120, 129. In September 1793 the poor-law overseers of Sunderland were expecting an increase of expenditure from £1,000 to £3,000 per annum in the next twelve months, as the dependents of impressed seamen fell to their charge (Clive Emsley, *British Society and the French Wars, 1793–1815* (1979), p. 40).

theoretically created a possible need for higher poor-rates. Sometimes compulsory insurance schemes were imposed by employers to help overcome this difficulty. In the Shropshire iron belt, as early as 1734, Richard Ford and Abraham Darby II agreed with their landlords, when renewing their lease of the Coalbrookdale works, that they would themselves be responsible for the upkeep in poverty of outsiders brought to work at the foundries. The scale of this responsibility later on can be seen from the fact that in the parish of Madeley in 1793 over 1,000 of the 3,677 inhabitants had settlements in other parishes. In the event, with the constant prosperity of the iron industry in the period up to the end of the great French wars, the need to meet such liabilities rarely arose.[39]

Various other data also indicate that restraints on movement under the law of settlement were very extensively avoided or evaded. One historian has remarked that 'up to a third of the population of some large towns . . . was known to be without a settlement there'. Whether immigrants had settlement certificates or not, action to remove them was rarely taken. Private charity or the support of friendly societies tided them over in time of need, or else the practice developed whereby the parish of settlement refunded sums paid out in relief by the overseer of the parish of residence. This latter common-sense arrangement ensured that an individual temporarily without work would nevertheless be able to remain in the district where his skills were likely once more to be soon in demand. Labourers seem to have ranged equally freely in rural districts, and farmers eager to keep good men connived at the neglect of the law. After 1793 wartime labour shortages doubtless helped to reconcile the authorities to this situation.[40]

The late eighteenth-century English Poor Law was open to abuse; it was sometimes inadequate; and it was sometimes callous in the treatment of individuals. The same could be

[39] Barker and Harris, *Merseyside Town*, pp. 145–7; Trinder, *Industrial Revolution in Shropshire*, p. 312. For employers' insurance schemes for their men, see p. 126.

[40] P. Corfield, *The Impact of English Towns 1700–1800* (Oxford, 1982), p. 100; Hill, *Georgian Lincoln*, p. 148; Oxley, *Poor Relief*, p. 41; Hampson, *Poverty in Cambridgeshire*, pp. 148–9, 268; Eden, *State of the Poor*, i. 298.

said after the reforms of 1834. Nevertheless, it provided a safety-net for the unfortunate, and the parsimony of rate-payers was often effectively checked by the pressure of conscientious parish clergy and the humanitarian impulses of enlightened justices. It seems probable that it contributed greatly to the degree of social peace in the country, and that without it the elements of instability would have been far more formidable. This conclusion is strongly reinforced by a brief consideration of the situation of the poor in Scotland, Ireland, and France.

II

The Scottish poor-law system to some extent developed similarly to that in England, and like the English rested upon the traditional parish organization.[41] The Scottish Acts of 1574 and 1579 almost exactly paralleled the English Act of 1572, though omitting the obligation to provide work for the able-bodied which was written into this and later codifying Elizabethan statutes. In Scotland relief was provided out of funds raised by fines and collections taken at church services, by fees charged for the use of hearses and mort-cloths at funerals, and to a small extent from charitable endowments. Such relief was controlled in rural parishes by the kirk sessions and in towns by the magistrates of the burgh. In practice there was less stress in Scotland on relief as a duty imposed by the secular authority, and more on its nature as a central social obligation of a Christian community: to this extent it resembled Continental rather than English patterns. Scottish statutes of 1663 and 1672 did create a poor-law

[41] For general outline see Sir George Nicholls, *A History of the Scottish Poor Law in connexion with the condition of the People* (1856). Contemporary comments include *The Correspondence of Jeremy Bentham*, vol. 3: *January 1781–October 1788*, ed. Ian R. Christie (1971), pp. 30–43; Rev. John McFarlan, *Inquiries Concerning the Poor* (1782); Rev. Robert Burns, *Historical Dissertation on the Law and Practice of Great Britain and particularly of Scotland with regard to the poor . . .* (2nd edn., enl., Glasgow, 1819). For later comment see Rosalind Mitchison, 'The Making of the Old Scottish Poor Law', *Past and Present*, 63 (1974), 58–93, and 'The Creation of the Disablement Rule in the Scottish Poor Law', in *The Search for Wealth and Stability. Essays in Economic and Social History presented to M. W. Flinn*, ed. T. C. Smout (1979), pp. 199–217; R. A. Cage, 'Debate. The Making of the Old Scottish Poor Law', *Past and Present*, 69 (1975), 113–18.

obligation to provide work for the unemployed and the vagrant population, using the resources of parish rates, but public resistance to the raising and spending of money in such ways had rendered the law largely inoperative. There was a deeply ingrained prejudice against giving public aid to the able-bodied, and some commentators declared outright (though they were not wholly correct) that such relief was not available.[42] The statutes had laid down an obligation to set up workhouses and houses of correction, but the refusal to raise funds caused these provisions to remain a dead letter.

Departure from legislative intention had also arisen during the century up to 1760, because the kirk sessions to some extent had lost control over poor-law administration to the heritors of the parishes. In the long run this development gave the whip hand to the ratepayers who were interested in economy. The legal provision that money might be raised by assessment if sufficient funds were not forthcoming in other ways was used as a pretext for depending solely on the alternatives, and even in face of the increasing difficulties up to the very end of the eighteenth century barely a hundred of the Scottish parishes had by then adopted the practice of raising a poor-rate.[43]

Within its limits the Scottish system in principle served the pauper much as the English did. Pensions were paid to the elderly and impotent; payments were made for the bedridden and insane; their rights were never in question, though the support given was far less generous than in England. Less regularly, the able-bodied were tided over difficulties with help on a minimal scale. As one contemporary observed, by comparison with English practice the poor 'were more frugally provided for', and it was this Spartan economy, together with a greater dependence on voluntary charity, which enabled most parishes to get by without collecting a rate.[44] As might be expected, it was in the big cities that

[42] *Bentham Correspondence*, vol. 3, p. 39.

[43] Nicholls, *Scottish Poor Law*, p. 106; Eden, *State of the Poor*, iii. ccxcvii.

[44] McFarlan, *Inquiries concerning the Poor*, pp. 160, 177. Since starvation produced irreversible physical and mental deterioration in numbers of the middle-aged, who then had to be supported as impotent, Scottish policy was more improvident than its champions would have allowed.

such economy was beginning to break down towards the end of the century. Poor-rates were being raised in parishes in both Glasgow and Edinburgh by the beginning of the 1780s, and during the harvest failure of 1799–1800 a number of parishes adopted this expedient. The kirk sessions of Duns, for example, followed the Speenhamland example and used parish funds to supplement wages, winning a case at law on the point when this practice was challenged in the courts.[45] There was a growing tendency in some districts to exclude support for the able-bodied altogether, but, contrary to some assertions, this had not become a general practice up to 1800.[46] However, insofar as it was adopted, it might well be argued that what saved the situation for Scotland was the relative freedom of job opportunity created by industrialization on both sides of the Border.

The situation of the poor in Ireland was far less favourable. During the formative decades of the English and Scottish systems, this country had still been in the throes of the conquests and plantations, and much of the legislation affecting the poor had been simply directed against vagabondage.[47] An Irish Act of 1635 provided for rate funds to build county houses of correction but did not authorize general rates to provide relief. This was still substantially the situation when the peculiarly pressing problems of the poor, first in Dublin (in 1703) and then in Cork (in 1735) were met by the creation of city corporations of the poor in charge of workhouses for employing and maintaining them. In both cases the Acts allotted very small resources of taxation to help with basic expenses. In Dublin this took the form of a local 3*d.* rate on houses, and the proceeds of the sale of licences for a specified number of hackney coaches and sedan-chairs. In Cork a duty was levied on coals and culme entering the port. In neither case did the funds go far to meet costs, and reliance was placed chiefly on charitable donations and on church collections. A further extension of these principles to the whole country followed in legislation of 1772, under

[45] McFarlan, op. cit., pp. 161–2; Mitchison, 'Making of the Old Scottish Poor Law', pp. 90–1.

[46] Mitchison, 'The Creation of the Disablement Rule'.

[47] Sir George Nicholls, *A History of the Irish Poor Law, in connection with the condition of the people* (1856), pp. 2–58.

which corporations of the poor were to be set up in every county and county of a city, with powers to receive donations and bequests and to hold property. These assets were to be used to finance the building of houses for the reception of the helpless poor and for keeping beggars and vagabonds under restraint. Rates to a maximum of £200 in a city or £400 in a county might be collected on annual assessments made by the grand juries. It was implicitly recognized that these would only meet a part of the cost of relief. Impotent poor were to be housed so far as funds would allow. Folk who were destitute but deserving were to receive badges permitting them to be licensed beggars; but begging without a licence was made a criminal offence. Only in the case of deserted children did Irish legislation in 1772 and 1774 specify that rates must be raised to provide such sums as were required to deal with the problem.

The system as reshaped in 1772 and 1774 remained theoretically in force until well into the nineteenth century. In practice, as a leading contemporary expert remarked, 'it does not appear to have been carried into effect except in a very few instances', and the Act of 1772 can be regarded as having been in general inoperative.[48] The provisions were totally inadequate. The reliance on voluntary donations for most of the funds needed ensured that they would fail financially. At the end of the eighteenth century the Dublin House of Industry was housing up to 4,000 destitute persons, which can have represented only a fraction of the very poor in a city with a population approaching 170,000. The foundling hospital attached to it seems to have been, at any rate up to 1796, a place where deserted infants were simply brought to die. Little effort was made to keep them alive. Between 1784 and 1796, out of 25,352 children recorded as received, over 17,000 died, either in the hospital or in the country places where they had been put out to nurse—a total which, even allowing for the high child mortality of the age, seems appalling.[49] The crucial weakness of the Irish system (like that of the French) was that no public provision of moneys adequate to deal with the problem of destitution was laid

[48] Nicholls, *Irish Poor Law*, p. 57.
[49] Constantia Maxwell, *Dublin under the Georges, 1714–1830* (1956), p. 160.

down in any enforceable public law. Save for the minorities sheltered in workhouses, relief was to come entirely from charity, much of it as a response to organized begging. Few among the many poor in Ireland could feel that those in charge of public affairs had any concern for their wretchedness or that any significant bond existed between them and the rest of the community. The safety-net provided by the Poor Law in England simply did not exist in Ireland. Its absence seems likely to have been one more negative factor in the general Irish situation tending towards a state of disorder and potential for rebellion in that kingdom.

There is a similar striking contrast in the situation of the poor between England and France in the period before the outbreak of the French Revolution.[50] Moreover, although the proportion of the population at risk in France may not have been so very different from that in Britain, economic conditions seem in some respects to have been more adverse. The French people faced a far steeper rise in grain prices relative to wages during the late eighteenth century, and the general deterioration of their condition was leading to a deceleration of the rate of population growth, associated with a rising death-rate, an appreciable increase in the numbers of destitute and of abandoned children, and a growth in rural criminality. Land shortage and indebtedness were depressing the lot of many of the peasantry. Epidemics appear to have been on the increase and to some extent at least were associated with starvation diet.

In the face of this deteriorating situation, no such safety-net sustained the French poor as was to be found in England, and to some extent in Scotland also. Modes of relief based entirely on a philosophy of Christian charity proved increasingly inadequate during the twenty or thirty years before 1789. Village charitable foundations were very limited. Over 60 per cent of the villages in every diocese——and in the Massif Central well over 90 per cent——had no such resources at all. Even where they existed these charities would make no appreciable dent on the surrounding poverty. The *hôpitaux générales* in the major towns provided a limited

---

[50] The following account is based on Olwen Hufton, *The Poor of eighteenth-century France* (Oxford, 1974).

extent of food and shelter for some of the aged, crippled, and orphaned members of the community, but their reliance on voluntary contributions put it out of their power to deal with more than a very small proportion of deserving cases, and only an individual nominated by a sponsor could get relief. The local *bureaux de charité*, which provided outdoor relief, again out of voluntary offerings, were similarly limited by lack of funds in their capacity to deal with the problems of poverty.[51] It has been calculated that in many areas of France, 'the total resources divided by the number of destitute would not have been sufficient in any one year to buy a single pound of bread for each hungry person'. In general the system made no provision for the aged and infirm who had no sponsor, or for the able-bodied poor who were not classed by the relief committee of a *bureau* as deserving of help.[52]

At a crisis the national government occasionally stepped in with aid, but the scale of this too was derisory in comparison with need. Funds allotted in connection with a crop failure in Brittany in 1785 provided perhaps one week's bread for some 2,000 destitute people in the district of Nantes. Government-sponsored workshops—the *ateliers-de-charité* —also had only a limited impact. At their peak in 1789 they were providing temporary work for about 31,000 men, women, and children, a scale of activity which could make little impression on a national problem of such magnitude.[53]

The dependence of the destitute on the charity of those who were capable of giving it depended in turn on the maintenance of prosperity and of a favourable balance between givers and recipients. As this balance gradually broke down under the strain of adverse economic circumstances, the solicitation of aid turned into blackmail and extortion, practised by beggars acting together in vagrant bands, and extended often to outright robbery which further sapped the resources of those initially capable of charity. The lack of any curb on the movement of people about the French countryside meant that an area where it was rumoured help might be available might be picked bare as by a swarm of

[51] Hufton, op. cit., pp. 132–67.   [52] Ibid., p. 176.
[53] Ibid., pp. 181–93.

locusts by an invasion of strangers. Crime, as an indispensable means of existence, became a way of life for large sections of the very poor in France.[54] Whatever the shortcomings of the English Poor Law it helped to ensure that no such situation developed in late eighteenth-century Britain. But it must be added that it was the relative prosperity of the British nation, and the increase of wealth through agricultural improvement and industrialization during the years from 1760 onwards, that enabled both the Poor Law and private philanthropy to rise to the occasion as they did.

In France charity was to bear the brunt of relief; any public provision was merely ancillary. In England it was the other way about. Public provision was the main support of the poor: charity played an ancillary role. This is not to say that philanthropy was relatively unimportant, for it must be recognized that the Poor Law had its limits of usefulness. Any serious food or unemployment crisis demanded heroic measures which were beyond its capacity. The data drawn together in Sir Frederick Morton Eden's investigation of the poor in the early 1790s are generally regarded as fairly reliable; and they reveal a salient circumstance about the bread crisis of 1795-6. In that year inflated poor-rates supplied about £5 million towards the relief of the poor, but charitable expenditure of various kinds provided at least £6 million——£6 million expended in a variety of useful ways, from the running of soup kitchens to the purchase of bulk supplies of foodstuffs, especially grains, and their distribution cheaply at subsidized prices.[55] Patrick Colquhoun noted a similar though not so large philanthropic effort in respect of the next major provision crisis in the years 1800-1. These surges of private support were of more than limited signficance.

<hr/>

[54] Hufton, op. cit., pp. 194 ff. Pages 219–317 are devoted to the discussion of crime as a means of self-preservation for the poor.

[55] Eden, *State of the Poor*, i. 465. Eden recorded his belief that the estimated figure of £6 million for charity was probably well below the correct figure. Manufacturers as well as landowners played their part in this work; and, indeed, the former might have particular obligation arising out of their responsibility for an influx of labour into parishes in defiance of the principles of the law of settlement. Thus for instance, in the industrial area of the East Shropshire coalfield landowners and entrepreneurs met at Ironbridge in 1795 and undertook to contribute funds for the purchase and distribution of foodstuffs at subsidized prices. Subscriptions from landowners, from iron companies, and from ironmasters,

In the first place, they took part of the burden off smaller ratepayers seriously squeezed by the increases of rates, whose financial position was not all that more secure than that of people who were falling back on public assistance. Eden noted that the flood of philanthropic aid often coincided with a situation in which little increase of poor-rate took place. Which of these associated phenomena was cause and which effect is by no means clear, but what is clear is that philanthropy met almost all the extra burden. Secondly, this philanthropy meant that the charge of supporting the poor in a crisis was passed to and shouldered by the wealthier members of the community, who were best able to bear it. In the third place, the whole performance in 1795-6 and again in 1800-1 was an impressive demonstration of the degree of social conscience and sense of responsibility among the propertied classes, and of their power of organization and willingness to step in at a time of crisis.

were of the order of one hundred guineas each. These donations were dwarfed into nothingness compared with the subscriptions raised in the same district the following year for the purchase of supplies of rice. This time two or three of the big firms contributed £1,500 or more each, and the leading entrepreneur, Richard Reynolds, gave £500 on his own account. Very similar efforts were made again in the autumn of 1800 (Trinder, *The Industrial Revolution in Shropshire*, pp. 380-1).

V

Defence of the Interests
of Working Men

I

The conflict and tension between employers and employees
—or between master and servant as the common phrase
went in the eighteenth century—long pre-dated the highly
industrialized society brought into being by the Industrial
Revolution. Till recently this circumstance has tended to be
obscured by the temptation for writers on social and
economic questions to see the nineteenth-century developments which followed modern industrialization as those of
absorbing importance for the present. The study of labour
organizations in the eighteenth century has only very
recently received attention in its own right.[1] And yet, as has
become clear from recent scholarship, such organizations
played a significant part in the lives of multitudes of craftsmen and artisans during the Hanoverian age.

On the face of it, societies of working men, trade combinations, trade unions, or what you will, are commonly associated
in our minds with stress and strife. It may appear paradoxical
that I propose to discuss them in the context of social
stability. Yet there is justification for this. In whatever ways
men combined, so as to attain some degree of security in
their lives, if, and so far as these activities were successful,
they took the sting out of human discontent and so contributed to social stability. They helped to achieve what was

[1] Of the two classic accounts, Sidney and Beatrice Webb, *The History of
Trade Unionism, 1661–1920* (1920), devoted about 70 pages out of over 700 to
the period up to 1800, Henry Pelling, *A History of British Trade Unionism*
(1963), a few opening pages only. Arthur Aspinall, *The Early English Trade
Unions: Documents from the Home Office Papers in the Public Record Office*
(1949), starts at 1792. The history of British trade combinations in the eighteenth
century has only begun to receive full treatment very recently, in R. C. Dobson,
Masters and Journeymen: a prehistory of Industrial Relations, 1717–1800 (1980),
and John Rule, *The Experience of Labour in eighteenth-century Industry* (1981).
See also the summary in John Stevenson, *Popular Disturbances in England,
1700–1870* (1979), chapter 6.

felt to be some sort of tolerable balance of interests between different sections of the community. Although workmen's organizations in the eighteenth century often encountered failure, nevertheless they also secured a sufficient degree of success to have these effects.

Broadly speaking, working men engaged in three different forms of mutual-help organization during that century—the friendly society, the trade union, and the co-operative. The scale of activity was inevitably small. It was based on the place of work, or on the district in which a number of men belonging to a particular craft were concentrated. But cooperation between one district and another frequently developed to an effective pitch, although nothing like national unions were as yet possible.

So far as yet appears from the evidence, before 1800 experiments with co-operatives were extremely limited and require only brief discussion. There are some traces of such activity among the textile workers of Lancashire. More clearly, co-operative associations appeared towards the very end of the century among the well-organized employees in the government dockyards. Evidence for Portsmouth is clear, something similar seems to have developed at Chatham, and it would be surprising if the idea was not also taken up in other government yards. In June 1796, faced with the aftermath of a year of bad harvests and high food prices, inhabitants of Portsea subscribed nearly £2,000 in order to establish a local fishery to supply themselves and the neighbouring towns with fish 'at moderate prices'. Dockyard employees at Portsmouth set up a 'United Society' for the purpose of erecting a windmill and building bread ovens, in order to supply themselves with flour and bread at a reasonable rate, independently of the local millers and bakers, who, as usual in these circumstances, were suspected of profiteering. This dockyard co-operative continued to function for the remainder of the war of 1793–1802, and by 1802 it had nearly 900 members.[2] Doubtless detailed investigation at

[2] Duncan Bythell, *The Handloom Weavers. A Study in the English Cotton Industry during the Industrial Revolution* (Cambridge, 1969), p. 182; Alasdair Geddes, *Portsmouth during the Great French Wars, 1770–1800* (Portsmouth, 1970), p. 20.

local level would turn up other examples, but it seems clear that co-operative activity did not at this time ease social relations on any significant scale.

No such dismissal is possible of the friendly societies, varieties of which flourished throughout the century.

At one extreme some of these organizations came near to being compulsory insurance schemes run by major employers, to cover their workers in cases of illness, unemployment, and old age. This was one means whereby industrialists could overcome the problem of the poor-law rules of settlement. It was a material point that, if the people they wished to attract as a labour force were to become settled in the parishes where their enterprises were located, there should be no question of their becoming a charge on the poor-rates: otherwise such an immigration would have been repelled by the poor-law authorities. The earliest known scheme of this kind was launched by Matthew Boulton for the employees of his Soho manufactory some time in the 1770s or early 1780s and subsequently extended to those working in his foundry. This was almost certainly the model for the scheme adopted by John Wilkinson in the 1780s. The general advantages of such arrangements to the new-style entrepreneurs are again attested by their introduction at Leeds by the leading flax-spinner, John Marshall. They were also taken up by Arkwright, the Strutts, and other East Midland industrialists. It seems likely that such societies run in connection with industrial undertakings were more widespread than the surviving evidence enables us to know with certainty.[3]

But most friendly societies were the spontaneous creations

[3] For the details of the very elaborate scheme set up by Boulton, see Erich Roll, *An Early Experiment in Industrial Organization, being a history of the firm of Boulton and Watt, 1775–1805* (1930), pp. 225–36; cf. W. G. Rimmer, *Marshall of Leeds, Flax-Spinners, 1788–1886* (Cambridge, 1960), p. 121; Roy Porter, *English Society in the eighteenth century* (1982), pp. 345–6; A. H. Dodd, *The Industrial Revolution in North Wales*, p. 373; R. S. Fitton and A. P. Wadsworth, *The Strutts and the Arkwrights* (1958), pp. 252–3; S. D. Chapman, *The Early Factory Masters. The Transition to the factory system in the Midlands Textile Industry* (Newton Abbot, 1967), p. 161. A variant form was developed at Bury by the elder Sir Robert Peel, who encouraged the continuance of the friendly societies he initiated for his work-people by allowing them 5 per cent interest on their funds, and by making periodic donations to swell their reserves (S. D. Chapman and S. Chassagne, *European Textile Printers in the eighteenth century. A Study of Peel and Oberkampf*, 1981, p. 56).

of the groups who benefited from them. Some proved lasting and successful: the enquiries of Sir Frederick Eden in the late 1790s disclosed a number in the north of England which had existed 'above a hundred years'. Many, however, were short-lived; and their members ran various risks from the dishonesty or incompetence of their elected officials, or from the failure in that age to understand sound actuarial principles. Unscrupulous officers could manipulate the rules of membership in such a way as to deprive, to their own advantage, some of the paid-up members of benefits for which they had contributed; control of grounds for expulsion was one of the issues underlying regulatory legislation in 1793. The primary object of providing benefits at times of adversity might also be defeated by the custom of sharing out the fund when it reached a certain level, or using some of it for anniversary or casual feasts. Many such societies were clubs providing occasions for conviviality as well as some sort of safeguard against disasters. Travelling through Cheshire in June 1792 Colonel John Byng found the Angel Hotel at Chester crowded out by a grand dinner party, and discovered it was a settlement meeting of the friendly society of the elderly women of the town, which maintained a fund for sick and old-age benefit and the cost of funerals. Insurance funds were also subject to other hazards. A number of Norwich societies lost their savings with the bankruptcy of a local brewer in whose business they had invested: in this case rescue came in the form of a public subscription. The social range involved in societies of this kind was wider than might be imagined: in Essex, for example, such people of the middling sort as lesser clergy ran their own benefit clubs.[4]

Friendly societies tended to be small: a membership of between 50 and 100 was probably typical. But there were

[4] Sir Frederick Morton Eden, *Observations on Friendly Societies for the maintenance of the industrious classes during sickness, infirmity, old age and other exigencies* (1801), pp. 3–5, 12–22; George Rose, *Observations on the Act for the Relief and Encouragement of Friendly Societies* (1794), p. 8; *Torrington Diaries*, iii. 122; C. B. Jewson, *Jacobin City. A Portrait of Norwich in its Reaction to the French Revolution, 1788–1802* (1975), p. 5; A. F. J. Brown, *Essex at Work, 1700–1815* (Chelmsford, 1969), p. 135. For instances of friendly societies in the London area investing their savings with the big breweries, see Peter Mathias, *The Brewing Industry in England, 1700–1830* (Cambridge, 1959), pp. 264, 277–8, 556–7.

great numbers of them, and, whether or not they had some industrial connection, they covered multitudes of people. In the mid 1790s, for instance, Nottingham had 51 societies with a total membership of about 2,000 individuals (about 7 per cent of the city's population). The 8,000 or so inhabitants of Lancaster supported no less than eighteen societies: as these averaged over 100 members each, they probably included more than half the adult male population. In 1803 the county of Essex, mainly rural, with a number of very small, but no very large towns, had no less than 353 societies with about 15,000 members. The passage of the Friendly Societies Act in 1793, sponsored by the treasury official George Rose, reflected the belief of many of those in authority in their great value as a source of social security, and its provisions were intended to strengthen their use for this purpose. Registration of such societies was voluntary under the Act. The advantage was extra security for the funds against bankruptcies of officials or defalcations. In return, societies which opted for the advantages of registration submitted their rules to the approval of the justices at quarter sessions and were expected to conform to guidelines which both safeguarded their individual members' rights within the society and provided that the funds were not used for other than strictly benefit purposes. These provisions meant that working-men's clubs which wished to use their funds indifferently for benefits and for the pursuance of labour disputes were ineligible, and so were those whose members wished to keep a freedom to engage in convivial expenditure. For these reasons not all friendly societies took advantage of the Act. But the actual registrations give some indication of the scale of the movement at the end of the century. According to one estimate in 1801, about 5,400 societies did register, and a further 1,800 were estimated not to have done so, making a total of some 7,200 societies, with about 648,000 members, and an annual financial turnover of almost £500,000.[5]

[5] Roger Smith, 'The Relief of Urban Poverty outside the Poor Law: a Study of Nottingham', *Midland History*, 2, no. 4 (1974), p. 215; Eden, *The State of the Poor*, ii. 310–11; J. R. Poynter, *Society and Pauperism: English Ideas on Poor Relief, 1795–1834* (1969), p. 38; Eden, *Observations on Friendly Societies*, pp. 6–9.

It was normal for such societies to provide help in case of sickness—so long as it was not self-inflicted; almost invariably, for instance, cases of venereal disease were ruled out. They also gave assistance at moments of social stress. For instance, the society of lead-miners at Alston Moor in the northern Pennines laid down in its rules in 1755 that members should receive 4s. a week during the first ten weeks of sickness or retirement. The society also prescribed a payment of £3 to a widow on the death of her husband, a sum which would meet funeral expenses and leave £2 or more for other immediate contingencies.[6] Despite actuarial hazards and other accidents which often brought such societies to a premature end, they did provide an appreciable amount of protection, mainly for people in the artisan or craftsmen classes. Men who were within the lower earning scale of the common labourer could rarely afford the level of contribution usually demanded, and in some cases were deliberately excluded by a financial bar: for instance, the Bristol Union of Carpenters, formed in 1768, refused to admit anyone who earned less than 10s. 6d. a week.[7]

The Bristol Union of Carpenters, however, was not just a benefit society. The line between the friendly society and the trade union was never very clear. Throughout the century there were many instances, of which this was one, of groups of craftsmen associating to accumulate funds which might be partly intended for benefit purposes but which might also be applied to the pursuit of labour disputes. It was this admixture of functions which the Friendly Societies Act of 1793 was partly intended to check: funds which might be used for strike purposes continued to have no protection at law. But it is doubtful if the Act made much difference, · for ways of evading it were not difficult to find. In the London area, there was a rich proliferation of such societies in many of the main crafts from early in the eighteenth century, and the trade element tended to be heavily emphasized. Numbers of such benefit societies were confined to

[6] C. J. Hunt, *The Lead Miners of the Northern Pennines in the eighteenth and nineteenth centuries* (Manchester, 1970), pp. 83–4.

[7] I. J. Prothero, *Artisans and Politics in early nineteenth-century London: John Gast and his times* (1979), p. 29. The common labourer's weekly wage was then in the region of 6s. a week.

members of a particular trade, and moreover to members who had served an apprenticeship, and at least one imposed restrictions on the employment of apprentices upon its members.[8] Two factors at least tended to impress a degree of stability and continuity upon such an association once formed: the maintenance of a roll of entitled members; and the periodical election of one or other trusted members as treasurers and as controllers of the triple-locked box in which such a society's fund was commonly kept. In London at any rate, the number of craftsmen in a particular calling was likely to be so large that they would be enrolled in a number of societies, not just in one; but this did not exclude joint action at a time of disputes with employers.

II

How effectively did trade societies and combinations defend the industrial interests of their members? How significant a factor may this have been in contributing to social stability?

In order to clear the ground before trying to deal with this question, it is worth noting first, that some groups of working people rarely engaged in industrial disputes and seem to have found no occasion for the formation of trade combinations. In some expanding areas of the economy, earnings and employment were sufficiently buoyant to eliminate incentive to organize: in others the mode of industrial organization had a similar effect.[9] Thus, although occasional disputes between employers and workmen occurred in the North Staffordshire pottery industry, there is no evidence of the existence of any unions before 1800, or, indeed, up to the year 1824.[10] Mining was expanding and developing in complexity throughout the later eighteenth century, but with the one exception of the North-East coalfield, undertakings were generally on a small scale and no direct master-and-servant relationship existed between the

---

[8] I. J. Prothero, op. cit., p. 33.

[9] On these areas of prosperity, see pp. 69 ff above.

[10] W. H. Warburton, *The History of Trade Union Organization in the North Staffordshire Potteries* (1931), pp. 27–8.

owners of pits on the one hand and the men who worked them on the other. Some variant of what may for short be called the 'butty' system was to be found almost universally in the Cornish tin and copper mines, the lead mines of the Pennines, the coal mines of the Forest of Dean, of Nottingham, and of Cheshire and South Lancashire. A gang-master and a small group of associates, making a team of five or six, or at most a little larger, entered into short-term contracts to drive shafts and to extract minerals, on terms which partly depended upon their skilled evaluation of the degree of profit likely to be won for themselves. From the miners' point of view the contract operated on similar principles to a lease. It preserved a degree of independence, and left them free to work for their own profit at times of their choosing. They were not in the dependent position of wage-earners. While the work was hard and often dangerous or unhealthy, the obligation of labour was less onerous than for many workers. In the lead mines of the Pennines, around 1800, the recognized working week was four days of six hours, which brought rewards satisfactorily higher than those of a common labourer. Usually men in the mining industry were not wholly dependent upon mine earnings, but drew part of their livelihood from the cultivation of smallholdings, and, in Cornwall, from participation in the seasonal pilchard fishery. One historian has observed that 'the Cornish miner . . . was noted for his backwardness in trade union activity', and another that no miners' unions appear to have been formed in the Lancashire–Cheshire region before 1794.[11] The iron-foundry workers were another group which seems to have been too prosperous during the late eighteenth century to be tempted into industrial organization: trade unions did not begin to emerge in the industry until the catastrophic depression of 1809.[12]

[11] Hunt, *Lead Miners*, pp. 34–55, 75–82, 122–3, 135, 138, 141, 147; John Rowe, *Cornwall in the Age of the Industrial Revolution* (1953), pp. 26–8, 166; John G. Rule, 'Some Social Aspects of the Cornish Industrial Revolution', *Industry and Society in the South West* (Exeter Papers on Economic History, no. 3, University of Exeter, 1970), pp. 105–6; T. S. Ashton and Joseph Sykes, *The Coal Industry in the eighteenth century* (Manchester, 1929), pp. 100–7, 111–12; J. D. Chambers, *Nottinghamshire in the Eighteenth Century*, p. 89; Esther Moir, *Local Government in Gloucestershire, 1775–1800* (1969), pp. 6, 8.

[12] H. J. Fyrth and H. J. Collins, *The Foundry Workers. A Trade Union History* (Manchester, 1959), pp. 10–15. See pp. 77–8, 81 above.

For quite different reasons two other major groups, though much in need of protection, lacked any trade organization in the eighteenth century: agricultural workers, who had no economic leverage and were closely enmeshed in the hierarchical social organization of their villages; and general labourers both in country and town, the nature of whose work gave them little opportunity to join forces with other men of similar interest.

Early trade unionism thus was not in the main associated with the expanding spheres of employment being opened up by the early Industrial Revolution. At least, this was not the case in either mining or metallurgy. Nor was it the case with textiles, where the strongest manifestations of trade-union activity were to be found among old-established crafts, particularly combing and shearing, but relatively little before 1800 among factory spinners or handloom weavers. More noticeably, trade-union organization developed effectively —and to the point where it could achieve at least a modicum of success in disputes with employers—among groups of relatively skilled workers where certain favourable conditions obtained. Earnings were sufficiently high to permit regular subscriptions; local concentration, or the grouping of men in workshops, as with compositors and pressmen, made co-operation easy. The heavy concentrations of manufacturing craftsmen in the London area made it a forcing-house for union development, but there were also important regional concentrations, like the stocking-weavers of the East Midlands, and the weavers of Lancashire and of the Clyde Valley. And before the eighteenth century came to an end, in some trades at least, the growth of a sense of common interest was leading to the establishment of systems of co-operation extending far beyond the area of the metropolis or of one particular provincial region.

The defence of interests against employers usually involved one or more of three interlinked issues: the rate of wages; the hours of labour; and the closed shop. The last of these issues had two main aspects: the limitation of numbers of apprentices, and the exclusion of unapprenticed labour. Such questions were constantly on the minds of the crafts-men who were members of 'box clubs' based at particular alehouses which acted as 'houses of call'. In London numbers of 'houses of call' existed for men in a large variety of different skilled occupations—hatters, smiths, carpenters, weavers, boot-and-shoe makers, metal-workers, bakers, tailors, plumbers, painters, glaziers, bookbinders, and others. The 'house of call' provided a venue where masters could seek workmen and where workmen could be hired according to the roster established by the club, so that work was shared out among those seeking it. Such clubs inevitably tended to adopt a coherent policy over the rates of pay offered to their members; and from an early date they were also concerned to try to prevent the dilution of labour by the masters' introduction of, or dependence on the labour of, an excessive number of apprentices. They also tried to insist that only trained men, who had served apprenticeship and belonged to the clubs, should be employed. Traditionally such groups of craftsmen could bring pressure to bear on their employers by one or other of two methods. Either they could invoke the jurisdiction of magistrates under the Elizabethan statutes, who might rule, for instance, that employers were offering a less than fair or customary wage and order them to mend their ways; or they could enter into direct negotiation associated with a threat of strikes. Social historians sometimes give the impression that the gradual move from the first of these situations of confrontation to the second marked a deliberate gradual abandonment of an old-time paternalist policy in favour of *laissez-faire* capitalism, as hard-faced employers increased their economic and political dominance. By mid-century the second of these methods of adjustment of interests was certainly gaining ground, but, contrary to the impression just referred to, this seems to have been at the initiative of the workmen, who found it served them better. In 1761 one London newspaper made the comment that 'fair wages and hours set by the tailors, curriers, wheelwrights, smiths, and shoemakers were generally more favourable than those enforceable in the courts'.[13]

In the late eighteenth century this seems to have remained the case with one at least of the two industrial groups which

[13] Quoted in Dobson, *Masters and Journeymen*, pp. 38–9.

continued to be given particular preferential treatment by Parliament: the silk-workers of Spitalfields and the London tailors. The Spitalfields Acts of 1773 and 1792 established a machinery for the enforcement of rates of pay, which in the first instance were left to be worked out by a joint meeting of masters and men. In the event of failure to agree the magistrates had an ultimate power of arbitration. In essence the Acts provided protection from undercutting, and as such were welcome to the great body of the masters as well as to the men. The London tailors received similar legal protection under an Act of 1768. But from the 1770s onwards they scarcely had any recourse to it, but made use of their own formidable bargaining power to force wages above the approved rates and then to push them up in line with inflation. In the 1790s they developed what one historian has called 'the strongest of all the London trades, with a secret and near military structure that took the masters thirty years to break down', and they won significant wage increases in 1795, in 1801, and on a number of later occasions. During the successful strike of 1801 the number of journeymen brought out was reputed to be about 15,000.[14]

This description of the London tailors highlights an important aspect—the two-tier nature—of eighteenth-century labour organization when involved in major confrontations with employers. The trade clubs at 'houses of call' were the basic units of association, but at times of crisis some overarching organization become necessary to co-ordinate the efforts of the members of the clubs. Such organization was not necessarily permanent, though it appears to have been in the case of the tailors and of some other London trades. But in London sometimes, and in the provinces as a general rule, trade-union activity in furtherance of a dispute could appear sporadically or occasionally among working groups of working people in certain trades and in certain localities, simply on the basis of their continuing association in their employment, and without the existence of any permanent organizational base. A crisis in relations with employers

[14] Alfred Plummer, *The London Weavers' Company, 1660–1970* (1972), pp. 324–9, 331; F. W. Galton, *Select Documents illustrating the History of Trade Unionism. i: The Tailoring Trade* (1896), pp. xiii–lx.

would generate the establishment of a temporary *ad hoc* committee of leading spirits, which would lapse as soon as the dispute was over. The network of mutual support was far more complex and spread far more widely than would have been expected, were continuous organization to be the criterion (as the Webbs suggested) of the existence of a trade union.[15]

In some trades something like a national network of contacts, capable of exploitation at need, was being established towards the end of the eighteenth century. This could sometimes be the consequence of a migration of workers. For instance, groups of calico printers moving from London to Lancashire seem to have taken with them their tradition of trade organization and maintained some contact with their old base. Wool-combers seem to have been a particularly peripatetic set of men, a factor which may account for their ability to co-ordinate action in their interest between places as far apart as Yorkshire and the South-West. In other instances it seems likely that widespread co-operation grew gradually out of the practice of tramping.[16] A system of itinerancy for those seeking work, supported by fellow craftsmen in other districts, seems to have begun in one or two trades early in the century and was well-established in a number of them before its close. Curriers and wool-combers appear to have established tramping federations by the middle of the century, hatters by the 1770s, leather-breeches-makers by the 1780s. The system served firstly to facilitate the search for work, secondly perhaps as a means of gaining experience and a measure of ability and of reward, and in the third place it could be used to give temporary relief to the finances of a local trade club if these were embarrassed as a result of a labour dispute.[17] Local clubs involved in tramping federations undertook to give support to each other's certified members, or to repay help given to them.

[15] See the discussion of this point in Rule, *The Experience of Labour*, pp. 149–51.

[16] On this subject see E. J. E. Hobsbawm, 'The Tramping Artisan', in his *Labouring Men* (1972), pp. 34–40; Rule, *The Experience of Labour*, p. 165; S. and B. Webb, *History of Trade Unionism*, p. 31 (on the wool-combers); *The Autobiography of Francis Place*, ed. Mary Thale (Cambridge, 1972), p. 113 (on breeches-makers). It is probable that the practice developed earlier and more widely than surviving evidence permits to judge.

[17] See the case of the leather-breeches-makers, p. 140 below.

In the 1780s an arrangement was familiar among the leather-breeches-makers, 'that a man who brought a certificate to any leather breeches makers' shop in the country would be sure of a day's keep, a night's lodging and a shilling to start again with the next morning, and in some of the larger towns a breakfast and half a crown in money to help him along'.[18] It seems very likely that the tramping system contributed effectively to the further growth of trade organizations. It tended to foster the affiliation or federation of trade clubs into larger bodies; it was a means whereby information about rates, conditions, and grievances could be circulated; it gave occasion for personal contacts to be established or renewed; and it permitted union leaders to escape victimization in a locality where they had made themselves unpopular with employers and find at least temporary work elsewhere. It could also facilitate the direct support of strikes in one area, by contributions raised from sympathizers in other districts.

Perhaps partly as a result of this development, co-ordination of protest and policy among men in particular crafts was becoming more noticeable in the late eighteenth century. Thus, in 1785, when the cordwainers of the Saffron Walden district took up a campaign against employment of non-apprenticed labour in the shoemaking trade and advertised a forthcoming meeting in the local press, they emphasized how their action was 'through the example of our brothers in London, Chelmsford, and many other towns in England'. When in 1800 the London calico printers agitated for repeal of the Combination Act of 1799, their action was clearly part of a well co-ordinated campaign which brought in petitions, suspiciously uniform in wording, from nearly a dozen important provincial towns and cities. In 1778 and 1779 the stockingers of the East Midlands had an agreed policy with stockingers in London about securing a regulation of wage-rates for various specific types of work. The home counties were the focus of a number of clubs of papermakers' employees, who entered into a series of effective combinations, picking off individual employers, in order to

---

[18] *The Autobiography of Francis Place*, ed. Thale, p. 113. For another example some years later, see the letter of the Bath shoemakers, of 10 Feb. 1804, printed in Aspinall, *Early English Trade Unions*, p. 78.

force up wages between 1784 and 1797; and soon after 1801 their connections were extending to Dorset and the North. Legislation against the paper-workers' unions in 1796 was of no avail, and they secured further advances of wages in 1801. In the Western Lowlands of Scotland, local combinations of cotton-weavers were affiliated into a Clyde Valley Weavers General Association in 1787. Though they failed in their immediate initial attempt to maintain wage-rates during a slump, in 1803 they successfully promoted legislation regulating the descriptions and the methods of giving out work, which eliminated some causes of disputes between them and their employers.[19]

The English shipwrights provide an informative and well-studied example of how successful an important group of workers could be in their dealings with their employers, even when the main employer was the government itself. Their role was an important one, both in the British economy in general, and in the business of national defence in particular. Towards the close of the century some 3,500 were employed in the various royal dockyards, nearly 2,000 in the private yards in the London area, and 2,000–3,000 more in small groups in the outports.[20]

In the campaign which the government's shipwrights opened for higher pay to meet inflation in 1772 (and on subsequent occasions), they displayed an impressive capacity to organize committees, delegations, and deputations to state their case. The Admiralty tried to meet their plea by arranging systems of task work, which would increase wages but also productivity. At the same time, the First Lord, the Earl of

[19] A. F. J. Brown, *English History from Essex Sources, 1750–1900* (Chelmsford, 1952), p. 206; Prothero, *Artisans and Politics*, p. 43; Chambers, *Nottinghamshire in the eighteenth century*, pp. 37–8; D. C. Coleman, *The British Paper Industry* (1958), pp. 252–301; Norman Murray, *The Scottish Handloom Weavers, 1790–1850*, pp. 185–6.

[20] Dobson, *Masters and Journeymen*, pp. 100–10; J. M. Haas, 'The Introduction of Task Work into the Royal Dockyards', *Journal of British Studies*, 8 (1969), 44–68; R. A. Morriss, 'Labour Relations in the Royal Dockyards, 1801–1805', *Mariner's Mirror*, lxii (1976), 341–2, and 'The Administration of the Royal Dockyards in England during the Revolutionary and Napoleonic Wars, with special reference to the period, 1800–1805', Ph.D. thesis, University of London, 1978, p. 146. On the shortage of shipwrights and other craftsmen in the 1770s, see R. J. B. Knight, 'The Royal Dockyards in England at the time of the War of American Independence', Ph.D. thesis, University of London, 1972, pp. 111–14.

Sandwich, tried to include as an intrinsic part of the package the abolition of the much-abused privilege of taking chips, that is, the waste pieces of wood left over after the shaping of ships' timbers. Everyone knew that this privilege was wantonly abused, sound timber being destroyed to provide the men's perquisites: Samuel Bentham, knowledgeable from his apprenticeship in the royal dockyards, once referred to 'an hour in the day, that is $\frac{1}{2}$ day in the week' being 'spent in cutting up and secreting of *chips*'.[21]

Many of Sandwich's proposals were adaptations of practices in the civilian yards. Nevertheless, they encountered fierce resistance. After two months of strikes during the summer of 1775, he had to make considerable concessions. With war threatening in America he was in no position to do otherwise, but it was also true that he believed the scheme would eventually make its way on its own merits (a belief justified in the event). He agreed that task work should be voluntary, not compulsory, and higher job-prices were offered to make it more attractive. The revised plan proved acceptable in three of the yards, Woolwich, Deptford, and Sheerness, but it was firmly rejected at Chatham, Portsmouth, and Plymouth, and not until the years 1782–8 did these yards fall into line. The disturbance had caused undermanning in all the royal yards during the first three years of the American War of Independence, the number of shipwrights not being restored to the 1775 level till 1778. The abuse of taking chips was not touched: the Admiralty proved insufficiently strong to abolish it until 1801. In this further confrontation the Admiralty was favoured by the ending of the war against Revolutionary France: in 1801 it was also able to resist a well-organized (and justified) agitation for advances in wage-rates, during which the men showed considerable resource in setting up a firm committee structure in all six yards, co-ordinating their agitation by post and messenger, and financing their delegates during a fortnight's stay in London. But the peace was brief, and war, as always, put the dockyard workers in a strong position. The perpetual shortage of shipwrights after the renewal of hostilities in

---

[21] *The Correspondence of Jeremy Bentham*, vol. 3: *January 1781–October 1788*, ed. Ian R. Christie (1971), pp. 138-9.

1803 produced a very different situation, in which yard workers won a series of concessions. In 1804 and 1805 the Admiralty accepted their complaints against work and pay routines in six out of seven instances. Wages were raised by some 20 to 30 per cent in 1805, and numbers of men sacked as troublemakers in 1801 were reinstated.

Skilled craftsmen in private shipyards also seem to have been able to defend their interests with some success. Bristol was the seat of a small shipbuilding industry—the poll-book for 1784 listed about a hundred shipwrights and anchor-smiths. During the American War wages had risen by about 20 per cent. In 1784 the shipbuilders sought to push them back down to the old figure, but in face of a determined strike they were obliged to go on paying the wartime rate. The London civilian shipbuilding industry went through a similar experience at the end of the French Revolutionary War. After a period of hectic prosperity and high bidding for scarce skilled labour, the Thames builders tried to bring wages down by some 30 per cent. Not all the various types of craftsmen were equally successful in holding their own, but the shipwrights at any rate were able to stand out for a wage only marginally less than the wartime level.[22]

Numbers of other examples can be adduced of strike action which was successful, either immediately or else ulti-mately, both in London and in the provinces. In some cases the strike was enforced with some degree of riotous violence. In 1768 the London seamen put a stop to all outward-bound shipping while they forced upon shipowners a wage-rate of at least 35*s*. a month (the Hudson's Bay Company had to concede 40*s*.). In 1783 they once again took action, in order to combat unemployment and falling wages, and held ship-owners to ransom by unrigging outward-bound ships until the latter agreed to replace all foreign seamen by English, at an advance in wages of 12*s*. a month. In 1787-8 a mass strike of 4,000 carpenters and joiners in London won a pay rise despite an attempt to crush it by indictments of the leaders for conspiracy—charges which the masters eventually decided it was better to abandon. In the spring of 1793 the

[22] Bryan Little, *The City and County of Bristol. A Study of Atlantic Civiliza-tion* (1967), p. 174; Prothero, *Artisans and Politics*, pp. 47–8.

250 or so members of the London Leather-Breeches Makers'
Benefit Society organized a strike for higher pay. On this
occasion Francis Place made his debut as a labour organizer,
arranging an exodus of the young unmarried men to live on
their tramping allowances in other parts of the country in
order to eke out the funds available as strike benefit from the
Society's coffers. Although the masters managed to overcome this strike with blackleg labour, they were sufficiently
shaken by it to bow to threats of a second strike two years
later. In 1795 the journeymen secured an agreement which
both maximized earnings by a rearrangement of work routines
and conceded the advance in pay from 22s. to 25s. which
they had demanded in 1793. About this time Place also
involved himself as secretary of a Benefit Society among the
London carpenters, which by the mere threat of strike action
was able to secure an increase in wages.[23]

London hatters brought similar successful pressure to bear
on their masters in 1772 and 1775. London bookbinders
mounted a successful strike for a reduction of hours in 1786
and repeated this success in 1794 when they threatened to
set up a bindery corporation of their own which would have
put the masters out of business. Compositors secured a series
of material concessions from the London master printers
by agreements of 1785 and 1793, embodied in an agreed
scale of prices, and won a further rise of about 15 per cent in
1800 on the score of the increasing cost of living: in none
of these three instances was the threat of a strike made
explicit, but the employers were well aware of the possibility
and reluctant to face it. The negotiation of the agreement of
1793 marked a new stage in the formal relationships within
the printing industry, for so far as is known this was the first
time when talks were carried on by formal committees representing each side.[24]

[23] George Rudé, *Hanoverian London, 1714–1808* (1971), pp. 193, 202;
Dobson, *Masters and Journeymen*, p. 132; *The Autobiography of Francis Place*,
ed. Thale, pp. 112–13, 116, 125–6; Place MSS, British Library Add. MSS 27834,
fol. 108, quoted in *British Working Class Movements. Select Documents, 1789–
1875*, ed. G. D. H. Cole and A. W. Filson (1951), p. 20. In 1802 another strike
raised the weekly wage of the leather-breeches-makers to 30s.

[24] Rule, *The Experience of Labour*, pp. 156–7; John Child, *Industrial Relations in the British Printing Industry. The Quest for Security* (1967), pp. 53, 62,
63; Ellic Howe, *The London Compositor* (1947), pp. 10–117 (a splendidly

London craftsmen were by no means always successful in their confrontations with employers, and resort to riot, when it occurred, was likely to prejudice their case. Nevertheless, by the 1780s and 1790s a system of negotiation and pressure, with at least some degree of ritualistic observance, had come into operation among those involved in a number of skilled trades in the capital, through which the aspirations of working men could often be at least partially satisfied, and by which the danger of a really explosive build-up of discontent was averted. Confirmatory evidence comes from the decade or so after 1800. The strength and self-confidence of these groups was a revelation to the provincial labour organizer Thomas Large, who visited London in 1812, and reported to his colleagues that the London carpenters had a fighting fund of £20,000, and that tailors, shoemakers, bookbinders, gold-beaters, printers, bricklayers, coat-makers, hatters, curriers, masons, and whitesmiths were all in a position to insist that no journeyman should receive less than 30s. a week, while many of their number were paid over three times this figure. It is surprising to find domestic servants in the metropolis also becoming successfully involved in trade-union activity. However, this was the case at least with that numerous but sought-after category, the footmen. By forming a combination and establishing a fund which would secure them maintenance during periods of unemployment, they freed themselves from the necessity of accepting whatever position was offered and were able to stipulate various favourable terms before taking a post.[25]

Similarly, many groups of working people in the provinces maintained or when necessary improvised machinery for adjusting relationships with employers, and showed considerable skill and success in exploiting their opportunities. One local historian, writing about the North-East of England, has observed that 'from an early date some of the more coherent groups of workers showed a very impressive capacity in the

full account of arrangements about job rates); *The British Working Class Movement*, ed. Cole and Filson, p. 108.

[25] E. P. Thompson, *The Making of the English Working Class* (1964), p. 238; J. Jean Hecht, *The Domestic Servant Class in eighteenth-century England* (1956), p. 86.

defence of their own interests, and in strike situations the workers' leaders often outclassed their employers in skill and ingenuity'. Another has remarked that by the late eighteenth century, 'union organization seems to have reached a scale and maturity on Tyneside unequalled anywhere else in the country': miners, keelmen, shipwrights, and seamen had long possessed their own very effective forms of collective bargaining.[26] These abilities did not always have to be constantly demonstrated. The miners of the North-East won a battle over the right to change jobs at the yearly hirings in 1765, but from then until the end of the century seem to have had no serious grounds for disputes with the coal-owners, and round about 1800 they were exploiting a favourable situation of labour shortage.[27] The Tyne keelmen, whose strength lay in their ability to bring the coal trade of the area almost to a standstill, by the solidarity of the strike they mounted in 1768 won significant wage concessions. Particularly conspicuous for its success was the Tyne seamen's strike for higher pay in 1792. The sailors on the colliery vessels which carried the coals to London and to foreign destinations could block the coal trade even more effectively than the keelmen, and in this instance they stood out against employers and magistrates to win a 20 per cent advance in wages, together with concessions about the rations supplied on board.[28]

Often the defence of the interests of provincial craftsmen was not associated with so great a degree of sustained organization as was to be found in London, but nevertheless quite large-scale movements could be improvised at need. A confrontation between Gloucestershire clothiers and weavers in 1765 involved several thousand journeymen, and culminated in a six-week strike, at the end of which the clothiers gave way to the men's demands. Forty-five years of

[26] N. McCord, *North East England*, p. 80; John O. Foster, *Class Struggle and the Industrial Revolution* (1974), p. 105.

[27] E. Welbourne, *The Miners' Unions of Northumberland and Durham* (Cambridge, 1923), pp. 21–3.

[28] J. M. Fewster, 'The Keelmen of Tyneside in the eighteenth century', *Durham University Journal*, xix (1957–8), p. 120; D. E. Brewster and N. McCord, 'Some Labour Troubles in the 1790s in North East England', *International Review of Social History*, 13 (1968), 366–74.

comparative peace followed this settlement, which in itself is perhaps a measure of the success won by the men. Then another crisis was to produce another such response. In 1802 and the years immediately following, the local trade societies showed themselves capable of creating a county association embracing altogether some 13,000 weavers, each subscribing $1\frac{1}{2}d.$ a week. This body was held together by monthly meetings in each parish and quarterly meetings at one or other of the main centres, and it collaborated with similar associations in Somerset and Wiltshire in a campaign against the spread of gigmills and the dilution of labour with apprentices.[29] Lancashire weavers may have found combinations less easy to sustain owing to the scattered locations and often casual nature of their occupation; but numbers of local societies were coming into existence during the 1780s and 1790s. Informal committees seem to have been established in major towns in the cotton-weaving districts of the North-West and of the Clyde Valley in Scotland, to organize the large-scale petitioning of the years 1799–1802. However, in general, the boom conditions which weavers enjoyed between 1780 and about 1796 gave them relatively little occasion for disputes with employers.[30] A string of reports to the Home Office during 1792 attests the ability of other groups of working people in the provinces to exact better terms from their employers—carpenters at Liverpool, shoemakers and others at Bristol, journeymen cutlers at Sheffield, and seamen in the east-coast ports.[31]

III

While it would be wrong to assume that members of trade combinations always obtained their demands in the period 1760–1800, or that they escaped altogether a degree of victimization by employers either through the use of the courts or by other means such as refusal of employment,

[29] Esther Moir, 'The Gentlemen Clothiers', in *Gloucestershire Studies*, ed. H. R. P. Finberg (1957), pp. 253–60; W. E. Minchinton, 'The Beginnings of Trade Unionism in the Gloucestershire Woollen Industry', *Transactions of the Bristol and Gloucestershire Archaeological Society*, 70 (1951), 127–41.

[30] Bythell, *Handloom Weavers*, pp. 177–85.

[31] Aspinall, *Early English Trade Unions*, pp. 2–14.

nevertheless the evidence just presented indicates a more balanced picture than doctrinaire enthusiasts for labour history have sometimes drawn. A grasp of this balanced situation is relevant to an understanding of the underlying stability of British society in the age of Revolution. There are also other ways in which it can be perceived. For instance, the general attitude of the law and of its administrators towards combinations was in fact ambiguous and reflected an element of quasi-acceptance. In theory the law was harsh. Any combination in restraint of trade attracted penalties under the law of conspiracy, which could be heavy, including sentences of up to seven years' transportation. Striking workmen broke the law if they left work unfinished. An Act of 1726 prescribed the death penalty for breaking knitting-frames. And yet accounts of labour disputes give rise again and again to comments upon the sympathetic attitude taken by gentry, magistrates, and officials, and a tender regard for men who found themselves before the courts. Furthermore, combinations to state grievances and to appeal for remedy within the law were in no way illegal, and in particular cases—those of the London tailors and silk-weavers—received statutory confirmation during this period.

Apart from this, employers had fewer advantages over workmen than has sometimes been allowed.[32] It is true that they were more free to combine—the law of conspiracy not operating in their case. They sometimes tried to overcome the problem of scarcity of labour by entering into agreements to require discharge certificates from previous masters before accepting men for employment (though the near-impossibility of sustaining such a system was made only too plain by the miners of the North-East in 1765). They could theoretically use the law of conspiracy against strikers—though in this case they had to persuade the magistracy to act—or prosecute them for leaving work unfinished. Employers in a number of lines of business could appeal to one or other of about forty statutes against combinations in specific trades which had been enacted over the years up to 1799.

[32] For the following discussion see in general, Rule, *The Experience of Labour*, pp. 172–86, and Dobson, *Masters and Journeymen*, pp. 130–3.

But appeal to the law was often muted. The effectiveness of proceedings against conspiracy was greatly blunted by the delays involved in bringing a case and having it heard before the next meeting of quarter sessions or of the assizes. Offenders had ample time to abscond. The expense of pursuing them was not worth while. The whole procedure was in any case costly. Employers were also loath to invoke legal sanctions against workmen when an industrial dispute was already over, and the likely consequences would be merely to create bad blood and make a return to normal working more difficult. It was frequently acknowledged that leaders of strikes were often men who commanded general respect among their fellows, and to prosecute them would merely turn them into martyrs. There was also the consideration that prosecutions for conspiracy could misfire with serious results. In 1772 ten men prosecuted at the instance of the Curriers' Company of London were found not guilty by sympathetic juries and were then able to bring actions against the Company claiming damages for assault and false imprisonment. Not only juries could be sympathetic, but judges also. Lord Chief Justice Kenyon, from the moment of his elevation to the King's Bench in 1788, seems to have shown a strong paternalistic attitude towards the underprivileged, and a desire to see conciliation succeed in industrial disputes; he may have influenced the peaceful settlement of a dispute involving the London carpenters in 1788.

Disputes were likely to arise out of a temporary depression in a trade and to be followed by a recovery. Thus, if opportunities for expansion of business were in the offing, the employers' best course was a full or partial concession of workmen's demands. Furthermore, under the conditions of wartime inflation and high food prices due to bad harvests, employers and the ruling classes generally tended to acknowledge the equity of working men's demands for higher pay in line with rising costs of living. All these considerations operated to check action by masters against journeymen, and frequently, even if action at law had been invoked, the need to restore good relations led to the abandonment of prosecutions or even the filing away of the record without sentence after a verdict of guilty had been found.

Apart from the special arrangements under the Spitalfields Acts and the London Tailors' Act, magistrates in the City of London and the metropolitan area were inclined to put themselves foward as mediators in disputes between masters and men. Middlesex justices voted in 1777 that under the Acts of 1562 and 1603 they had a right to settle wages of labourers, craftsmen, and artificers, and they offered to enforce negotiated agreements—a role which they continued to fulfil spasmodically up to the end of the century. Newcastle dignitaries acted as conciliators in a keelmen's dispute in 1771 and in a conflict in the local sugar-bakers' trade in 1774. Mediation in the Tyneside seamen's dispute of 1792 was successfully conducted by a local JP who was also one of the Members of Parliament for Newcastle. The authority of the magistrates to act as final arbiters in disputes between employers and workmen was built into the Combination Act of 1800 and was invoked and used on a number of occasions in the years immediately following. In 1801, after a strike of over 15,000 journeymen tailors in the metropolis, the Recorder of London, acting in accordance with the Act of 1768, awarded an advance in wages which was a compromise between the men's claim and the employers' offer. Around the turn of the century there is also evidence from Scotland of the willingness of the authorities to intervene on behalf of the journeymen. At Edinburgh in 1803, compositors, drawing attention to the fact that wage-rates had not been altered since 1785, made representations that the rising cost of living justified an advance of about 30 per cent. Faced with a refusal by the master printers, they appealed to the Court of Session. The Court carefully examined the figures put forward by both sides and gave judgement in their favour, awarding rises calculated to bring the purchasing power of wages back into conformity with the pre-existing scale.[33]

The attitude of the magistracy is also clear from the numerous instances when prosecutions against strikers involved in riots often resulted in derisory sentences or in

[33] Dobson, *Masters and Journeymen*, chapter 6 *passim*; McCord, *North East England*, p. 81; Aspinall, *Early English Trade Unions*, pp. 33-4; Ellic Howe, *The London Compositor*, pp. 248-50.

no sentences at all. In 1779 after an orderly campaign to secure an Act of Parliament to regulate wages in the hosiery industry had failed, the journeymen in the Nottingham area sought to coerce recalcitrant employers by widespread rioting and destruction of property. The losses incurred by some of the hosiers were considerable. Nevertheless, only insignificant fines and brief terms of imprisonment were handed out to captured ringleaders, and in one instance a public apology was considered sufficient redress for an assault upon a magistrate. Liverpool was the scene of a major riot over unemployment and wage reductions at the beginning of the American War of Independence, in which mobs of up to 3,000 sailors reduced the town to complete disorder and at one point mounted an attack on the Exchange with two cannon seized from a whaler. Troops had to be called in to restore order. Nevertheless, only twelve ringleaders were indicted at the next assizes, true bills were found against only eight, and all were discharged upon their agreeing to enter the navy.[34]

The Acts against labour combinations in 1799 and 1800 made little difference to the situation in practice. These Acts did not forbid workmen from associating to improve wages and conditions of work—indeed, in one respect, by laying down machinery for arbitration, they encouraged this. What they proscribed was the use of strike action for such a purpose. They purported to make action against strikes more effective by permitting employers to bring a prosecution themselves for summary trial before justices of the peace, instead of relying on the time-consuming and expensive process of a crown indictment; though the scale of punishments available to magistrates exercising summary jurisdiction in this way was less severe, the maximum possible sentence under the Acts being three months' imprisonment.

In fact there was little recourse to the Acts. An employer was likely to find that an initiative would prejudice his interest in various ways. He would lose the goodwill of his

[34] Chambers, *Nottinghamshire in the eighteenth century*, pp. 40-1; R. B. Rose, 'A Liverpool Sailors' strike in the eighteenth century', *Transactions of the Lancashire and Cheshire Antiquarian Society*, 68 (1958), 85-90. A joint strike of sailors and shipwrights reduced the town to a state of riot again for seven weeks in 1791 (ibid. 92.)

journeymen, and he might be left the victim of competition by other masters who would rather profit from his difficulties than stand by him against his employees. In the East Midlands hosiery area, for instance, the effect was negligible. During the twenty-five years from 1800 during which the Acts were in operation, at least fifty 'illegal' unions were operating in Nottingham, engaging in disputes and in negotiations with employers; at least fifteen strikes took place, but only five prosecutions were undertaken. At Leicester the magistrates adopted a policy of 'salutary neglect' and when compelled to act passed lenient sentences.[35] Numbers of trade combinations in London continued to function without serious interference and effectively upheld the interests of their members.[36] The master millwrights of London complained that the Acts 'had no effect at all among engineers and millwrights in restraining combinations'.[37] That is a verdict which was echoed by contemporaries in government circles and has been almost unanimously endorsed by historians. On the other hand, the paternalistic provisions of the Acts—the clauses establishing a system of arbitration, with ultimate powers of award vested in the magistrates if the arbitrators nominated by the two sides failed to agree —were invoked on several occasions in the first few years after 1800. They only lapsed in the years of depression after 1809 when it became clear that arbitration could put employers out of business altogether and destroy chances of future employment.[38] Whilst the operation of the Combination Acts, strictly speaking, lies outside the period under

[35] M. I. Thomis, *The Town Labourer in the Industrial Revolution* (1974), pp. 138-9; and *Politics and Society in Nottingham, 1785-1835* (Oxford 1969), pp. 51, 53, 60-2, 65.

[36] Above, pp. 139-41.

[37] James B. Jeffries, *The Story of the Engineers, 1800-1945* (1945), p. 12.

[38] E. P. Thompson appears to have allowed ideological preconception to overtake grasp of facts when he wrote of the Combination Acts that 'their novelty consisted in this; in the inclusive nature of their prohibition of *all* combinations; and in the fact that, unlike legislation in the earlier paternalistic tradition, they included no compensatory protective clauses' (*The Making of the English Working Class*, p. 504). Both statements are incorrect. Nor was he correct (ibid.) in attributing Acts which clearly arose out of industrial considerations to a motive of 'intimidating 'political reformers'—a confusion over the Corresponding Societies Act of 1799, which was directed against undoubtedly *revolutionary*, not reformist, organizations.

consideration, it provides retrospective evidence confirming the general tolerant attitude of society towards trade-union activity in the late eighteenth century.

Much of the foregoing material reinforces the emphasis which social historians of the eighteenth century have begun to lay on the innately stabilizing nature of trade combinations. Dr Dobson has written, for instance, that the 'unending exercise in negotiation' typical of much labour–employer relationship during the century was an essentially conservative activity. The basic aim of most of these combinations was to maintain an existing balance of reward—to check the efforts of those who in seeking change, improvement, greater profits, would disturb the sober prosperity and well-being of the rest; in other words, fundamentally, to resist change. It was therefore usual, though not universal, for journeymen and a large proportion of masters to find a common interest on one side of an industrial dispute. Union activity was not always founded on an assumption of conflicting interests between classes—between masters and men, between capital and labour. Thus, the Midland Stockingers' Association which agitated for statutory regulation of wages in the trade in the late 1770s included delegates of the more moderate master hosiers, who were willing to have such an arrangement, not least because it would hold their most aggressive competitors in check. Lancashire weavers similarly sought the cooperation of 'fair-trading' masters, when they mounted a campaign for parliamentary regulation in 1799. In these situations the objective of the men was usually not to increase their reward but to maintain the level they enjoyed —to maintain it against erosion of purchasing power as a result of high food prices or inflation, or against the efforts of masters suffering through trade depression to lower wages or dilute labour.[39]

Apart from this essentially conservative function, trade combinations had a stabilizing social effect in other ways. They provided an arena for a ritualistic working-out of the element of combativeness in human nature. They provided

[39] Dobson, *Masters and Journeymen*, p. 153; Prothero, *Artisans and Politics*, pp. 37–8; Chambers, *Nottinghamshire in the eighteenth century*, pp. 37–8; Aspinall, *Early English Trade Unions*, pp. 21–4.

a safety-valve for human discontent, not least because they held out the prospect of a reasonably satisfactory degree of success. Combinations also provided a social milieu—a social context—in which people could purposefully play out their lives, a context within which they could be assured of some degree of security through entitlements of social and financial support when in need of it, and also at other times feel the satisfaction and fulfilment of giving such support. In offering social status, friendship, and a social role, the trade club did for its members many of the things done for others by the church or chapel; while in some cases, as in the Gloucestershire textile industry, the two overlapped, in other instances they did not. In any explanation of the non-revolutionary nature of British society in the age of revolutions, the trade combinations, it seems to me, must find a place.

IV

One other aspect of the working people's defence of their interests needs to be set in context here: the food riot.

Riot was a fairly common phenomenon in eighteenth-century Britain and occurred in numerous different connections. In mid-century it constituted one form of protest against militia service. In some large towns like Coventry rioting at parliamentary elections was almost invariable. Violent demonstrations with destruction of property were occasionally stirred up by mindless religious fanaticism against Roman Catholics, as in the case of the Gordon Riots of 1780 in London, or against Unitarian radicals, as with the Priestley Riots in Birmingham in 1791. A riot might occur as a by-product of agitation in favour of a particular manufacturing interest, as when the Spitalfields silk-weavers besieged the Duke of Bedford's town house in 1765 during their campaign for protective tariffs against French silks. As already mentioned, they occurred not infrequently in support of industrial disputes, when violence was used to coerce men into strikes, to deter blacklegs, and to bring employers to comply with demands. The propensity of the Northumberland miners to destroy pit-head gear for this purpose led to the passage of no less than eight statutes directed against this mayhem between 1747 and 1816, with little result. East Midland weavers, and spinners in various districts, engaged in machine-breaking during the late 1770s.[40] But this kind of behaviour was more often found among very numerous bodies of the semi-skilled, such as sailors and weavers, and was not typical of the skilled craftsmen in the clothing, building, and other trades, who relied on the forms of strike pressure already discussed. The food riot stood in a different category. Each such affair was a response to a particular set of circumstances, varying from one case to the next, though having a certain common ground; and this type of action could involve and be a defence of the interests of lower levels of society incapable of making use of trade combinations as well as of those who were involved in them.

Food riots became more frequent in the second half of the eighteenth century as a result of a combination of factors, of which the two most fundamental seem to have been climatic and demographic. After 1760 the British Isles appear to have been afflicted by more inclement weather, leading at intervals to deficient harvests, than had been common during the previous thirty years. At the same time the expansion of population and of demand for foodstuffs created a sellers' market for farmers, millers, and wholesalers. It set up a situation in which improvement in and increase of agricultural output no more than kept up with the country's growing requirements. In the early eighteenth century England and Wales had exported a marginal surplus of wheat, and adequate supplies for the home market had kept prices low and steady. From the 1760s this ceased to be the case. There was never any crisis of subsistence; but in the new circumstances slight shortages, even strictly local ones, could push up prices in particular localities. There was a constant temptation for farmers, millers, and wholesalers to engross supplies, or to hold them off the market, or to sell them elsewhere, in hopes of realizing higher prices. Apart from price fluctuations induced in this way, there was a long-term secular rise in the price of grains during the second

---

[40] E. J. E. Hobsbawm, 'The Machine Breakers', in his *Labouring Men* (1971), pp. 6–17.

half of the century, which took place not in a gradual imperceptible progression, but in jumps, particularly in the 1760s and 1790s. Recent writers have emphasized that overall blanket explanations, such as the sense of 'moral economy' of English crowds, are insufficient, and that to some extent, the causes of riot differed from place to place according to specific local circumstances. Thus, miners in Cornwall, who had a particularly strong local group organization, were especially sensitive about food prices, owing to the local excess of demand over supply and the temptation to local farmers to ship their grain to the more profitable markets in the London area. By contrast, some areas of the country were little affected. But wherever fears of shortage developed, or an unexpected rise in prices occurred, the response of the aggrieved populace was the food riot.[41] The worst years during the late eighteenth century were the mid 1760s, the early 1770s, the mid 1790s, and 1799–1800.

The usual target of condemnation by food rioters was an excessive price charged in shops or markets for staple foodstuffs, usually flour and bread, sometimes cheese, less fre-

[41] There is now a large and informative literature on food riots in eighteenth-century England. A good starting-point is the article by R. B. Rose, 'Eighteenth Century Price Riots and Public Policy in England', *International Review of Social History*, 6 (1961), 277–92, to be followed by E. P. Thompson, 'The Moral Economy of the English Crowd in the eighteenth century', *Past and Present*, 50 (1971), 76–136. John Stevenson, *Popular Disturbances in England, 1700–1870* (1979), chapter 5, provides an excellent general account. The food riots of the 1760s receive extensive treatment in Walter J. Shelton, *English Hunger and Industrial disorders. A study of Social Conflict during the first decade of George III's reign* (Toronto, 1973), and those of the 1790s in John Stevenson, 'Food Riots in England, 1792–1818', in *Popular Protest and Public Order. Six Studies in British History, 1790–1920*, ed. J. Stevenson and R. Quinault (1974). A number of regional studies have also appeared, including Alan Booth, 'Food Riots in the North West of England, 1790–1801', *Past and Present*, 77 (1977), 84–107; R. A. E. Wells, 'The Revolt of the South West, 1800–1: a study in English popular protest', *Social History*, 6 (1977), 713–44; 'Dearth and Distress in Yorkshire, 1793–1802', *Borthwick Papers*, no. 52 (1977); and 'Counting Riots in eighteenth-century England', *Bulletin of the Society for the Study of Labour History*, 37 (1978); D. E. Williams, 'Midland Hunger Riots in 1766', *Midland History*, 3 (1975-6), 256–97; John G. Rule, 'Some Social Aspects of the Cornish Industrial Revolution', in *Industry and Society in the South West* (Exeter Papers in Economic History, no. 3, University of Exeter, 1970). There is also material on the attitudes of the authorities in Tony Hayter, *The Army and the Crowd in Mid-Georgian England* (1978), and John Stevenson, 'Social Control and the Prevention of Riots in England, 1789–1829', in *Social Control in Nineteenth-Century Britain*, ed. A. P. Donajgrodzki (1977), pp. 27–50. Further evidence can be found in almost any recent study of the social and economic history of particular localities.

quently meat or other supplies. R. B. Rose has suggested that such riots may be divided into four types. In some cases, relatively few in number, they were simple looting expeditions. In others the object was to check the removal of grain or other comestibles from the district on the suspicion that this would create a local scarcity and famine prices. A third variety had as its aim the coercion of market dealers and shopkeepers into selling at fixed prices (usually what was regarded on past experience as the 'normal' or 'fair' price). The fourth was intended to secure the same object by putting pressure on magistrates to fix 'fair' prices. To these types of riots may also be added another, that directed against farmers or millers, and usually accompanied by threats of the firing of barns or storehouses, with the purpose of coercing them into the release of stocks of grain, cheese, or flour suspected of being held back from the market in order to force up the price.

The investigation of these riots by historians seems to indicate that they scored a relatively high degree of success. The authorities were frequently inclined to believe that forestalling and engrossing by suppliers were largely to blame, and the laws against these practices were sometimes invoked, even—in 1766—in a royal proclamation issued by the government. Magistrates and gentry often took practical steps to see that increased supplies of foodstuffs were brought to market, with the object of moderating the price and preventing scarcity. Thus, in 1756, local Shropshire magnates, Sir Thomas Whitmore and Sir Richard Acton, instructed their tenants to sell wheat at Bridgnorth market at a fixed maximum price and agreed to compensate them with rebates of rent. In September 1800 twelve Devonshire landowners took the extreme step of publicly threatening their tenants with the non-renewal of leases unless they immediately sent their produce to market. On some occasions crowds seized wagon-loads of foostuffs suspected of being intended for shipment elsewhere and insisted on their sale at a 'fair' price at the local market. Urban magistrates played their part in trying to prevent forestalling and engrossing, and in some centres, as for example Coventry, co-operated on occasion with the leaders of crowds to get stocks moved from warehouses to market stalls or shops for sale at popularly approved rates.[43]

Although legal authority was sometimes invoked, and troops were sometimes brought in to restore law and order when riots got entirely out of hand, rioters were on the whole treated with sympathy and leniency. Magistrates were well aware of the limits upon using force in an unpopular cause, when the goodwill of militia, and even of regular soldiers, would be in doubt. They gave a sympathetic response to delegations demanding the imposition of fair prices. They avoided punitive action as far as possible, and when sentences had to be imposed on leading rioters they were usually light. Magistrates exerted pressures to satisfy popular feeling. Also they stepped in with their own resources and with the use of their political authority to defuse riotous situations. Subscriptions were organized to subsidize the sale of foodstuffs at popular prices or to aid the poor in other ways: newspaper reports show that during 1766-7 numbers of gentry in the Midlands contributed donations for this purpose of £50 to £100, and smaller sums were collected by tradesmen in various towns.[44] In the 1790s, and especially in 1800-1, the government itself became more directly involved in the organization of methods of relief, by encouraging importation of grain, by strengthening the powers of local authorities to provide relief—this by the Parish Relief Act of December 1800—by encouraging the free play of market forces to overcome hoarding, and not least by insisting upon the use of food substitutes to overcome the wheat shortage.

Thus, in one way or another, the poor who engaged in food riots did gain a considerable measure of satisfaction. Taken into their hands supplies of foodstuffs in markets *were* immediately distributed at traditional, not inflated, prices. Cheap price agreements *were* imposed, sometimes over a period of weeks till a shortage was expected to be ended, as a result of either acceptance of the mob's diktat or of a ruling by local magistrates. Hoarders *were* forced

[43] Rose, article cited, p. 286; Wells, in *Social History*, 6, p. 721; Williams, article cited, pp. 264-6.

[44] Williams, article cited, pp. 269-70, 278-9.

to open their stores, and artificial scarcities were brought to an end. And when the crisis was beyond immediate local control, the central government did step in with further effective measures. The modes of proceeding, and the results, ensured that food riots did not become protests against the existing system of supply as such. Their object was to make the system work in its traditional mode, according to a familiar pattern of prices and supply, and to eliminate what were regarded as aberrations. There was nothing revolutionary in their nature. This was an essentially conservative process.[45]

[45] Cf. John Bohstedt, *Riots and Community Politics in England and Wales, 1790–1810* (Harvard U.P., 1983), published after this text had been prepared.

VI

The Intellectual Repulse
of Revolution

I

Revolutions—as those who seek to establish formulas to explain them never weary of stressing—require a renegade minority of the élite to give leadership and a discontented mass to provide destructive brute force to be applied against the existing regime. Both elements were present in France in the 1780s, flowing into the power-vacuum left by the collapse of monarchical government to combine in spontaneous combustion. Both elements were also present in Ireland in the 1790s. Here, however, the flames were smothered by a combination of counter-revolutionary action on the part of the authorities and of irreconcilable incompatibility between an Ulster-based leadership and a southern Catholic mass.[1] In Britain no power-vacuum developed, and it can be contended that neither a renegade élite nor an insurrectionary mass was present in sufficient force to constitute a danger to the established order.[2]

Of these two necessary elements, it can be argued that the élite is the more important. The mass will respond to slogans and leadership. It is the élite that derives a driving force from the flame of its convictions, the élite which formulates the objectives and fabricates the slogans to win support for them, and which provides organization and momentum. Some survey of the beliefs and attitudes of the British élite in the

[1] Pages 14–25 above.

[2] The French visitor, Rochefoucauld, was much struck during his sojourn in in England during 1784 by the general satisfaction of Englishmen with their system of government. Noting the contrast with his own land, he wrote: 'How many thousands of Frenchmen will deem their own imperfect' (*A Frenchman in England, 1784*, ed. Marchand, pp. 115–16). 'You have not', wrote a French correspondent in 1793, 'the same mass of abuses to change—you have not the same mass of folly and vice to struggle against—your people are neither so generally ignorant nor ferocious as the French populace—and . . . you have not amongst you that shocking *inequality* which disfigured human society in France' (quoted in *The Monthly Review, or Literary Journal Enlarged*, xiii (1794), p. 62).

1780s and 1790s is therefore important to our theme. The rise of a renegade élite requires stimulus from a profound discontent and disquiet about the existing state of affairs; and whatever elements of material interest may be present, these are likely to derive greater momentum from intellectual rationalization. The degree of influence achievable through such rationalization depends considerably on the defensive intellectual strength sustaining the contemporary system thus brought under attack.

The intellectual defences of the Hanoverian regime were formidable and were energetically sustained. In one respect British conservatives were carrying on a war of ideas on two fronts in the 1790s. They were combating propaganda in favour of parliamentary reform, and they were contesting any suggestion that the French Revolution formed a model to be copied or admired. In another respect, however, these two fronts fused into one, at least from the conservative viewpoint, because parliamentary reform itself, or at least some versions of it, might be expected to have a revolutionary effect. The political system would no longer work as before if the representation was radically changed. And not only would such a change be likely to have repercussions on the social order but, if Thomas Paine were taken as representative of radical thought, then this was what ought to happen; this was the intended result. Opposition to reform and to the Revolution had therefore a dual aim: the preservation of the existing constitution and the preservation of the established social order.

The line of approach of the conservative polemicists was partly determined by a further factor: the ambiguity in the French Revolution itself. Superficially the Revolution was an embodiment of acceptable Enlightenment ideas. The French Declaration of Rights of August 1789 seemed to stand four-square on an acceptable foundation of natural-rights theory. It also invited defence on utilitarian grounds. But underneath the surface the Revolution was steadily being transformed into something different: it was moving in the direction of totalitarian democracy. The individual was swallowed up in the mystic concept of the nation, and a legislative assembly once elected became the unchallengeable arbiter of the fate of all. Such a metaphysical identification of ruler and ruled created a Leviathan far more dread than anything conceived by Hobbes, a sovereign assembly or a sovereign revolutionary junta unrestrained by any consideration of individual rights or claims.

It was in this connection that an unbridgeable ideological gulf yawned between British conservative political thought and the stark facts of the French Revolution. This was something that radical critics failed to grasp. Good British admirers of the Enlightenment took the Revolution at its face value and could not or would not realize that it was betraying the very principles for which they stood and for which they thought it stood. The blindness of such men need not surprise us. We have had plenty of experience in our own century of the West's adulation of the Bolshevik revolution in Russia despite its barbarities; experience of the way in which men can be mesmerized by the projected vision of what they wish to believe rather than the reality. This radical failure of perception gave a further twist of inconsequence to much of the polemical discussion that filled British book-stalls in the 1790s and which took place within the two Houses of Parliament.

II

In the decades before the French Revolution, although a fair amount of argument controverting radical ideas found its way into print, much of it was merely directed to particular questions and did not constitute a coherent body of conservative argument, let alone of basic political theory. A number of writers—Josiah Tucker, Francis Basset, Soame Jenyns, and Lord Rivers—recapitulated defences of the presence of placemen in the House of Commons, which by that time were fairly commonplace.[3] They defended the system of constitutional checks and balances which prevented arbitrary action by any one focus of power in the state. They emphasized the connection between property and political stability, and they countered the pressure from

[3] H. T. Dickinson, *Liberty and Property. Political Ideology in eighteenth-century Britain* (1977), pp. 275-9.

the Wilkites in London to stress the role of MPs as delegates of their constituents by laying emphasis on the 'virtual representation' practised within the British system and the duty of MPs to think in terms of national, not sectional interests.[4] Much of this defence of the existing constitution was on pragmatic and practical grounds.

But there were also more deeply rooted intellectual defences against reform, even if they were not always fully articulated, and the growing heat of controversy during the two last decades of the century gradually brought them to the surface. This circumstance is important to the present theme. It indicates, as has recently been suggested by one leading scholar in the field, that there is a fallacy in the common assumption that the radical reformers in Britain won the intellectual argument but were defeated by the force at the disposal of their opponents. On the contrary, Professor Dickinson has written, 'it can be argued and argued quite strongly that the radicals were defeated by the force of their opponents' arguments and by the climate of conservative opinion among the politically conscious, not simply by recourse to repressive measures and the forces of order'.[5]

For statement of this conservative philosophy it is customary to turn to Edmund Burke, and Burke, indeed, cannot be ignored. But for a more systematic exposition of the intellectual tradition upon which Burke and other conservative writers of the 1790s drew, it is worth first considering the political thought of William Paley. Paley's book, *The Principles of Moral and Political Philosophy*, published in 1785, was not, as was Burke's *Reflections on the Revolution in France*, a *pièce d'occasion*. It was indeed written in the wake of Christopher Wyvill's county association movement but it did not address itself to the particular issues raised by that agitation for reform. It was a systematic treatise. It had an immediate impact and won remarkable acclaim. Crisp,

[4] Among the conspicuous champions of this idea was Edmund Burke, not only in his address to the electors of Bristol in 1774, but also in other communications to them (*Works*, i. 442-9, and ii. 1-54, 127-68).

[5] Dickinson, *Liberty and Property*, p. 272. I agree with this judgement, but I think that the grounds of it are more complex and compelling than Professor Dickinson makes clear.

clear, and accurate in style, penetrating in argument, and
devoid of any clerical obscurantism, it went through five
impressions in four years and into a further, corrected edition
in 1790. Within a year or so of the first publication, it was
adopted as a standard examination text in the University
of Cambridge—one of those occasions in the eighteenth
century when 'the other place' seems to have stolen a march
on Oxford—and it seems fair to assume that over the following years it came to have a certain conditioning effect upon
the outlook of part at least of the political class.[6] It is evident
that it provided a quarry for arguments paraded by anti-
revolutionary publicists after 1789.

Paley's discussion of the origin of political society rested
on a basis of such anthropological information as was then
available, relating to primitive societies in North America
and Africa, and stressed the element of paternal authority in
the small family groups which it could be presumed were
gradually aggregated into larger communities with settled
government. He noted that military leadership was also likely
to give rise to political authority. Nevertheless, he argued that
in the last resort political obedience was voluntary, since 'in
all cases, even in the most popular forms of civil government,
the physical strength resides in the governed'. Despite this
strength men remained in their obedience. In some cases
this might be due to reason or to immediate self-interest, but
Paley attributed it for the most part to prescription, and he
saw in this the operation of the utilitarian principle. 'Nor',
he wrote, 'is it to be wondered at, that mankind should
reverence authority founded in prescription, when they
observe that it is prescription which confers the title to
almost everything else', particularly to every form of
property right. The importance of prescription as a social and
political cement dictated caution about innovation, for
innovation was likely to foster instability.[7]

Paley dismissed theories of contract (so repudiating

[6] *The Works of William Paley, DD. With a Biographical Sketch of the Author*,
ed. and introd. by D. S. Wayland (5 vols., 1837), i, p. xv.

[7] *The Works of William Paley, DD, and an account of the life and writings of
the author*, by the Rev. Edmund Paley, AM (4 vols., 1838), iii. 224–31; The
italics are Paley's. Following references are to this edition which, unlike that of
1837, presents all the text of the *Principles* within one volume.

Locke) as a fiction containing within itself insuperable difficulties. Contract was historically unidentifiable. There was
no escape from a contract once entered into, and so logically
no right of rebellion—a right which Paley was prepared to
justify: the argument that a contract might be broken by a
ruler, releasing his subjects from allegiance, he thought to be
'captious and unsafe'. Political obedience, he argued, reduced
itself to a question of expediency which every man in a
political society had to judge for himself.[8] His gloss, that
reasoning from expediency revealed 'the will of God' on the
matter, while placing politics within his general theological
context, perhaps saved the phenomenon of natural law,
without however making it integral to his argument. The
ruling consideration in his view was what most conduced
to the advantage of the community, submission or rejection
of existing authority. On the one hand public interest must
overrule individual or sectional interest: 'The interest of the
whole society is binding upon every part of it.' But within
this definition of purpose Paley was prepared to allow, for
instance, that a calculus of utility could justify the rebellion
of colonies against a metropolitan state: 'When, by an
increase of population, the interest of the provinces begins
to bear a considerable proportion to the *entire* interest of the
community, it is possible that they may suffer so much by
their subjection, that not only theirs, but the whole
happiness of the empire, may be obstructed by their union.'
Adjustments in relationships, even independence, might then
be justified. Paley's conservatism, like Burke's, was perfectly
compatible with the recent revolution in North America.[9]

Paley stood on common ground with radical reformers
when he defined civil liberty as the absence of any restraint
at law, except such as conduced 'in a greater degree to the
public welfare.' He also agreed that it consisted 'not merely
in an actual exemption from the constraints of useless and
noxious laws and acts of dominion, but in being free from

[8] As a reviewer in the Foxite *Monthly Review* pointed out in 1790, this
reasoning kept Paley's ideas about popular sovereignty in line with mainstream
liberal political speculation: 'expediency must require all power to originate with
the people and ultimately to revert to them' (*The Monthly Review, or Literary
Journal Enlarged*, ii (1790), pp. 85–8).

[9] Paley, *Works*, iii. 232–42.

the *danger* of having such hereafter imposed or exercised'. Civil liberty necessitated the presence of some set of institutions which could block the exercise of power to the detriment of individual freedom. Within this general definition could be subsumed systems of separation of powers, rule of law, taxation only through representation, government by consent even if only through virtual representation, freedom and purity of elections, and popular control of the army. 'That people, government and constitution is the *freest*, which makes the best provision for the enacting of expedient and salutary laws.' His encomiums on 'mixed government' reveal his feeling that in many respects the existing British system represented the most effective line of defence for liberty, although he was by no means entirely uncritical of it, remarking for instance, that a wide 'democratical' participation in government could have an important formative effect on the moral character of the populace as well as securing greater respect for the lower ranks of society from the higher.[10]

But if Paley did not exclude all improvement, in other respects his arguments traversed the ideas of most reformers of his day. He dismissed as fictitious any conception of an original 'pure' constitution, to the principles of which it was necessary to return. Cartwright and Paine were equally rebuffed. In Paley's view, no original constitution ever existed as a historical datum: 'No such plan was ever formed, consequently no such first principles, original model, or standard, exist.' On the contrary, the constitution had 'grown out of occasion and emergency'. Such reasoning had obvious logical implications for the consideration of reform. On this subject Paley felt that 'the habit of reflection to be encouraged, is a sober comparison of the constitution under which we live—not with models of speculative perfection, but with the actual chance of obtaining a better'. Innovations could have bad as well as good effects, and the former were often unforeseen. In his view the criteria of improvement must lie in the attempt in the mixed system of British government 'to unite the advantages of the several simple forms and exclude the inconveniences'.[11] This view held obvious implica-

<hr>

[10] Paley, Works, iii, 250-61.　　　[11] Ibid., 262-5.

tions in store for the future when the nature of the French Revolution came under debate.

Paley made perfunctory acknowledgements of the illogicalities within the electoral system which produced the House of Commons, but he defended it vigorously on grounds of expediency. He believed it provided a form of virtual representation for 'each order and profession of men in the community', who were 'interested in the prosperity and experienced in the occupation of their respective professions'. The bias in favour of great landed estate and other forms of wealth, plus the variety of interests, was a safeguard that Members of Parliament would neither combine in sinister interests themselves nor come under external dictation. A degree of common interest in good legislation was secured by the circumstance that 'the representatives are so intermixed with the constituents and the constituents with the rest of the people, that they cannot, without a partiality too flagrant to be endured, impose any burthen upon the subject, in which they do not share themselves'. He regarded the publication of parliamentary debates and proceedings as a further safeguard.[12] Even if it was true, as he accepted, that one half of the MPs were elected by the people, and the other half secured seats by purchase or through nomination by great landed proprietors, nevertheless he treated proposals for reform with extreme reserve. He dismissed the view that representation was a natural right: 'We consider it so far only as a right at all, as it conduces to public utility; that is, as it contributes to the establishment of good laws, or as it secures to the people the just administration of these laws.' Who elected the MPs was of less importance: what mattered was that the men elected should be most likely to promote the general interest. This, he thought, the present system did: 'Does any new scheme of representation promise to collect together more wisdom, or to produce firmer integrity?' The merits of the existing system, he believed, provided 'just excuses for those parts of the present representation which appear to a hasty observer most exceptional and absurd'. He considered—and writing in the wake of the general election of 1784 perhaps not without some justification—that:

[12] Ibid 266-7.

The present representation, after all the deductions, and under the confusion, in which it confessedly lies, is still in such a degree popular, or rather the representatives are so connected with the mass of the community by a society of interests and passions, that the will of the people, when it is determined, permanent, and general, almost always, at length, prevails.

Writing in the context of the ideas circulated by the county association movement of the early 1780s and the speculative propaganda of the Westminster Committee, Paley's reasoning led him to support only a limited measure of 'economical reform', a direct reduction of the patronage of the crown, of 'superfluous and exorbitant emoluments of office'. This would be in line with the general principles of the mixed constitution. But he defended strongly the presence of placemen and of a government 'interest' in the two Houses of Parliament.[13]

III

Paley's book was the fruit of tranquil reflection in his study. Far otherwise was the contribution to the debate of Edmund Burke, which grew out of passionate involvement in the crisis occasioned by the French Revolution. Yet both drew upon the same intellectual tradition, a fact only superficially obscured by the incandescent imagery of Burke's majestic prose and oratory. Burke's defence of conservative politics against parliamentary reformers and French revolutionaries was never articulated in a coherent treatise. It emerged piecemeal in response to discussions of particular circumstances. It had nevertheless a basic consistency founded upon fundamental principles. This was typical of the man. In 1790, when the *Reflections on the Revolution in France* were in course of composition, Burke's son wrote to Philip Francis of his knowledge, 'from an intimate experience of many years', that:[14]

my father's opinions are never hastily adopted; and that even those ideas, which have often appeared to me only the effect of momentary

---

[13] Paley, *Works*, iii. 274–80.
[14] *Correspondence*, ed. Copeland and others, vi. 92.

heat or casual impression, I have afterwards found, beyond a possibility of doubt, to be either the systematic meditation perhaps of years, or else if adopted on the spur of the occasion, yet formed upon the conclusion of long and philosophical experience, and supported by no trifling depth of thought.

Burke's ideas have been convincingly classed as a form of historical utilitarianism. A case can be made that he subscribed to the classical form of the theory of natural law. There are many references to it scattered through his writings. He accepted the idea of an immutable law of divine origin, anterior to positive law, which described the nature of moral duty and provided a criterion of justice in the social order. Revealed religion was part of the evidence of this law, and the emphasis this set on moral duty meant that 'rights' were not to be regarded in isolation. But Burke's natural law appears very often as merely the icing on the cake. It has no integral part in his trains of argument, which are based on empirical observation. As other writers have pointed out, there is inconsistency between his metaphysics and his epistemology.[15] For him the real test of institutions lay not in theory but in practical experience, and ideas about 'natural rights' or unhistorical contracts were nothing to do with the case. The key, in his opinion, was the actual behaviour of men in political society. 'You have theories enough concerning the Rights of Man', he told a French correspondent in November 1790, warning him: 'It may not be amiss to add a small degree of attention to their nature and disposition. It is with Man in the concrete, it is with common human life and human actions you are to be concerned.'[16] To know and understand what had actually happened in the past was vital. Forms of political organization evolved through a process of prolonged trial and error over many generations, during which their institutions underwent a test of utility, defects were eliminated, and necessary modifications were made.

[15] Alfred Cobban, *Edmund Burke and the Revolt against the Eighteenth Century. A Study of the Political and Social Thinking of Burke, Wordsworth, Coleridge and Southey* (1928), pp. 75-7; P. J. Stanlis, *Edmund Burke and the Natural Law* (Ann Arbor, 1965), *passim*; Carl B. Cone, *Burke and the Nature of Politics. The Age of the French Revolution* (1964), pp. 318-19; Michael Freeman, *Edmund Burke and the Critique of Political Radicalism* (Oxford, 1980), p. 28.

[16] *Correspondence*, ed. Copeland and others, vi. 46.

No single best model existed. The experience of different political communities could lead them to different solutions of the basic problem of constructing a polity which served the best interest of men.[17] This interest was not to be found in the guarantee of particular 'rights', but in a social system in which order, duty, and justice were fused to the best advantage of its members in conformity with the rules of the divine order. While no existing system was likely to be perfect, and while it would be naturally subject to further evolutionary change, there was a presumption that, on balance, the main features of it were justified, *because they were there*. Thus for Burke natural law became identified with prescription, and the doctrine of prescription dominated his speeches and writings on this theme.

Burke's consistency—and thereby the deep-rooted nature of the intellectual tradition on which he drew—can be clearly demonstrated over the whole period from his concern with the American imperial crisis in the 1770s until the years of his denunciation of the French Revolution.

Take, for instance, his magnificent analysis in 1775 of the American colonists' preoccupation with liberty.[18] Of the six reasons for it which he adduced, five related to the development of the colonies since their foundation: one only stood apart as different in character, the geographical remoteness of the colonies from the centre of imperial power.

'First', Burke pointed out, 'the people of the colonies [were] descendants of Englishmen.' They had migrated at a time when the 'great contests' in England were over the questions of the control of taxation, and they had carried with them the awareness that this was a crucial issue: without popular control of money grants through representatives, 'no shadow of liberty could subsist'. The active role of popular representative assemblies in the colonies had reinforced this conviction. The psychology on which it rested had been buttressed by the dissenting Protestant faiths prevalent in the northern colonies, a religious outlook 'the most adverse to all implicit submission of mind and opinion

[17] *Correspondence*, ed. Copeland and others, vi. 45–6.
[18] *The Works of Edmund Burke* (Bohn Library, 8 Vols., 1894–1900), i. 464–9 (speech on conciliation).

. . . a persuasion not only favourable to liberty but built upon it'. This spirit had been at its height in the mid seventeenth century both in England and among the migrants who established the New England settlements. Although many colonists in the south belonged to the Church of England, there another circumstance sharpened their attachment to the principles of freedom, the presence of Negro slavery: 'in such a people, the haughtiness of domination combines with the spirit of freedom, fortifies it, and renders it invincible'. The colonists' inheritance of the English legal tradition, their study of the law, and their litigiousness also helped to explain their attitude, and their isolation across the Atlantic helped to foster it. 'From these six capital sources,' Burke declared, 'of descent; of form of government; of religion in the northern provinces, of manners in the southern; of education; of the remoteness of situation from the first mover of government; from all these causes a fierce spirit of liberty had grown up. . . . What in the name of God shall we do with it?'

Burke's whole argument here was in essence historical. It implied that the American colonies, while still parts of the British Empire, were also the product in their own right of generations of political evolution. Indeed, a year earlier, in his speech on American taxation, Burke had given utterance to an even more forthright recognition of the colonial communities: 'For my part I never cast an eye on their flourishing commerce, and their cultivated and commodious life, but they seem to me rather ancient nations grown to perfection through a long series of fortunate events, and a train of successful industry, accumulating wealth in many centuries.'[19] The colonies had their own prescriptive rights, and Burke's perception of the American Revolution was that it was a conservative movement in defence of them.[20] British violation of these rights did, in his view, justify the Declaration of Independence.[21]

Burke used similar arguments when opposing parliamentary

[19] *Works*, i. 403.
[20] Cf. his statement to this effect in 1791, *The Parliamentary History of England*, ed. W. Cobbett and T. C. Hansard (36 vols., 1806–20), xxix. 395.
[21] *Works*, v. 469.

reform in May 1782, and in doing so expressed his total opposition to doctrines of natural rights.[22] 'Our constitution', he declared, 'is a prescriptive constitution; it is a constitution whose sole authority is that it has existed time out of mind'; and he argued that prescription was 'the most solid of titles, not only to property, but, which is to secure that property, to government'. Each complemented and supported the other. Prescription was supported by presumption: 'It is a presumption in favour of any settled scheme of government against any untried project, that a nation has long existed and flourished under it.' The government a nation enjoyed was in effect one it had chosen; for 'a nation is not an idea only of local extent, and individual momentary aggregation; but it is an idea of continuity which extends in time as well as in numbers and in space'. Such a form of government was 'a deliberate election of ages and generations . . . made by the peculiar circumstances, occasions, tempers, dispositions, and moral, civil, and social habitudes of the people, which disclose themselves only in a long space of time'. Roundly he accused the proponents of natural rights of false circular reasoning:[23]

On what grounds do we go to restore our constitution to what it has been at one given period or to reform and reconstruct it upon principles more conformable to a sound theory of government? A prescriptive government such as ours never was the work of any legislator, never was made upon any foregone theory. It seems to me a preposterous way of reasoning, and a perfect confusion of ideas, to take the theories which learned and speculative men have made from that government, and then, supposing it made on those theories which were made from it, to accuse the government as not corresponding with them.

Reformers, Burke maintained, were seeking to impose their own limited wisdom and partial preconceptions, in place of the accumulated practical wisdom of the nation gradually accreted over centuries: 'they wish us to . . . prefer their speculations . . . to the happy experience of this country of a growing liberty and a growing prosperity for five hundred years'. Not the least of the advantages that had accrued was the balanced constitution, which held monarchy, aristocracy, and a 'tumultuous and giddy people' alike in check—in

[22] *Works* vi 144–53.   [23] *Works*, vi. 148.

other words it had guaranteed the rule of law. Under such a system the individual, while free, could not use his freedom to the damage of others: 'there is an order that keeps things fast in their place; it is made to us and we are made to it'.

Many of these points of argument were to reappear, presented with more cogency, more grace, and more force, in Burke's *Reflections on the Revolution in France*. He stressed the interlocking, interdependent nature of a political society, which secured the protection of the law to all its members: 'The constituent parts of a state are obliged to hold their public faith with each other, and with all those who derive any serious interest under their engagement, as much as the whole state is bound to keep its faith with separate communities. Otherwise competence and power would soon be confounded, and no law be left but the will of a prevailing force.'[24] British liberties were claimed 'as an *entailed inheritance* derived to us from our forefathers and to be transmitted to our posterity, as an estate specially belonging to the people of this kingdom, without any reference to any other more general or prior right'.[25] Historical utilitarianism as the foundation of government was spelled out in one of the most famous and most eloquent passages in the Burke canon:[26]

Society is indeed a contract. . . . But the state ought not to be considered as nothing better than a partnership agreement in a trade of pepper and coffee, calico or tobacco, or some other such low concern. . . . It is to be looked on with other reverence; because it is not a partnership in things subservient only to the gross animal existence of a temporary and perishable nature. It is a partnership in all science; a partnership in all art; a partnership in every virtue, and in all perfection. As the ends of such a partnership cannot be obtained in many generations, it becomes a partnership not only between those who are living, but between those who are living, those who are dead, and those who are to be born.

In Burke's own view—though this was in no way essential to the main thrust of his argument—additional respect

---

[24] *Works*, ii. 294–5.   [25] *Works*, ii. 306.

[26] *Works*, ii. 368. To subscribe to the idea, as one or two writers have done, that Burke here embraced the idea of a social contract, seems inappropriate; for though he used the word 'contract' in this passage, the political entity he proceeded to describe had no connection with 'contract' in the common use of the term.

should be shown to the fruits of such political evolution, since these evolving states were a part of the divine order. Laws thus evolved by the wisdom of the generations were the nearest approximation men were capable of to the law of God.[27] This did not mean, however, that he condoned despotism and the destruction of liberty, which to him was the very negation of that law.[28] Nor did Burke believe in a die-hard conservatism that would make the removal of abuses and oppression impossible. His record on America and on economical reform gave the lie to that. In an early passage in the *Reflections*, he stressed the need for adaptive mechanisms: 'A state without the means of some change is without the means of its conservation. Without such means it might even risk the loss of that part of the constitution which it wished the most religiously to preserve.' Such a mechanism, he maintained, had operated in the English Revolution of 1689.[29]

IV

To contemporaries then, and to us now, the clash between Burke and Paine over the French Revolution epitomized the confrontation between conservatism and revolution. In considering that confrontation two points concerning intellectual strategy need to be kept in mind. In the first place, each man based his arguments on a different premiss—Burke on natural law and historical utility, Paine on natural rights— and neither admitted the validity of the other' premiss. In the second place—and this, I suspect, is a circumstance that is generally overlooked—Burke and Paine had quite different perceptions of the French Revolution. A convincing case can be made out for the conclusion that Paine's perception was a figment of his imagination based on superficial information

[27] On the basis of this and other supporting passages, some writers have claimed Burke as one of the originators of the metaphysical theory of the state (G. H. Sabine, *A History of Political Theory* (1939), pp. 617–19; C. E. M. Joad, *Guide to the Philosophy of Morals and Politics* (1947), pp. 573–5). But Burke's concern with men as they were suggests this view should be treated with reserve.

[28] For Burke's concept of law, see Cobban, *Burke and the Revolt against the eighteenth century*, pp. 41–4.

[29] *Works*, ii. 295–6.

and preconceived notions, whereas Burke's penetrated to the heart. In making this assertion, I am not denying the fact that Burke's understanding of some of the immediate realities in both France and Britain was faulty, and that in particular he exaggerated the extent of convinced egalitarian republicanism in Britain. But on the crucial issue of the theoretical basis of revolutionary action in France he was right, and had made the correct assessment long before anybody else.

Paine, with his American experience, shared the misconceptions of many British observers, that the French Revolution was cast in the mould of 1689 and 1776, and that it would issue in representative government and a rule of laws. It would, that is, put into practice the political ideas of the Enlightenment. Given the initial emergence of the French national assembly and the issue of the impeccable French Declaration of Rights, which looked like the entrenchment of the liberties of the subject, hitherto at the mercy of an autocratic monarchy, perhaps this impression was understandable. These were the results which Paine expected to flow from Frenchmen's exercise of their natural rights to frame a government for themselves, to cashier rulers who had abused their trust, and to choose new governors.

In this spirit of optimism Paine confidently set out to justify the Revolution against Burke's strictures in the *Reflections*. Theories of prescription he rejected outright. Condemning all historical precedent as contentious and contrary, he insisted on reaching back beyond history to the ultimate beginnings of human society: 'If any generation of men ever possessed the right of dictating the mode by which the world should be governed for ever, it was the first generation that existed, and if that generation did not do it, no succeeding generation can show any authority for doing it nor can set any up. . . . Every generation is equal in rights to the generations that preceded it, by the same rule that every individual is born equal in rights with his contemporary.' This 'illuminating and divine principle of the equal rights of man', which Paine attributed to God's creation, was the basic axiom on which he reared his own reasoning about the state. He defined these equal rights in traditional terms as 'all the intellectual rights or rights of the mind, and also all those rights of acting as an individual for his own comfort and happiness, which are not injurious to the natural rights of others'. Civil rights were in his view founded upon these natural rights: men entered society to obtain the greater security for them which society and government could provide.[30]

To Paine, taking developments at their face value as they appeared at the end of 1790, the French Revolution appeared to be accomplishing the creation of an effective constitutional system, which, in his opinion, the British state had never achieved. The existing National Assembly—in his words, 'the personal social compact', composed of 'the delegates of the nation in its *original* character'—was a constituent body, discharging the task of framing a constitution. Future assemblies would be legislatures with defined and limited authority, operating according to the forms and principles of the new constitution. With what can only be described as unconscious irony, given the turmoil into which French government was to fall during the next four years, Paine contrasted these constitutional limitations with the sovereign freedom claimed by the Parliament in Britain, much to the disadvantage of the latter. 'A government on the principles on which constitutional governments arising out of society are established cannot have the right of altering itself. If it had it would be arbitrary'—and in his view arbitrary was exactly the description of the British Parliament. With enthusiasm Paine pointed out that every Frenchman paying a tax of sixty sous or more was to be an elector under the new constitution, and contrasted this with the illogical and anomalous franchises in the English constituencies; also, that the number of representatives for any place would be in ratio to the number of taxable inhabitants; that the constitution prescribed biennial elections of the National Assembly; that it excluded officials and pensioners from the assembly. Here, it seemed, was a blueprint for an independent legislature representing the people to hold the royal executive government in check, protect taxpayers from excessive financial exactions, and prevent any invasion

[30] Thomas Paine, *Rights of Man*, ed. Henry Collins (Harmondsworth, 1969), pp. 88, 90.

of their liberties. What could be better? 'Much is to be learned from the French constitution', Paine concluded.[31]

Burke's understanding of the French Revolution was very different and much closer to the mark. His correspondence of 1789 displays his growing anxiety as the restraints of civilization in France appeared to snap. In September he recorded his impression that the National Assembly was powerless and acting under the dictatorship of lawless elements outside its walls. In October he remarked to his son: 'the elements which compose Human Society seem all to be dissolved, and a world of Monsters to be produced in the place of it'. In November, it seemed to him that 'The National Assembly is nothing more than an organ of the Will of the Burghers of Paris, and they are so because the feelings of the Burghers of Paris do not differ much from those of the generality of the French nation'. Social obligation, and the rule of law which underpinned it, were crumbling: 'The moment *Will* is set above Reason and Justice in any community, a great question may arise in sober minds, in what part or portion of the community that dangerous dominion of *Will* may be the least mischievously placed.' Here Burke put his finger on the crucial issue; for in truth, the political theory of the revolutionaries gave them no key to a solution of that problem, indeed obscured from them that there was any such problem at all; and many heads were to roll in consequence. By the beginning of 1790 Burke's worst fears were being realized: 'As much injustice and tyranny has been practised in a few months by a French democracy as in all the arbitrary monarchies in Europe in the forty years of my observation', he wrote. The members of a democratic majority 'would think everything justified by their warm good intentions—they would hurt one another by their common zeal—counsel and advice would be lost to them'. All this, Burke saw, was a total repudiation of British political experience. Ideas of balance, of restraint, of representation, were being thrown aside.[32]

These fears inspired the *Reflections*. Contrary to the

---

[31] Ibid., pp. 94–7.
[32] *The Correspondence of Edmund Burke*, ed. Copeland and others, vi. 25, 30, 36, 42, 96.

accusations of Paine and numbers of other pamphleteers in 1791, the *Reflections* was not a condonation of the *Ancien Régime*. It was a condemnation of the way the French had gone about replacing it. France indeed needed a reformed system of government, but this should have been evolved on the basis of the old, with due attention to the principles of justice and morality revealed in the nation's historical experience. It was clear to Burke that this was not happening. 'Upon a free constitution there was but one opinion in France', he wrote in the *Reflections*. 'The absolute monarchy was at an end. . . . All the struggle, all the dissension, arose afterwards upon the preference of a despotic democracy to a government of reciprocal control. The triumph of the victorious party was over the principles of a British constitution.'[33]

Considering the general blindness of British intellectuals to what was happening in France, this was an extraordinarily perceptive observation. It is wholly in line with the penetrating diagnoses of modern scholars such as Talmon, Cobban, and Furet.[34] However much Burke had gone overboard with emotive passages, such as that concerning Marie Antoinette, which exposed him to much contemporary derision, he had seized upon the destructive, murderous, self-contradictory central feature of the Revolution, to which his critics were wholly blind. Before long, even if many of them could not follow his line of reasoning, nevertheless, after the September Massacres and the Terror, some at least of them, though not Paine, came to a sickening realization that some kind of rottenness lay at the heart of the Revolution, and in the fullness of time a few, such as James Mackintosh, made their recantation.[35]

[33] *Works*, ii. 406. It was unrealistic of Burke to expect an English-style revolution in France—disintegration had gone too far—but this in no way invalidates his analysis of the type of revolution which emerged.

[34] Pages 21–5 above.

[35] Then, and later, many found the true explanation difficult to grasp. Alexis de Tocqueville, seventy years later, remarked in a letter: 'There is moreover in this disease of the French Revolution something very strange that I can sense, though I cannot describe it properly or analyse its causes. It is a *virus* of a new and unknown kind. . . . Despite all my efforts I cannot lift the veil that covers it. I can palpate it as through a foreign body that prevents me from grasping or even seeing it.' Quoted in François Furet, *Interpreting the French Revolution*, p. 163 n.

This was not the only issue over which the shafts loosed by Paine against Burke missed their mark. Part of the common ground among eighteenth-century political thinkers of whatever hue was that the people had an ultimate right to resist tyrannous government. To Paine the matter seemed crystal clear. If governors rode roughshod over the people's natural rights, the people could rise and overthrow them and establish a new, legitimate government. Paine thought Burke denied this. The stridency with which he attacked Burke's doctrine of prescription tends to obscure the degree to which Burke himself reserved the ultimate right of rebellion, while reprobating the inherent violence and anarchy which he, earlier than anyone, correctly sensed to underly the French Revolution. Like Paley Burke believed in an ultimate right of resistance and acknowledged that in the last resort the people might exercise their rights of sovereignty in defence of their liberties. In a draft address to George III in 1777 he wrote: 'Sir, your throne cannot stand secure upon the principle of unconditional submission and passive obedience', and he proposed to remind the king of the nature of the Revolution of 1689. 'The people at that time re-entered into their original rights; and it was not because a positive law authorized what was then done, but because the freedom and safety of the subject, the origin and cause of all laws, required a proceeding paramount and superior to them. At that . . . period, the letter of the law was superseded in favour of the substance of liberty.'[36] But such a right of rebellion was only to be exercised *in extremis*, and the occasion itself would arise out of a historical situation just as much as did any feature of an established system of government. To Burke the line at which resistance became justified was 'faint, obscure, and not easily definable', and for those who contemplated it, 'the prospect of the future must be as bad as the experience of the past'. Since no guidelines in the form of natural rights existed, men would be guided by events: 'Times and occasions, and provocations, will teach their own lessons. The wise will determine from the gravity of the case;

[36] *Works*, v. 473. It has been noted that 'at least five separate rebellions against authority can be cited' as meeting with Burke's 'specific' approval (Cobban, *Burke and the Revolt against the eighteenth century*, pp. 55, 100).

the irritable from sensibility to oppression; the high-minded from disdain and indignation at abusive power in unworthy hands; the brave and bold, from the love of honourable danger in a generous cause.' Resistance, however, would be a last resort.[37] For it would be a rending of that intricate and complex web of moral and political lore which any society gradually constructed over the generations and to which a degree of reverence should be given.

Against this view Paine opposed the pert assertion:[38]

Every age and generation must be free to act for itself, *in all cases*, as the ages and generations which preceded it. The vanity and presumption of governing beyond the grave is the most ridiculous and insolent of all tyrannies.

No man with legal training; no one reared in the traditions of classical learning and knowledgeable in the political thought of the ancients; no British politician, aware of the historical development of government in his own country, could think for a moment that Paine's dogma disposed of Burke's. Burke was not denying that every age and generation must be free to think and act for itself. He accepted the proposition that if the general wishes of the people were clearly known, then they should prevail, and he had swallowed the bitter gall of a public dismissal of his party in 1784.[39] What he insisted was that any present generation should not wantonly jettison the hoarded wisdom of its forefathers. It would court disaster if it did so. Those who, like Paine, proposed to discard the rubbish of centuries and return to what they thought were first principles, would inevitably throw out the baby with the bath-water. A civil and political community was far too complex an entity for a group of new brooms to start, *tabula rasa*, and erect an alternative system from first principles. Their capacities

---

[37] *Works*, ii. 304 (*Reflections*).

[38] *Rights of Man*, ed. Collins, pp. 63–4.

[39] *Correspondence*, ed. Copeland and others, iv. 220: 'It would be a dreadful thing if there were any power in this country of strength enough to oppose with effect the general wishes of the people'; iv. 228: 'I most heartily wish that the deliberate sense of the kingdom . . . should be known. When it is known it must be prevalent'; v. 154: 'The people did not like our work; and they join'd the Court to pull it down.'

would fall far short of the task. Burke had already answered Paine's assertion in advance, when he wrote: 'We are afraid to put men to live and trade each on his own private stock of reason; because we suspect that this stock in each man is small, and that the individuals would do better to avail themselves of the general bank and capital of nations and of ages.' This, Burke suggested, not wholly accurately, had been done in England in 1689.[40] Though Paine merely implied it, and did not say so, it was naïve of him and of other writers, citing American experience in support of their sweeping justifications of revolution, whether in France or elsewhere, to assume that events had proceeded otherwise in the United States after 1776. To the former colonists the solid foundations of English constitutional law, custom, theory and practice, which underpinned post-revolution American government, far outweighed the novelties dictated by the change to an independent, republican state. In his grasp of these truths Burke, with the ballast of his erudition and political experience, showed far more common sense than the author of *Common Sense*; furthermore, it was a common sense instinctive and bred in the bone of members of the British political class, even of many who did not at first share his acute perception of the ideological monster rearing up in France against the ideals of the Enlightenment.

In an important sense, because Paine misread, while Burke understood, the nature of the Revolution in France, the paper war between them did not articulate the ideological gulf which yawned between the Revolution and British conservatism and, indeed, between it and many British reformers. For radicals in the British and American tradition, and for British politicians generally, the sovereignty of the people was essentially a negative force. It would come into play in order to stop those in authority from committing arbitrary and tyrannous acts, from violating the just rights of the citizen, and to ensure that men wielding power acted within the restraints of the rule of law. On this point, fundamentally,

---

[40] *Works*, ii. 359, 304. Another writer, Robert Nares, made the point in a different way, when he wrote: 'In law-making speculative judgment is fallible and the best test of good laws is experience' (*Principles of Government deduced from reason supported by English experience and opposed to French Error*, 1792).

Burke and Paine were at one. The main thrust of Burke's conservative argument after 1790 lay in its recoil, on behalf of the English tradition, against the new doctrine of the sovereignty of the people emerging on the Continent, the positive, active, unfettered national will of the French Revolution. To Burke such an inevitable extrapolation of the doctrine of natural rights led unavoidably to anarchy, to tyranny, and to total social and political disaster.[41] In France popular sovereignty threatened to become a nightmare. Such uncontrolled political volition, unrestrained by any sanctions of law or custom, was worse than Stuart prerogative. The fire in the minds of men unleashed by the French Revolution was, to Burke and to those who took his point, the fire of Hell.[42] But this was a matter not understood by most of Burke's critics during 1790 and the years immediately following, who continued to accuse him of reneging on the principles of 1689 when, in reality, he was condemning something of an entirely different nature.[43]

[41] Michael Freeman places this belief of Burke's within the context of his understanding of the theory of natural law (*Burke and the Critique of Political Radicalism*, *passim*, and esp. p. 238).

[42] For example, William Cusac Smith, *Rights of Citizens* ... [1791], pp. 48–56, 71, 115–18; Charles Francis Sheridan, *An Essay upon the true Principles of Civil Liberty and of Free Government* (1793), pp. 25–31, 51; [Anon.] *Thoughts on the New and Old Principles of Political Obedience* (1793). Sheridan wrote: 'The doctrines of the day, respecting the absolute, unlimited and illimitable sovereignty of the people, teach only a transfer of despotism from the prince to to the nation—the destructive and detestable *principle* is the same. As well might it be expected that aggregate folly should produce true wisdom as that aggregate despotism should produce civil liberty.'

[43] The nature of this misunderstanding is best grasped from the cumulative denunciations of Burke reviewed in the *Monthly Review*, vols. i–ix, for the years 1790–2.

It is only if the nature of Burke's target is clearly grasped, that the significance of an episode in Fox's career a few years later becomes fully intelligible. At Fox's birthday celebrations on 24 January 1798, the chairman, the Duke of Norfolk, called on the assembly to drink 'our sovereign's health—the Majesty of the People'. He was promptly dismissed from his lord lieutenancy. In May Fox took the opportunity to champion Norfolk at a meeting of the Whig Club by giving the toast, 'The Sovereignty of the People of Great Britain'. He was thereupon struck out of the roll of the Privy Council. Though these verbal gestures probably were not so intended, they looked like declarations of attachment to French doctrine with all its demagogic implications. This partly explains the indignation they aroused in government circles; and those writers who have condoned Fox's action fail to grasp the point—e.g., Loren Reid, *Charles James Fox. A Man for the People* (1969), pp. 354, 356, and references cited thereto.

Burke made no direct reply to Paine—Paine's pique at this is obvious in the opening passage of Part II of the *Rights of Man*. But others did. Burke himself may have felt the less inclination to do so because of the methodical onslaught on Paine's central premises published in November 1791 by a young Irish lawyer, William Cusac Smith.[44] The main themes of Smith's essay may conveniently round off this inevitably incomplete sketch of the development of anti-revolutionary thought in Britain during the 1790s.[45]

Smith had little difficulty in showing that Paine had seriously misrepresented parts of Burke's arguments and was himself also guilty of inconsistencies. He made fun at some length of the disharmony between Paine's assertions that one generation could not bind the next and his apparent insistence that once a constituent assembly had drawn up a constitution, future representative assemblies were bound by the constraints laid down. More telling were his attacks on Paine's separation of the generations and his reliance on the doctrine of natural rights.

To abstract one generation from others was, Smith argued, unrealistic. This 'ideal being', a human generation, was not 'the link of a chain which we may disconnect and consider singly; it is a particle of fluid inseparably clinging to those around it in the stream of general existence'. The young, he went on, constantly had a natural deference towards the old, and the preservation of rights in society in general could be thought of as similar to the system of family settlement, in which both the older and the younger generations concur.[46]

Like Burke Smith saw in this social arrangement a mechanism for adjustment and improvement, and in this context a sovereign legislature (which Paine condemned) was perfectly adapted to effect such changes as might accord with

[44] *Rights of Citizens; being an Inquiry into some of the consequences of social union, and an examination of Mr Paine's Principles touching Government* (1791). Smith submitted this work when he asked and received Burke's leave to dedicate it to him, and Burke then praised its arguments as constituting a far more methodical approach to the issues than he himself had ever attempted (*Correspondence*, ed. Copeland and others, vi. 302-5).

[45] For a fuller survey of conservative thought in the 1790s see T. P. Schofield, 'English Conservative Thought and Opinion in response to the French Revolution, 1789-1796', Ph.D. thesis, University of London, 1984.

[46] *Rights of Citizens*, pp. 13-20.

the general opinion of the community. 'It is', he wrote, 'by these alterations and general improvements that generations are connected in their acts, as in their existence.' Establishments inherited from the past were justified by the concurrent approbation of past ages, and piecemeal improvement testified to the continuing approval of them by the community. Smith noted that such adjustments often came by way of legal judgements in the courts. Impulsive changes by a particular generation were to be avoided. Smith observed that opinions altered rapidly, and this warranted 'a certain degree of hesitation and distrust of them'. In the event of a dispute about the forms of the constitution, who was to decide, he asked, and answered in Burke' vein: 'The living or the dead? Both if you please, the living profiting by the experience of the dead.' And again: 'The counsel which a people can have is that of their ancestors; and is to be sought for in the institutions transmitted through ages to them.'[47]

But Smith's main thrust was at the revolutionary interpretation of 'natural rights'. Here, he insisted, Paine's argument was flawed, since the civil rights which existed in society were different from and might in fact be quite contradictory to 'natural rights'. Civil rights entrenched inequalities which were not natural, particularly in relation to property. This made nonsense of Paine's assertion that natural rights were retained in the social state and that civil power could not from its nature be applied to invade natural rights retained by the individual. *Pace* Paine, until society had established property rights, no such rights existed. Indeed, the assertion of property rights was in conflict with natural rights insofar as it denied certain fruits of nature to others in favour of the possessor. From this assertion of property rights sprang rights of redress, of judging and of punishing, all of which were civil and not natural rights.[48] Moreover, Smith argued, the inequalities which were perceived in society and which were safeguarded by civil laws were themselves perfectly natural. 'Social regulations', he wrote, 'balance that inequality which is the work of nature, by establishing an equality which is the work of convention. The equality of savage man is the

---

[47] *Rights of Citizens*, pp. 27–32, 38–44, 47.
[48] Ibid., pp. 21–4, 77–90, 94–6.

chaos of the species. A regulated and subordinate inequality is the fair creation, which nature, working with human passions, and human reason, has produced.'[49] The leveller was to be reprobated because he deliberately sought a return to the chaos of savage equality.[50] The irrelevance of theories of natural rights, which Burke merely stated as a dogma, Smith thus presented on the basis of reasoned argument. Finally, Smith attacked the outcome of natural rights theory —the tyranny of the majority—partly along Burkeian lines, but he also added an unashamedly élitist argument. Majorities, he argued, were less likely to be guided by moral principles. 'I cannot', he wrote, 'persuade myself to be a warm stickler for the rights of the *many*, whilst I remember that the virtuous are the few.'[51]

A full exploration of the conservative British political literature of the 1790s is a major undertaking, far beyond the scope of these lectures.[52] However, the writings of Paley, Burke, and Cusac Smith provide a reasonably representative spectrum of the ideas which were circulating in opposition to the advocates of radical reform and of revolution. The metaphysical bases of this body of thought were, perhaps, at least to a more modern observer, relatively unconvincing. It can be maintained that they depended upon arbitrary selection of assumptions based on Christian doctrine or on classical theories of morals and politics—the main strength of these assumptions lying in their correspondence or identification with what were seen to be the admirable existing practices of the system of British government.

This scepticism about conservative metaphysics points to the fact that the more compelling theme of conservative thought was a deep-rooted pragmatism, spilling over into historical utilitarianism, born of centuries of experience of the slow evolution of the English common law. This tradition had fostered an instinctive hostility to the violent or arbitrary exercise of authority by whatever source, be it kingship, military tyranny, or an ephemeral majority. Eighteenth-century conservative thought valued consensus rather than majority rule—a principle still observed much more than

---

[49] Ibid., pp. 107-9.   [50] Ibid., p. 110.   [51] Ibid., p. 71.
[52] See note 45 above.

we may sometimes think in British government today regardless of the party in power. At the core of this conservative thinking lay reverence for the rule of law in civil society. Such rule of law was the direct counter to the tyrannous, arbitrary exercise of political power, and was seen as the only safeguard for the life, liberty, and property of the individual. In claims to protection under the law all men were or should be equal. But this did not justify demands for equality in other respects. All human experience suggested that the varying actual inborn abilities and characters of different individuals made differences in the acquisition of property natural, not unnatural. Nor did equality before the law entail such equal political rights as universal enjoyment of the franchise. Indeed, French experience after 1789 suggested that an equal franchise, leading to the tyranny of the majority, could destroy the far more valuable principle of equality before the law. Thus, in the 1790s, British publicists summoned up the lessons of history, of pragmatic experience, and of utility, in defence of their existing system of government. In doing so they appealed to and rallied the instinctive support of the great majority of the British political nation.

VII

The Churches and Good Order

I

If one religion only were allowed in *England*, the government would very possibly become arbitrary; if there were but two, the people wou'd cut one another's throats; but as there are such a multitude, they all live happily and in peace[1]

There is a general assumption—it is not wholly wrong, though sometimes presented without the due reservations— that the Christian Churches in Britain in the eighteenth century formed one of the bulwarks of political and social stability. This view was certainly held by many of the ruling class at the time, who believed with Edmund Burke that 'in a Christian Commonwealth the church and the state are one and the same thing, being different integral parts of the same whole'.[2] Churchmen actively supported the state. Clerics, including clerical magistrates, took a leading part in promoting the nation-wide political reaction against radicalism and revolution which swept the country after 1792. Manchester and Birmingham provide notable examples of clergy whipping up mobs against those whom they chose to designate as Jacobins.[3] During the 1790s the development of the Sunday School movement increasingly reflected a desire to bring

[1] Voltaire, *Letters concerning the English Nation* (London, 1733), p. 45 (letter VI). I am indebted to Dr Stephen Conway for the location of this reference.
[2] Quoted in N. Sykes, *Church and State in England in the eighteenth century* (Cambridge, 1934), p. 379. Cf. E. R. Norman, *Church and Society in England, 1770–1970* (Oxford, 1976), pp. 18–19. While Burke in this context was probably more concerned with the question of human obligations within the community, it was also the case that the legal positions of Church and state were inextricably intertwined (G. F. A. Best, *Temporal Pillars. Queen Anne's Bounty, the Ecclesiastical Commissioners, and the Church of England*, Cambridge, 1964, chapter II).
[3] E. C. Black, *The Association. British Extraparliamentary Political Organization, 1769–1793* (Cambridge, Mass., 1963), pp. 233–74; Austin Mitchell, 'The Association Movement of 1792–3', *Historical Journal,* 4 (1961), 56–77; R. B. Rose, 'The Priestley Riots of 1791', *Past and Present*, 18 (1960), 68–88; John Money, *Experience and Identity. Birmingham and the West Midlands, 1760–1800* (Manchester, 1977), pp. 219–38; Frieda Knight, *The Strange Case of Thomas Walker* (1957).

young people of the rising generation under the influence
of the Churches, not only for their spiritual good but also to
inculcate a sense of resignation and acceptance of their lot in
the world. From Lecky onwards a number of writers have
stressed the importance in this regard of the Methodist movement, which was emerging on the fringe of the Established
Church. Biographers of John Wesley emphasize his personal
commitment against revolution in America in the 1770s and
the legacy of loyalty to the established government which he
passed on to the Movement at his death.[4] The thesis that
Methodism was an anti-revolutionary force has been pushed
to its extreme in the work of E. P. Thompson, who lays
stress on two particular lines of argument. He suggests that
in the first place Methodism offered an opiate for people's
discontent in this world by encouraging their belief in a
better life in the next, and is thus led to describe Methodism
as 'the Chiliasm of despair'; and he sees Wesley's insistence
on the Puritan work-ethic as conditioning the working people
to be docile and unquestioning wage-slaves to capitalist
employers.[5]

In fact, the role of the Churches in promoting social and
political stability was by no means so simple and clear-cut,
nor perhaps quite so significant, as is sometimes suggested.
A considerable field of investigation requires attention; and
if we are to understand the influence of organized religion
on the eighteenth-century British community, it is necessary
to consider some fundamental questions regarding popular
attitudes. We cannot even begin to do this unless, by a major
effort of historical imagination, we try to grasp the world-
view of people living prior to the intellectual revolution
represented by Lyell and Darwin and by modern biblical
criticism. Our cosmological perceptions have been so revo-

[4] For example, Maldwyn Edwards, *John Wesley and the eighteenth century.
A Study of his social and political influence* (1933), chapters i–vi. To the end of
his life Wesley was guided by an inherited late Stuart High Church attitude
towards the powers that be. In June 1775 he wrote: 'All my prejudices are against
the Americans, for I am an High Churchman, the son of an High Churchman, bred
up from my childhood in the highest notions of passive obedience and non-
resistance' (Historical MSS Commission, *Eleventh Report, Appendix, Part V: The
Manuscripts of the Earl of Dartmouth* (1887), pp. 378–9).

[5] E. P. Thompson, *The Making of the English Working Class* (1964), pp. 350–
400.

lutionized by the development of geological, biological, and astronomical knowledge during the last century and a half, that it is extremely difficult to project ourselves into the state of mind of folk in a society whose members generally regarded the biblical writings, *in toto*, as of divine inspiration, and for whom the biblical chronology was the only one available. In Christian Europe in the late eighteenth century —except for a handful of speculative thinkers like Kant and Buffon, and the relatively small circles of intellectuals who read their works—even those people who were fully educated by the standards of the day had no cosmological conception other than that the universe had been created by divine action nearly six thousand years ago and that the world had been peopled according to the story handed down in Genesis. The bounds of the plausible were quite different from those of our own time.[6] For many the world remained a mystical, magical place, in which instances of divine intervention might still occur; and although during the century there had been a rationalist reaction away from this notion among the educated, both lay and clerical, for ordinary people belief in the supernatural retained its appeal.[7]

To men and women in the grip of this world-view, organized religion—whether of the Church or of the Chapel—appeared to have an immediate relevance to their lives which it is difficult for most people nowadays to imagine. In the first place it could provide spiritual consolation and resource. As A. D. Gilbert has phrased it, 'by its putative capacity for invoking supernatural support, consolation, and reconciliation in this world, and through the prospect of other-worldly salvation', it could 'satisfy basic human aspirations for transcendental meaning, emotional security, or spiritual assurance'. Associated with this function, though not identical with it, was

[6] The move away from the eighteenth-century world-view is well presented in Alan D. Gilbert, *Religion and Society in Industrial England. Church, Chapel and Social Change, 1740–1914* (1976), pp. 175–87, especially 184 ff. For a convenient brief summary of the revolutionary cosmological ideas of Kant and Buffon, see Stephen Toulmin and June Goodfield, *The Discovery of Time* (1967), pp. 159–64, 175–83. Failure on the part of historians to make the necessary effort of mental readjustment can lead to quite unreal, not to say naïve, discussions of the role of religion in eighteenth-century society (*vide* John O. Foster, *Class Struggle and the Industrial Revolution*, 1974, pp. 26 ff.).

[7] Cf. J. H. Whiteley, *Wesley's England* (1938), pp. 72–9.

the support given by ritual or ceremonial routines. 'Non-recurrent' rites and ceremonies, such as baptism, confirmation, and marriage, and recurrent rites and services geared partly to the seasons, partly to the Christian year, might be felt as contributing 'to the maintenance of communal solidarity at times of individual and social crisis' and periodically reaffirming the cohesion of the social group.[8] Organized religion served social as well as religious purposes, although the line between the two was difficult to draw, and an evangelical leader like John Wesley would have denied on principle that such a line existed. In a number of different ways membership of a religious group provided a framework for the life of the individual, and did so in an age when fewer institutional alternatives were available than would be the case today. The fact that there existed several different religious affiliations to which men might turn, not one single monopolistic national Church, may itself have been of particular importance. Hostility to the Church of England could express itself within alternative religious fellowships. The presence of Dissent and of Methodism may well have contributed to save the country from the atheistic type of anticlericalism generated by established Churches on the Continent.[9]

For in the arena of religion all was by no means peace and harmony. In the 1780s and 1790s the Established Church was defending itself not only from renewed pressure from the dissenting sects but from a Methodist Movement in the process of separating itself from the Church and detaching parts of its actual or potential congregation in the process, and from an Evangelical movement within itself which many churchmen regarded as exhibiting many of the most objectionable characteristics of Methodism. This charge against the Evangelicals was not wholly justified, for its clerics were in general university trained and well-educated men, very different from the lay preachers and ministers of the Methodists. But there was this much truth in it, that the

[8] Gilbert, *Religion and Society in Industrial England*, pp. 69–70, 75.

[9] This suggestion was advanced over a century ago by Leslie Stephen (*History of English Thought in the eighteenth century*, Harbinger edn., 2 vols., 1962, i. 75). Cf. E. R. Taylor, *Methodism and Politics, 1791–1851* (Cambridge, 1935), pp. 4–5.

Evangelicals displayed a similar unseemly enthusiasm to the Wesleyans, demanded proofs of a 'second birth', and denied the virtue of full Christianity to any who did not profess this experience (including their fellow clergy). To the scandal of orthodox clergymen this seemed to deny the significance of a central Anglican rite, that of baptism. The tensions between High Churchmen and Evangelicals which developed during the 1790s were rendered the more acute by the fact that the latter, unlike the Methodists, had a formidable basis of lay support among members of the ruling class, and in Hannah More and William Wilberforce at least two propagandists of the highest talents. Their objects were, in the most extended sense of the term, to create a godly nation. In a manner similar to Wesley they believed everyone should be brought to direct his or her conduct according to the will of God (which inevitably meant according to their interpretation of it).

In relation to the main question of the stability of British society, one can view in various ways this rivalry between Church and Evangelicalism. We may—bearing the later religious census of 1851 in mind—be tolerably sceptical about the effects on the mass of the people of the clerisy's constant harping on resignation to the privations of life in this world. Up to 1800 the influence of the Evangelical movement among the upper ranks of society was still fairly limited, but the stimulus it gave to their involvement in social welfare work on behalf of the lower classes probably had some stabilizing effect upon society as a whole. The point that is most speculative, but which deserves consideration is, did the Evangelical movement absorb, in a manner relatively innocuous to social stability, the kind of revolutionary drive and zeal which elsewhere produced political breakdown? The Evangelicals displayed something of the same kind of 'excess of certitude' which swept revolutionary leaders like Robespierre into disaster. But their energies were deployed in a field of activity bounded by certain orthodox moral and spiritual considerations; and although they often showed little charity towards orthodox churchmen or others who got in their way and were not above descending at times into sharp practice and deceit in the pursuit of their objectives, they were confident that their schemes for infiltration of the Church were providentially destined to succeed and so remained completely committed to the preservation of the existing social and political order. Political revolution was anathema to them: none were hotter against the spread of the ideas of Thomas Paine. In this connection, as in others, it may be argued that the pluralistic character of British society gave it an enormous capacity to absorb pressures of internal conflict generated by the ideals and aspirations of dissident groups, without this seriously menacing the nation's political stability.

II

In the view of its own leaders, and of the governing class as a whole, the established church of England had a preponderant if not an exclusive claim to discharge the spiritual and social functions outlined above.[10] In some areas where it held a dominant position the Church still did effectively provide part of a familiar and accepted framework of local existence. Broadly speaking its organization was least defective in the southern parts of the country. Although these districts could furnish examples of parishes which were either too small and poor to be properly viable or else too large for a clergyman to keep in touch with all his parishioners, in many instances the relatively small extent of the parish ensured both that the parson could establish personal relations with everyone and that the church was within fairly easy reach of all. In East Anglia and Essex the average area of a parish was little over three square miles; everywhere else south of the Trent—Cornwall excepted—it was less than five, and the Vale of York constituted a northerly enclave of the same type.[11] In many of these parishes social and religious cohesion was effectively buttressed by the alliance between parson and

[10] Pages 185–6 above.
[11] Gilbert, *Religion and Society in Industrial England*, p. 100, table 5.1. Even so the situation was not uniformly ideal. At least one heavily industrialized parish in Gloucestershire had a population of ten thousand in the 1790s, and the same county affords an example of an indifferent estate owner, perpetually absent, 'who neither knows nor cares whether there is a church in it' (Esther Moir, *Local Government in Gloucestershire*, 1969, pp. 122, 19).

landowner, and the position of the clergy was enhanced further by their secular social responsibilities. In association with the parish officers nominated by the parish meeting the incumbent looked after the needy under the statutes relating to the Poor Law and often had a major responsibility for administering charities.[12] Increasingly, in some districts, the vicar or rector of a parish was himself a principal landowner, uniting the roles of priest and squire and often serving on the bench—for instance, at the beginning of the nineteenth century nearly a third of the Oxfordshire JPs were clergymen, though some of these were members of the University not holding a benefice. This doubling of roles could sometimes be a source of strength, though it also had serious disadvantages, especially in creating a common target for secular and religious discontent.[13] In older static urban centres the Church's organization on the ground seems to have remained adequate. For instance, in Norwich, with a population of just under 40,000 at the turn of the century, apart from the cathedral there were some twenty churches in which weekly services were held and another fifteen where they were conducted once a fortnight.[14]

Anglican organization was least strong in the northern districts, where economic developments were working the greatest changes in society during the second half of the eighteenth century. In Yorkshire the average size of parishes was between nine and ten square miles, and there were great extremes between the thickly churched Vale of York on the one hand and the extensive upland parishes in the west of the county, where the industrial population was rapidly

[12] Arthur Warne, *Church and Society in eighteenth-century Devon* (Newton Abbot, 1969), pp. 148–54; Diana McClatchey, *Oxfordshire Clergy, 1777–1869* (Oxford, 1960), pp. 123–9.

[13] McClatchey, op. cit., pp. 178–90. In Gloucestershire on the other hand clergymen constituted only a handful (sixteen in 1800) of the two to three hundred men named in the commission of the peace. Twenty-two leading active justices bore the brunt of the work of the Bench; seven of them were clergymen (Moir, *Local Government in Gloucestershire*, p. 53). William Cobbett's comment of 1802 upon the clergy, that 'their aggregate influence is astonishingly great', reflected perhaps his greater familiarity with the southern counties (quoted in Norman, *Church and Society*, p. 32).

[14] C. B. Jewson, *Jacobin City. A Portrait of Norwich in its Reaction to the French Revolution, 1788–1802* (1975), p. 135 and map opposite p. 52.

increasing. Halifax parish extended over roughly a hundred square miles, with a scattered population of some forty thousand.[15] The parish of Sheffield and its five outlying townships had a population of only fifteen or so thousand in 1736 but had risen to 45,000 by 1801.[16] Leeds parish extended over more than thirty square miles, taking in thirteen villages and an indeterminate number of hamlets as well as the borough itself; and the borough alone housed over 50,000 people by 1801.[17] The diocese of Chester, which included the heavily industrialized areas of eastern Cheshire and South Lancashire, as well as extending over Westmorland and some districts of north-west Yorkshire, presented its clergy with quite intractable problems.[18] The average size of its parishes was approaching twenty square miles, but this norm was far exceeded in some of the most thickly populated districts. The Cheshire parish of Prestbury extended over ninety square miles. Its magnificent parish church, almost a small cathedral, was situated in a village, while the neighbouring towns of Macclesfield and Congleton, with a joint population of 14,000 in the 1770s, were served only by two of its ten chapels of ease. The South Lancashire parish of Prescot, the most extensive in the hundred of West Derby lying inland from Liverpool, contained fifteen townships each similar in size to a southern parish.[19] The parishes of Bolton, Bury, and Middleton all had outlying townships at distances of from eight to twelve miles from the parish church; that of Bolton extended some twenty miles from north to south. Manchester parish covered some fifty-three and a half square miles and embraced nineteen adjacent townships: the refusal of the clergy of the collegiate church to assume any responsibilities outside the town itself, with its population of around 40,000 in 1778, was hardly indicative

[15] Gilbert, *Religion and Society in Industrial England*, p. 100, table 5.1.

[16] E. R. Wickham, *Church and People in an Industrial City* (1957), p. 20.

[17] *A History of Modern Leeds*, ed. Derek Fraser (Manchester, 1980), pp. 24, 48.

[18] John Addy, 'Bishop Porteus's Visitation of the Diocese of Chester, 1778', *Northern History*, 13 (1977), 175–98, is the basis for statements which follow, unless otherwise indicated. Addy's analysis is a model of its kind. For the average size of the parishes, Gilbert, loc. cit.

[19] G. W. Oxley, 'The Permanent Poor in South-West Lancashire under the Old Poor Law', in *Liverpool and Merseyside; Essays in the economic and social history of the port and its hinterland*, ed. J. R. Harris (1969), p. 20.

of zeal but was no doubt realistic.[20] Unwieldy parishes were also the norm in the two most northern bishoprics, Carlisle and Durham.[21] Even where growing urban parishes were not extensive in area, through sheer weight of population they were slipping out of the Church's control, often to the advantage of the dissenting sects. Between 1769 and 1797 the number of dissenters' meeting-houses in Hull increased from five to ten. The established Church obtained its third place of worship only in 1791. Joseph Priestley alleged in 1791 that since his taking up residence in Birmingham ten years before, seven meeting-houses had been built and three more were then under construction. Not one Anglican church or chapel had been erected during that period.[22] However reasonably adequate the ground organization in the southern and eastern parts of England, in the North and North-West the Church was far from effectively equipped to discharge either its spiritual or its social responsibilities. In Cornwall also, some of the western parishes were over-extensive, and the mining industry had created new centres of population in outlying areas beyond easy reach of the older villages and their parish churches.[23]

From the 1780s onwards various bishops' charges indicate that the Bench was not unaware of the serious weaknesses produced by this state of affairs and of its contribution to the problem of plurality and non-residence, but reform was beyond its powers. Private property rights in advowsons and parish livings had become so firmly defined—leading, incidentally to a considerable diversion of parish revenues into lay hands—that only drastic action by the legislature could achieve the necessary recasting of the system. There was no sign that at this time the political class accepted the need for such sweeping reform. Even much later, in the 1830s, when the point had been taken, the grave difficulties

[20] Leon S. Marshall, *The Development of Public Opinion in Manchester, 1780–1820* (Univ. of Syracuse Press, 1946), p. 36.

[21] Gilbert, loc. cit.; cf. C. J. Hunt, *The Lead Miners of the Northern Pennines*, p. 232.

[22] *Tours in England and Wales by Arthur Young selected from the Annals of Agriculture* (1932), p. 185; *The Monthly Review, or, Literary Journal Enlarged*, iv (1791), p. 429.

[23] W. J. Rowe, *Cornwall in the Age of the Industrial Revolution* (1953), pp. 39, 66.

besetting parish clergy seem not to have been fully grasped by either lay or clerical leaders.[24]

An equally serious problem for the Church was deficiency in manpower, and this despite considerable concern in the upper levels of command. George III took his responsibilities as supreme governor of the Church of England seriously, and was neither unaware nor wholly unappreciative of evangelical fervour. He showed a close interest in its leadership and vitality. True, political considerations could never be excluded completely from the choice of men for the episcopal bench. The great landed families claimed their share of the ecclesiastical spoils. The Church, like the army, needed protection from the worst effects of the patronage system. This could not always be given; but within the limits of eligible candidatures which were not politically exceptionable, the king made constant efforts to secure suitable appointments. Ministers involved in recommending to bishoprics were required to consult the Archbishop of Canterbury before submitting a name for the king's final approval. His correspondence about these appointments abounded in injunctions, 'to find a man of exemplary conduct to be brought upon the bench', 'that a man of learning and of exemplary life' should be recommended, or that he wished to prefer such a 'clergyman who for private character as well as orthodoxy and learning, might seem best qualified'.[25] In 1805 he insisted upon the elevation of Manners Sutton to Canterbury against the stubborn desire of William Pitt to secure the primacy for his old tutor and close supporter, Bishop Pretyman Tomline.

Nor did the king's interest cease with the appointment of prelates. He was concerned about performance from the highest to the lowest. On one occasion he sternly rebuked Archbishop Frederick Cornwallis, after receiving 'authentic information that *routs* had made their way' into the Primate's palace. 'My sentiments', he wrote, 'hold those levities and vain dissipations as utterly inexpedient, if not unlawful, to pass in a residence for many centuries devoted to divine studies, religious retirement, and the extensive exercise of

[24] Norman, *Church and Society*, pp. 90-1; Best, *Temporal Pillars*, pp. 171-2.
[25] Sykes, *Church and State in England*, p. 399.

charity and benevolence . . . a place where so many of your predecessors have led their lives in such sanctity as has thrown lustre on the pure religion they professed and adorned'; ending with the valediction he clearly felt to be necessary: 'May God take your Grace into his Almighty protection.' In 1801 he took heed of the state of the Irish episcopal Church lately united with the Church of England by the Act of Union. When the Earl of Hardwicke, newly appointed Lord-Lieutenant of Ireland, was about to set out for Dublin, the king enumerated among his duties the general supervision of the Church, and wrote: 'another most necessary measure is the encouraging the residence of the clergy . . . and the attending to the calling on the bishops by their examples as well as precepts to enforce it, the obliging them to keep their cathedrals in good repair and having the choir services performed with great punctuality and decorum.' The universities also drew his fire. When in 1770 Lord North was elected Chancellor of Oxford, the king wrote: 'I am certain this will stimulate you to recommend on vacancies none but men of character for the Regius Professorships and I can assure you that I shall expect all those I shall appoint to perform such duties as the Heads of Houses shall require of them.'[26]

But the influence the king could exert was limited, and the late Georgian Church suffered from various inbuilt short-comings of personnel which were to require far greater pressures to remove during the course of the following century. The aristocracy could not be denied a share of top posts. One First Minister, George Grenville, frankly declared 'that he considered bishoprics as of two kinds; bishoprics of business for men of abilities and learning, and bishoprics of ease for men of family and fashion'.[27] The great disparities of income between sees—some yielding over £3,000 a year whilst a group at the bottom were worth £600 or less—established a ladder of preferment leading sometimes to unseemly scrambles for advancement and to embarrassing

[26] J. H. Jesse, *Memoirs of the Life and Reign of King George the Third* (3 vols., 1867), ii. 58; A. Aspinall, *The Later Correspondence of King George III* (5 vols., Cambridge, 1962–70), iii. 533; Sir John Fortescue, *The Correspondence of King George III* (6 vols., 1927–8), ii. 400.

[27] Quoted in Sykes, *Church and State in England*, p. 157.

obligations between prelates and politicians. Nevertheless, on the whole the bishops were an able and conscientious set of men. This was as well, for a burden of leadership fell on the episcopate all the greater because the suspension of the Convocations, which continued throughout George III's reign, deprived the Church of any dynamic impulse from the lower ranks of the clergy. Moreover, the bishops needed determination and staying power to perform their ecclesiastical duties. The inextricable intertwining of Church and state cut seriously into the time and energy they had available for their pastoral cares. Six to eight months' residence in London each year during the parliamentary session was almost *de rigueur*, leaving only four or five summer months for visits to their sees. Episcopal visitations took place normally once in three years only, but this rather remote supervision was supplemented by a stream of information and returns on paper, and by the archdeacons' annual visitations. Towards the end of the eighteenth century the revival of activity by rural deans in some of the southern and western sees testified to renewed efforts to improve Church organization.

It was widely agreed that at parish level the great fault was clerical non-residence, and bishops never wearied of inveighing against it in their charges. No less than 7,358 incumbents were recorded as non-resident from the total of 11,194 benefices returned in 1809, and local studies suggest that for some time the figure had been getting worse.[28] The main reason undoubtedly was the inadequacy of parish endowments, but short of some major intervention by Parliament in the financial affairs of the Church, which was never on the cards at this time, it was difficult to see what could be done. The situation was not quite so bad as the bare figures suggest, for these concealed such circumstances as the holding in plurality of neighbouring small parishes which in point of size were mere hamlets incapable singly of producing a livelihood for a clergyman. Lack of a suitable residence forced some non-resident incumbents to live near to but just outside

[28] Locally the picture might appear even blacker. In the bishopric of Worcester in 1782 only 82 out of the 212 rectories, vicarages, and curacies (*c*. 39 per cent) had resident incumbents (*The State of the Bishopric of Worcester, 1782–1808*, ed. Mary Ransome, Worcestershire Historical Society, new series, vol. 6, 1968, p. 14). Cf. McClatchey, *Oxfordshire Clergy*, p. 31.

their parish bounds.[29] But aside from these instances, which less seriously affected clerical ministry, the Church accepted a wide range of excuses for non-residence—schoolmastering, university fellowships, chaplaincies to the great, membership of cathedral chapters—which were sometimes occasions of abuse, and which, even if there were financial justifications, had undesirable results. About 1809 over a thousand parishes were without any pastoral care. One in seven of the Devon parishes investigated in 1779 were in the care of resident stipendiary curates, a class of cleric generally among the most underpaid and overworked: in order to live, curates themselves had to practise pluralism. In Chester diocese Bishop Porteus was perturbed to find in 1778 that many of the clergy were men of insufficient education and that numbers of them had only advanced as far as deacon's orders.[30]

The overall general effect, over the whole country—not only in the North—was to reduce the clerical impact on parish life well below the level that the bishops thought desirable, not merely in respect of the holding of church services, but in regard to the multifarious activities of the clergy in relation to charities, sick-visiting, moral policing, unofficial arbitration of disputes, and education. In rural areas celebration of communion tended to be near the minimum prescribed by the canons of 1604—not more than four or five times a year.[31] Degrees of care or neglect produced remarkable variations in the proportions of communicants to population in different parishes: the record in the mining area of the Mendips before Hannah More took a grip upon it seems to have been appalling.[32]

[29] In Oxfordshire, for instance, about one in six of the parishes had no vicarage or parsonage (McClatchey, *Oxfordshire Clergy*, p. 19).

[30] Warne, *Church and Society in eighteenth-century Devon*, p. 42; John Addy, 'Porteus's Visitation', pp. 180, 195–6. Gloucester diocese seems in some ways to have been better managed. At the visitation of 1776 only ten holders of benefices were recorded as non-resident (four of them Oxford dons). But the great majority of incumbents held two or three parishes, residing themselves in the more important and putting in a curate to serve the other(s) (Moir, *Local Government in Gloucestershire*, pp. 26, 55).

[31] Warne, pp. 45–6; McClatchey, p. 86; Ransome, p. 9.

[32] Thus the Devon parish of Slapton with 200 families had only 32 communicants, Churston with 43 families had only three or four; in both the parson

Where the resident clergyman backed by the landowner held a firm grip upon his parish, the people could be kept at least formally loyal to the Church, but this situation did not always obtain, and contemporaries were well aware that the Church was losing its hold. There was, for instance, a steady long-term decline in the number of Easter communicants at Sheffield parish church, from 850 in 1764 to 340 in 1780, and to little over 200 by the end of the century—this in a town which had doubled its population during that period. Bishop Butler, investigating figures for church attendance in his diocese of Hereford between 1747 and 1792, discovered so alarming a decline that he refused to make the details public. 'Scarcely any of the poor come to church', John Venn observed in 1793, shortly after taking up his appointment as rector of Clapham. An address from the clergy of Manchester and Salford to the inhabitants of these two towns, published in the local press in November 1796, complained that at least two-thirds of the population failed to attend Sunday services, and was echoed in 1799 by Bishop Cleaver of Chester, who stigmatized a parish where 'above 40,000 persons . . . pass the Lord's day without attention to public worship under any mode whatsoever'. A survey of some Lincolnshire parishes published in 1799 disclosed that less than one in three of the population had anything to do with the church and only one adult in six could be regarded as a communicant. This religious indifference in a rural county with a cathedral city was not a recent phenomenon either. During the militia riots of 1757, when the magistracy in general was set at defiance by the populace, the Dean of Lincoln thus reported the response to a colleague's sermon on the obedience due to civil government:

was non-resident. In others, on the other hand, more than one person per resident family took communion (Warne, pp. 45–6). Wilberforce's visit to the Mendips in 1789 led him to discover that 'the vicar of Cheddar lived at Oxford; the curate lived at Wells; the thirteen adjacent parishes were without a resident curate; the only clergyman in the district was the vicar of Axbridge, of whom Hannah More wrote: "He is intoxicated about six times a week, and very frequently is prevented from preaching by two black eyes honestly earned by fighting" ' (G. R. Balleine, *A History of the Evangelical Party in the Church of England*, 1933, p. 154). In Cheddar parish, within ten years the efforts of Hannah More raised average church attendance from 50 to 700 and the communicants from 15 to 120 (Gilbert, *Religion and Society in Industrial England*, p. 74).

' "Aye", said his hearers, "he fetches that doctrine out of a book which our governors do not believe in, and why should we?" ' One church historian has concluded that in many districts fewer than 15 per cent of the population regularly went to church or were communicants.[33]

Such figures obviously have implications for any judgement about the role of the Church as a social bond in the age of revolution. Why had this decline in its influence taken place? Some historians now tend to put forward class distinction as an explanation, and it is possible that this may have played a part. There are indications that some of the lower clergy were rising in the social scale and becoming more closely connected with the landed class. In some areas career prospects were increasingly favourable. The financial status of clergymen in some parishes was greatly improved through the processes of enclosure, often involving a commutation of tithe which added to the glebe or the extension of tithe to hitherto uncultivated lands. Higher rents came in from building leases in some of the industrial areas of the North and Midlands.[34] There is a possibility also—hardly considered as yet, it seems, by historians—that the Evangelical Revival kindled a sense of mission among an increasing number of recruits to the priesthood from the upper classes

[33] Wickham, *Church and People in an Industrial City*, p. 55; R. A. Soloway, *Prelates and People. Ecclesiastical Social Thought in England, 1783–1852* (1969), pp. 50-2, 306; Michael Henning, *John Venn and the Clapham Sect* (1958), p. 116; G. B. Hindle, *Provision for the Relief of the Poor in Manchester, 1754–1826* (Manchester, 1975), p. 119; H. O. Alves, 'The Painites. The Influence of Thomas Paine in four provincial towns, 1791-1799', Ph.D. thesis, University of London, 1981, pp. 226-7; John Addis, 'Porteus's Visitation', pp. 181-2; Hill, *Georgian Lincoln*, p. 107—in 1791 Colonel John Byng lamented the thin attendance at services in the Minster, ibid., p. 48; Norman, *Church and Society*, p. 9. Norman concludes that the drift away from formal religion was not particularly associated with movement to towns but had previously occurred in the rural parishes from which the townsmen came (pp. 50-1). Cf. the extremely low figures of regular communicants in the Oldham area (about 4 per cent of population in 1789) cited in John Foster, *Class Struggle and the Industrial Revolution. Early Industrial Capitalism in three English Towns* (1974), p. 29.

[34] W. R. Ward, *Religion and Society in England, 1790-1850* (1972), pp. 9-10; Gilbert, *Religion and Society in Industrial England*, pp. 80-1; McClatchey, *Oxfordshire Clergy*, pp. 101-21. In Worcester diocese in Bishop Hurd's time, 205 of the serving clergy were identified as sons of gentry, and a further 122 as sons of clergymen. Only 62 were described as of plebeian origin (but the status of a further 121 was not specified). *The State of the Bishopric of Worcester*, ed. Ransome, p. 8.

of society. Nevertheless, some reservations must be expressed. Much the larger proportion of the parish clergy of the late eighteenth century came from the ranks of small farmers and tradesmen, if indeed their fathers were not clergymen themselves, and their financial standing was not greatly removed from that of many of their parishioners. One of them remarked that men of his type could make a better living as upper servants in a genteel family or in a variety of miscellaneous occupations: 'A journeyman in almost any trade or business, even a bricklayer's labourer or the turner of a razor-grinder's wheel, all circumstances considered, is better paid than a stipendiary curate.'[35] There is need for caution in attributing abstention from church-going to class distinctions of this kind. And even where it occurred, there remains the difficulty of assessing the impact and personal influence of the parish clergyman by way of his parish visitations, sick-visiting, and charitable activities, which by tradition were not confined to the mere circle of his communicants. The effect of class distinction on attendance was probably far more pervasive in connection with the established eighteenth-century practice of reserved pews and pew rents. Poorer folk relegated to a limited number of places at the back of a church were likely to feel themselves present on suffrance and not fully welcome as members of the local Christian community.

It is perhaps more clear that the Church's slackening hold on its constituency was due in part to its theology. Its teaching was becoming too refined and remote for the popular taste. Whilst the more extreme effects of rationalism— Deism and Unitarianism—were eschewed by mainstream Anglicanism, nevertheless 'natural religion' entered as a kind of bedrock into late eighteenth-century Anglican theology, affecting both the tone of intellectual discussion and the common approach of the clergy to their role. Among the theologians, William Paley, it has been said, 'represented the consummation of the apologetic and evidential studies

---

[35] Quoted in Sykes, *Church and State in England*, p. 228. For further illustrations of the difficulties of the curates, who carried a substantial part of the burden of parish work, see A. Tindal Hart, *The Eighteenth Century Country Parson (circa. 1689 to 1830)* (Shrewsbury, 1955), pp. 14–22.

of the epoch with singular clarity and force'.[36] His exposition
drew into harmony the rationalistic elements of 'natural
religion' derived from observation of natural phenomena and
religion as revealed in the New Testament writings. Such
theology combined acceptance of miracles in the past with
a present which was ordered and predictable. It set at a distance the immanence of the divine, the idea of constant
supernatural involvement in human affairs. For Paley, just
as the intricacies of a watch demonstrated the existence and
purposes of a watch-maker, so the phenomena of nature as
well as the Scriptures argued the purposes of a Creator who
had set the universe in motion, to operate according to the
natural laws which human observation might discern and the
rules which Scripture might furnish for human behaviour.
He reflected the prevailing Latitudinarianism in his belief
that credal formulas and articles of subscription should be
as few and all-embracing as possible. Paley's system also
included other concepts typical of his generation—a belief
in divine beneficence, which led in turn to virtual rejection
of the doctrine of original sin and to the idea that the purposes of Christian belief included the promotion of
happiness, in this world and the next. In some degree, owing
to earlier publication, he forestalled Bentham as one of the
first Utilitarians.

Ideas of this nature, widely disseminated throughout the
Church, tended to shape in certain ways the view of their
role held by its servants. The members of the clergy tended
to be seen as ministers giving instructions, guiding their flocks
in their duty towards God and their neighbours, by exhorta-
tion and by active example, but not striving to instil into
them a sense of mystical personal contact with a transcendent deity. They sought, it has been said, the *via media*
between superstition and fanaticism—between the beliefs
either that God revealed himself to external experience in
the modern world, or that he revealed himself by internal
experience.[37] Emotion, mysticism, and dogma were carefully
eschewed. One contemporary critic of eighteenth-century
sermonizing remarked: 'The name of Christ is scarcely ever

[36] Sykes, *Church and State in England*, p. 379.
[37] Stephen, *History of English Thought in the eighteenth century*, ii. 286.

heard, nor any of the characteristic doctrines of His holy religion. The watchword, or catchword . . . is Morality.' Perhaps associated with this circumstance was the fact that the degree of dedication to the clerical profession often fell short. There were probably few men in the service of the Church like the vicar of Axbridge, who was sometimes incapable of functioning in the pulpit on account of two black eyes 'honestly acquired in fighting'. But there were more, perhaps, who lacked the full commitment necessary, and struck what they thought was a reasonable balance in their activities—like, for instance, the incumbent of Thaxted, Essex, in the 1760s, who recorded: 'Every morning I visited the sick and the poor and, to the utmost of my abilities and powers, aided them: every afternoon I rode out to Easton, Dunmow, Ashdon and some of the neighbouring seats, where I agreeably spent my time with those whose integrity and good sense might be of service to me in my further progress through the world.' The copious diaries of James Woodforde, the rector of Weston Longueville near Norwich, dwell mainly on five major topics, of which the first was his food, the second his social engagements among the gentry, and clearly fifth and last, church affairs and his duties as a parish priest. The last was discharged in a spirit of earnest goodwill but not spiritual zeal. 'His theology', it has been said, 'was based on a profound belief in divine benevolence and the need for humanitarianism in Man.' This was a far cry from the obsessive religion of those who were beginning to react against the Church's apparent complacency.[38]

III

For herein lay at least in part the source of the discontent which, well before 1760, had sparked off the Evangelical Revival, a movement which infiltrated both the Church of England and Dissent but found its most dramatic manifestation in the rise of Methodism. As the tone of the Church grew more rational and formalistic—a trend reflected also among the Nonconformist sects—so it failed to satisfy

[38] A. Tindal Hart, *The Eighteenth Century Country Parson*, pp. 41-2, 51-2; Brown, *Essex at Work, 1700-1815*, p. 157; note 32 above.

a minority whose psychological make-up sought satisfaction in a sense of immediate communion with a transcendent deity, and for whom the experience of believing in—to the point of 'knowing' with a deep inward emotional fervour and certainty—the Christian doctrine of redemption through Christ afforded a sense of personal salvation. This sort of religious enthusiasm has been penetratingly analysed with particular reference to John Wesley by Ronald Knox. In Knox's words, the enthusiast 'sees what effects religion can have, sometimes does have, in transforming a man's whole life and outlook', and demands that this become 'the average standard of religious achievement'. Wesley had in his mind 'a picture of the early Church visibly penetrated with super-natural influences', and believed it still existed in this mode for those who had grasped its truth. Furthermore, in Wesley's view, the experience variously described as 'conversion', 'new birth', or 'salvation' meant an immediate and imminent sense of contact with the divine, which the individual thus graced should actively work to maintain; or, as a Methodist historian has expressed it, 'the individual who achieved salvation was not merely purged of sin but entered into an unbroken fellowship with God'.[39] Under these circumstances religious practices were no longer merely a matter of outward forms and observances but 'an affair of the heart', a series of all-consuming commitments to the search for or the maintenance of this exalted state, a state realized by the individual through 'an inward experience of peace and joy'.[40] What

---

[39] Maldwyn Edwards, in *A History of the Methodist Church in Great Britain*, ed. R. E. Davies and E. G. Rupp (2 vols., 1965–78), i. 61.

[40] R. A. Knox, *Enthusiasm. A chapter in the History of Religion with special reference to the seventeenth and eighteenth centuries* (Oxford, 1950), p. 2. For the Anglicans, the nature of evangelical zeal is perfectly illustrated in John Venn's biographical note on his father, Henry Venn: 'He required (according to the ideas which he had imbibed from the mystical writers) a measure almost of perfection in man; and exalted the standard of holiness to a degree to which it was scarcely possible that the frail children of men could ever reach. . . . He kept a diary, in which he endeavoured to record the very slightest alienation of thought from the love or fear of God. . . . This he deeply lamented before God, and, with fervent prayer, requested that every thought of his heart might be brought into captivity to the Law of Christ' (*The Life and a selection from the letters of the late Rev. Henry Venn, MA*. Drawn up by John Venn and edited by Henry Venn, 1839). For further examples from John Venn's writings, see Hennell, *John Venn and the Clapham Sect*, pp. 205–7.

Wesley offered to his followers was not merely the consolation of an assured blessed life in the hereafter but a hope of beatitude in this. The person who arrives, or hopes to arrive, by whatever means, at that sense of virtue and of peace with himself and with the world, is *ipso facto* uninterested in secular revolution.

This was perhaps the bedrock of the considerations that led most Wesleyan Methodists (and, indeed, other evangelicals) to shun political radicalism during the revolutionary age. The Wesleyan was not in any way a quietist. He believed in the improvement of the world around him. The evangelical faith that Wesley preached was deeply concerned with the here and now as well as with the Christian vision of the life to come. Wesley was the very reverse of an anchorite: he believed religion to be an intensely social affair, and the well-spring of social regeneration. He held that individuals who had gone through the experience of 'conversion' underwent a transformation of personality in this world and accepted an entirely new role within it. In the evangelical idiom, all thought and action became thought and action in the service of God and not of self. 'Conversion' thus had fundamental implications for the conduct of life in human society. All this set Methodists entirely apart from social reformers or revolutionaries of the Painite variety; for part of Wesley's dream was a transformation of human society through a transformation of human nature. This is an ideal which Marxism has since stood on its head, with the adoption of the assumption that human nature can be changed by an alteration of the institutions within which human society operates. But for Wesley (and generally speaking for all evangelicals) the reform of institutions was irrelevant. The only necessary —and in his conviction perfectly achievable—thing was the reformation of human nature by bringing people into a state of grace, and all the necessary desirable consequences for life in this world would follow.[41] It is easy to suggest that this was as hopelessly unrealistic as is the Marxist alternative. But

[41] Wellman J. Warner, *The Wesleyan Movement in the Industrial Revolution* (1930), pp. 56–69; Maldwyn Edwards, *John Wesley and the eighteenth century*, pp. 147, 180–1. For reflections on comparable attitudes within the Church of England, see Norman, *Church and Society in England*, pp. 38–40.

the point with which we are here concerned is the way in which numbers of people towards the end of the eighteenth century were thinking and the effects this had upon their actions.

The spiritual approach to life of Methodism was not the only circumstance linking it with conservative political attitudes. It has been observed that the Methodist societies also overcame the problem of 'anomie'—the breakdown of established social values and systems—which was typical of human experience in the expanding industrial districts at a time when labour was becoming increasingly mobile and operating in new social and economic environments.[42] Methodism, like other religious organizations and also like non-religious societies such as the Freemasons, gave companionship, social connection, status, and a sense of belonging. Its hierarchies of local helpers, from preachers and class leaders downwards in each district, provided opportunities for service and for self-distinction within the community. In this, too, it proved a conservative force. Moreover, a Methodist society provided an instrument of social cohesion in which class distinctions—at least up to the end of the century, if not later—counted for relatively little, although the range of differences in incomes among members might be considerable. The selective nature of the membership facilitated the practices of mutual help which Wesley from the first had stressed as one of the essential features of the Christian life and which he had linked intimately with his stress on the work-ethic. To Wesley the obligation to work hard and add to the fruits of the earth was closely tied to the Christian obligation to cherish and support less fortunate neighbours; in his early days he had come very near to advocating a communistic form of life in the Methodist societies. Inherent in early Methodist teaching was the duty to give to charitable uses all but the minimum earnings required to sustain family life. The truly 'converted' individual thus perfectly naturally fulfilled his role and helped to improve the quality of life in this world. By Wesley's death this principle was being watered down to an obligation to make generous gifts for alms, even to the extent of half one's income, and the

[42] Gilbert, *Religion and Society in Industrial England*, pp. 87-93.

obligation was very generally honoured. The generous practice of charity between members of Methodist societies provided an important degree of social security for their members: it was noted that they rarely were forced to become dependent upon the Poor Law.

Also significant for the development of a conservative ethos was the fact that, within certain limits, though hardly in the way Wesley expected or approved, desirable consequences for life in this world did follow from the acceptance of Methodist evangelicalism and its apparatus. At least, they followed for some Methodists, for those who, upon the whole, were the most important lay section of the movement; and this was not without political significance. Sobriety, diligence, and responsibility were qualities stressed by the Methodist preachers as some of the indicators of a meaningful pursuit of salvation, and were becoming increasingly noted as typical hallmarks of the Movement by the 1780s and 1790s. In a real sense the Movement seems to have created itself in this image by something akin to a process of natural selection. Various writers have noted that throughout much of the eighteenth century the turnover of membership was considerable.[43] Numbers of those who were initially attracted into Methodist societies afterwards fell by the wayside, unable or unwilling to rise to the standards of behaviour it required. Whatever the social elements of its composition, the Wesleyan Movement as a result of this process was assuming by the end of the century something of the character of an élite. It was heavily weighted with people who wished for a passionate religious involvement and who were possessed of the qualities of sobriety, diligence, and responsibility.

This brought further consequences which had implications for the Methodists' political attitudes. People of this sort prospered. At the very least, there was a tendency for them to rise above the bare level of poverty, in which others at the bottom of the social pile found themselves through inability to manage their lives in a disciplined fashion. In many cases Methodists attained a modest affluence and some achieved considerable wealth. As early as 1797

[43] Knox, *Enthusiasm*, p. 461.

a Methodist minister could write that 'the Methodists are become a numerous and respectable body . . . many are persons of fortune, respectable tradesmen and men of good repute'.[44] Methodists were folk whose qualities gave them an advantage in the exploitation of the economic advantages of the early Industrial Revolution. Successfully engaged in this way, they had a stake in the established order and no incentive to interest themselves in radical or revolutionary designs.

In fact, the whole question of the relation of Methodism to radicalism and revolution needs reassessment in the light of the social composition of the movement. It is sometimes loosely stated that the bulk of Methodist membership at the end of the eighteenth century was to be found among the poor, but this term is somewhat imprecise. Certainly Wesley had always stressed that it was to this section of the community that his mission was directed. Now figures available for the first three or so decades of the nineteenth century suggest that almost 63 per cent of Methodist strength came from those described as 'artisans' and another 24 per cent from 'labourers', miners, and unspecified occupations.[45] But not all artisans were 'poor' in any contemporary sense, and the term itself is not precise. Apparently it includes hand-loom weavers, but we have recently been told that these were for the most part not 'skilled labour'; and at least up to about 1800 many of them were securing very good earnings.[46] But the minority of more well-to-do members of a society, who may have a little more information, and a little more leisure, and the influence that comes from the extra support they are able to give, may have a more than proportionate effect in setting the tone of the organization to which they belong—

[44] *A History of the Methodist Church in Great Britain*, ed. Davies and Rupp, i. 308. Cf. the observations of Joseph Sutcliffe, *The Review of Methodism* (1805), summarized in Maldwyn Edwards, *John Wesley and the eighteenth century*, p. 183. It has been observed of that leading northern centre of Methodism, Hull, that 'there is no reason to suppose that the direct influence of religion was spreading rapidly among the working class in the late eighteenth century. Surviving evidence shows a predominantly middle-class participation' (Gordon Jackson, *Hull in the eighteenth century. A Study in Economic and Social History*, Oxford, 1972, p. 298).

[45] Gilbert, *Religion and Society in Industrial England*, p. 63, table 3.1.

[46] Duncan Bythell, *The Handloom Weavers. A Study in the English Cotton Industry during the Industrial Revolution* (Cambridge, 1969), pp. 50–61, 98–100, 130–2, 271.

and a small but significant membership above the artisan class was emerging by the time Wesley died in 1791. The early nineteenth-century statistics just cited suggest that about 13 per cent of the Methodist membership was supplied by manufacturers and merchants, by shopkeepers, and by farmers, and at least a few of these were men of substance, including by 1812 at least two Members of Parliament.[47] This element was probably rather smaller before 1800, but it was nevertheless probably influential, including as it did many of the trustees who held the title-deeds of chapels and presenting Wesley with a serious problem towards the end of his life regarding the independence of the preachers. And it may have been larger than these estimates allow. In Sheffield at any rate, there are indications that not only the elements of the middle class but also a substantial number of prosperous Methodist artisans had set themselves on the upper side of the social barrier dividing those who paid pew rents from those who did not.[48]

IV

E. P. Thompson's picture of Methodism in the age of revolution has been described as 'arguably . . . the most perceptive available',[49] but it suffers from a number of lacunae and unsoundly based judgements. Perhaps the most serious is the failure to take the imaginative leap into the minds of eighteenth-century men and women, whose cosmological perception was intimately bound up with the Old and New Testaments and who, by that circumstance, were conditioned to respond willingly and enthusiastically to Wesley's message of hope for divine intervention in their affairs. Thompson's attribution of the Methodist commitment to the work-ethic to three factors—direct indoctrination, the Methodist

[47] Gilbert, *Religion and Society in Industrial England*, p. 63, table 3.1; David N. Hempton, 'Thomas Allan and Methodist Politics, 1800–1840', *History*, 67 (1982), 13–15.

[48] Pew rents financed the construction of the first Methodist chapel built in Sheffield in 1780 and it appears that less than half the seats were 'free'. In the second chapel opened in 1804 pew rents were charged on all but 350 of the 1,500 seats available (Wickham, *Church and People in an Industrial City*, pp. 57–8).

[49] Gilbert, *Religion and Society in Industrial England*, p. 87.

community sense, and what he calls 'the psychic consequences of the counter-revolution' (whatever that may mean)[50]— recognizes neither the religio-social stress on this point of all the Christian confessions,[51] nor the attractions of the practical benefits which many Methodists found the more disciplined life dictated by the Movement would bring. Nor does it take into account the way in which the Movement, sifting out those who did not conform, turned itself into an élite voluntarily committed to the social values as well as the religious values for which its founder stood. The constant purging of those unable to adhere to the high standards of religious discipline set by the Movement ensured that only those remained members for whom that discipline, however totalitarian it was, was nevertheless acceptable. The Methodists' belief in social improvement through reformation of character by means of divine grace is overlooked. Thompson is scathing about the 'psychological atrocities' and the 'appalling system of religious terror' by which children were conditioned to accept the work-ethic.[52] He does not perceive that this was not confined to Methodism and that it was a common feature of life long before 1800. W. J. Warner's prosopography of the early Wesleyan preachers reveals that many of them as children went through similar experiences in family backgrounds which pre-dated Methodism and often were within the ambience of the Established Church. The agonies of nervous depression endured before experience of 'conversion' by William Wilberforce show how educated adults could suffer similar stresses.[53] As for psychic disturbance—the hysteria sometimes displayed by converts at Methodist meetings—one must wonder whether many of these evidently unstable individuals remained within the Movement for long.

Thompson's contention in respect of Methodism (but it is one which, logically, one must consider in relation to all evangelical religion at the end of the eighteenth century) that 'there is a sense in which any religion which places

[50] *The Making of the English Working Class*, pp. 375-81.
[51] Norman, *Church and Society in England*, pp. 32-3.
[52] *The Making of the English Working Class*, pp. 374, 377.
[53] Warner, *The Wesleyan Movement in the Industrial Revolution*, pp. 249-56; John Pollock, *Wilberforce* (1977), pp. 32-9, 44-8.

great emphasis on the after-life is the Chiliasm of the defeated and the hopeless . . . the Chiliasm of despair', was implicitly refuted by writers before him and has encountered a dismissive reception from others since.[54] It was the judgement of W. J. Warner in 1930 that the suggestion that 'the teaching . . . was focussed upon other-worldly interests, important for the present only in the relation of a means to an end', was not upheld by 'a careful scrutiny of the records. . . . No exclusively other-worldly emphasis dominated the early Wesleyan societies. . . . The secular record of Wesleyans is a final refutation of the charge.'[55] A. D. Gilbert has commented that 'evangelical nonconformity [Methodist or otherwise] echoed the aspirations rather than the despair of the working classes': it was not the most 'defeated' and 'hopeless' sections of society which were drawn into it.[56] For the late eighteenth century, at any rate, neither economic nor political circumstances fit Thompson's picture. Many of the working people in the textile industry who were moving over to Methodism in considerable numbers in the 1790s were making a respectable, even a comfortable living out of their calling; not until after 1800 did the fall in wages hit this group with serious effect.[57] Cornwall with its large population of independent miners and fisher-folk became one of the strongholds of Methodism in the late eighteenth century; this was a time when first the tin-mining and then the copper-mining industries experienced a series of prolonged and profitable booms.[58] Thompson suggests that religious revivalism took over just at the point where 'political' or temporal aspirations met with defeat.[59] But this contention overlooks the fact that revivalism had been going on for forty years before the economic dislocations and political jarrings of the 1780s and 1790s. The active rank and file who sustained

---

[54] *The Making of the English Working Class*, pp. 381-2, 388, 391.

[55] *The Wesleyan Movement in the Industrial Revolution*, p. 59.

[56] *Religion and Society in Industrial England*, p. 83.

[57] Bythell, *Handloom Weavers*, pp. 98-100.

[58] W. J. Rowe, *Cornwall in the Age of the Industrial Revolution* (1953), pp. 166-76. Apart from a short, sharp slump in 1789-90, tin prices rose steadily during the 1780s and 1790s, and while technical difficulties caused a falling off of tin-mining after 1798, copper production nearly doubled between 1794 and 1809.

[59] *The Making of the English Working Class*, pp. 388-90.

the Methodist Movement in the localities were not folk who just reacted spasmodically to wayside preaching when times were bad. The choice made by over 90 per cent of the Wesleyan Movement in 1796 in favour of a hierarchical as against a democratically controlled system, with its overtones of hostility towards political democracy also, reflected positive commitments of social and religious principle, not a despairing retreat.

Far from being a force of repression, the Methodist Movement offered a religious and social package highly attractive to thousands of people. In this it was not alone, though it was perhaps the most successful of the groups involved. Evangelicalism within the Established Church also had its appeal. Occasionally an influential layman lent his hand to this work, exploiting the very weaknesses of the system to forward the movement. Early in George III's reign the Earl of Dartmouth, the stepbrother of the Prime Minister, Lord North, used his considerable influence with well-disposed lay patrons, and was responsible for a number of appointments of evangelical clergymen, including that of Henry Venn at Huddersfield.[60] A more organized group exploiting lay patronage for this purpose emerged during the late 1780s and the 1790s, when William Wilberforce and the members of the Thornton family came together in the loose association which soon gained the name of the Clapham Sect.[61]

Despite the hostility of many of the bishops and clergy Anglican Evangelicalism won a following among the public both in London and in various provincial districts. In the City it exploited two peculiar opportunities. For some time episcopal sanction had been given to the establishment by lay patrons of proprietary chapels as a means of supplementing the inadequate parish church facilities. During the second half of the eighteenth century an increasing number

---

[60] Michael Hennell, *John Venn and the Clapham Sect*, p. 21; Dartmouth's recommendation was accepted by the patron, Sir John Ramsden, 3rd baronet. Other men for whom Dartmouth secured preferment were Thomas Robinson (Leicester), James Stillingfleet (Hotham), Matthew Powley (Dewsbury), and John Newton (Olney). Balleine, *History of the Evangelical Party*, p. 58.

[61] A. Armstrong, *The Church of England, the Methodists, and Society, 1700–1850* (1973), pp. 79, 129, 131-2. The founder of the Clapham group, John Thornton, left eleven advowsons in trust for this purpose at his death in 1792.

of these proprietors appointed evangelical clergy. Also, over the years private benefactors had endowed lectureships at various of the City churches, appointment being vested in the parishioners. In some instances these chose evangelical clergy as lecturers despite the opposition of the incumbent and parish officers. Although, at the turn of the century, evangelical clergymen were excluded from all but three of the livings in London, they were reaching considerable audiences through their Sunday afternoon lectures and ministering to large congregations in the proprietary chapels.[62]

Outside London, although Methodism had a particularly strong grip in the Bristol area, this was also the centre of an Anglican evangelical revival.[63] Evangelicalism also became strongly established in Yorkshire. The influence of Joseph Milner, headmaster of Hull grammar school and afternoon lecturer at the parish church, caused Hull to become a notable evangelical centre, and various zealous and energetic clergymen planted the standard in the Pennine valleys.[64] The drive could not always be sustained. When, for instance, illness forced the retirement of Henry Venn, causing Huddersfield to be left without an evangelical incumbent, a large part of the congregation transferred its allegiance to the Methodists or to dissenting evangelical groups. Nevertheless, the information amassed by G. R. Balleine indicates that at the end of the eighteenth century the evangelicals within the Church of England were relatively far stronger in Yorkshire than in any other part of the country. Balleine also establishes the point that, in general, evangelical clergy, partly through their pertinacity and force of personality, partly through the appeal of the optimistic doctrine they taught, were able to attract and hold large congregations in districts where general indifference had previously prevailed.[65] From the 1780s the work was pushed forward with increasing momentum by such leaders as Isaac Milner and Charles Simeon, who sent out from Cambridge a steady stream of young ministers trained in the new spirit. By the turn of

[62] Balleine, *History of the Evangelical Party*, pp. 61-3.
[63] Ibid., pp. 90-2.
[64] Ibid., pp. 64-81; see also Gordon Jackson, *Hull in the eighteenth century*, pp. 291-9.
[65] Balleine, op. cit., chapter IV.

the century there were perhaps between three and five hundred evangelical clergymen serving in the Established Church. But their reception from unsympathetic colleagues and superiors had often been harsh and frustrating, leading sometimes to enforced resignation from benefices in which their efforts had begun to show positive results.[66]

A similar phenomenon is apparent in the history of Protestant Dissent.[67] During the early eighteenth century all sections of Dissent—Baptists, Congregationalists, and Presbyterians—had been affected by the prevailing latitudinarianism, and the reaction against enthusiasm, and had been suffering a steady decline.[68] In Chester diocese, the visitation returns seem to confirm that this process was continuing as late as 1778.[69] Among the Presbyterians, who were least affected by the evangelical revival and whose rationalist approach to religion was carrying many inexorably into the Unitarian camp, this process of decline continued into the opening years of the nineteenth century. By contrast, the wave of evangelicalism within the Congregational and Baptist Churches brought them a significant increase in membership during the 1790s. Both sects derived fresh momentum from the inflow into their ranks of enthusiasts who had been influenced by evangelicals within the Church of England, by Wesley and his preachers, and by men like George Whitefield, preaching an evangelical gospel outside both the Church and the Wesleyan Movement. Of this influx the Congregationalists seem to have taken the lion's share. Not only did this recruitment have its effect in terms of numbers, but it tended also to temper, though not destroy, the Calvinistic spirit of these sects, and to submerge concern with doctrinal niceties under the pervading current of evangelical enthusiasm: in this respect these Churches experienced a change of theological emphasis comparable with that discernible within the evangelical wing of the Church of England. As with the Methodists, the earnestness

[66] Gilbert, *Religion and Society in Industrial England*, p. 74.

[67] On this subject see in general Henry W. Clark, *History of English Nonconformity* (2 vols., 1911–13), ii. 205–8, 234–5, 245–57; Gilbert, *Religion and Society in Industrial England*, pp. 71 ff.

[68] Gilbert, op. cit., pp. 35–6.

[69] John Addy, 'Porteus's Visitation', pp. 188–9.

of evangelicalism tended to foster material success among the Dissenters. In 1805 a knowledgeable traveller recorded his impression after touring the manufacturing districts, that the commerce of the country was principally in the hands of persons attached to evangelical faith in one form or another.[70]

Granted the existence of this evangelical revival, extending in varying degrees through all the Churches at the end of the eighteenth century, what can be said about its steadying effect upon society at that time?

So far as the masses were concerned, the effect was probably negligible. The numbers caught up by the revival before 1800 were relatively small. According to the most recent reassessment of the data, Wesleyan Methodists increased from about 37,000 in 1781 to 77,000 on the eve of the Kilhamite secession of 1796, and numbered 87,000 in 1801, at which time the Kilhamite New Connection had about 5,000 members. In the decade 1790–1800 the total of Baptists and Congregationalists rose from about 46,000 to about 62,000.[71] The number of evangelical Anglicans seems impossible to assess, especially given the degree of mobility between the different Churches. Possibly it might be another 60,000—more than that seems unlikely, but such a figure can be no more than an intelligent guess. On this basis it may be said that in all about 200,000 persons, many being of the poorer sort, were influenced by evangelicalism during the revolutionary decade of the 1790s. Even given the local concentrations found in parts of Yorkshire and elsewhere, they amounted to only a very small part of the population. Evangelicalism had scarcely dented the very large numbers—perhaps half the population in some districts and sometimes even more—who were no longer connected with any Christian Church.[72]

Possibly more significant, though the extent of it seems

[70] *A History of the Methodist Church*, ed. Davies and Rupp, i. 60.

[71] Gilbert, *Religion and Society in Industrial England*, p. 31, table 2.2, and p. 37, table 2.4. As Baptists and Congregationalists kept less careful records, their strength may be underestimated.

[72] See p. 210 above. Gilbert's figures, plus the estimate for the Anglicans, suggest that evangelicals in 1801 amounted to rather less than 4 per cent of the adult English population.

impossible to judge, was the effect of evangelicalism upon the educated and half-educated minority, which in any society can form a natural recruiting ground for the leadership of revolutionary movements. It may have diverted the energies of some potential radicals from political to spiritual channels. Even although, overall, the movement influenced only a limited number of people, its impact on 'subordinate élites' could be considerable.[73] If enthusiastic idealists were brought to believe that the world could be set to rights by the winning of men to a state of holiness, then they were likely to be not merely indifferent to political radicalism but horrified by the anti-clerical turn taken by it in France during the 1790s.[74] Some historians perhaps have not looked sufficiently hard in this direction for explanations of the vehement reaffirmations of loyalty to the established order made at that time by Methodist leaders.

What seems clear, despite the weakness of the Church Establishment and the limited influence of evangelicalism in the 1790s, is that religion made a far greater appeal than secular radicalism to the thinking active minority in the nation. For some the satisfaction was spiritual. For others it was a degree of social self-fulfilment, the lack of which might otherwise have provoked political discontent. Numbers of people of the artisan and lower middling classes gained status, self-respect, and the satisfaction of a sense of service performed, as a result of the local leadership roles which fell to them in the Methodist and Dissenting Churches. By legitimating self-improvement and economic endeavour, evangelicalism provided a guide for successfully meeting the challenge of the Industrial Revolution, and so may, at least for some,

[73] Through his preoccupation with the working people, E. P. Thompson misses this possible impact of Methodism as a force counter-working middle-class sympathy towards revolution; nor is this point picked up by one of his chief Methodist critics (J. H. S. Kent, 'Methodism and Revolution', *Methodist History*, 12, no. 4 (1973–4), 136–44).

[74] There was, that is to say, a far more positive element in the conservatism of the evangelical movement than the mere political quietism derived from the seventeenth-century Anglican tradition (note 4 above). It is a notable circumstance, that the most uncompromising clerical radicals of the 1790s, men like Joseph Priestley, belonged to the Unitarian group, who called for reforms in a spirit hostile to both the existing political and religious order. This was the section of Dissent which remained virtually untouched by the evangelical revival and was unsympathetic towards it on theological grounds.

have averted a potentially dangerous build-up of frustration and political discontent.[75]

[75] In 1813 a hostile critic of the Methodists wrote that 'the immediate temporal advantages which people of the lower classes feel as soon as they enter the society, must be numbered among the efficient causes of its rapid and continual increase'. Quoted in Gilbert, *Religion and Society in Industrial England*, p. 92.

Conclusion

It is a matter of fact, that the British people avoided a revolution in the 1790s. The margin by which they did so has been a matter of some debate. It is possible that the absorbing interest of some historians in radical or revolutionary movements and in trends towards popular forms of government may have swayed them in the direction of assuming that the nation's susceptibility to revolution, its closeness to the brink of a collapse of the old order, were more real than in fact was the case. There can be no mathematical precision about such judgements. But what seemed advisable to me, when I undertook this study, was some survey of factors on the other side of the equation—factors which established grounds for the British people's acceptance of the existing framework of society and government; factors which might be either positive or inertial in character. The more of these that might be traced, the less surprising the emergence of British society undisturbed from the stormy years at the end of the eighteenth century.

Among the fundamental advantages of the British nation in those years was an absence of acute class or caste division, or of excessively privileged groups whose situation was intolerably provoking to others. Social jealousy sometimes found expression but it was confined to a relative few. The infinite gradations in society often noted by contemporaries made some degree of success in emulation relatively easy for men of talent and ambition. They also facilitated the establishment of links of common interest and common concern, which countered the frictions arising from differences of rank. These social circumstances had their economic counterpart in the spread of the general concern among high and low to make profitable use of capital. This spirit linked together in common interest people of different ranks of society and facilitated the accumulation and the use of small packets of capital by men scattered over a fairly wide social spectrum. The consequent growth of private capitalist enterprise, often on a relatively small scale, with the accompanying significant expansion of output, employment, and domestic purchasing power, contributed further to social stability. It created a situation in which increasing numbers of people could confidently hope to improve their material circumstances, even if, as sometimes happened, the process suffered temporary setbacks owing to bad harvests or interruptions of trade. The idiosyncrasies of the unreformed parliamentary system did not prevent significant interest groups from securing attention to their concerns. 'The Lobby' was already a well-entrenched part of the governmental system. If authority sometimes thwarted the subject, at other times it gave aid and support.

In other ways also British society displayed a closely integrated quality. Englishmen were intensely clubbable. Such involvement extended through all ranks of society, except perhaps the lowest. Friendly societies and trade clubs provided mutual support and a degree of social security in times of crisis. Religious affiliations among the Methodists and the various Nonconformist sects brought social support as well as religious fellowship. In numerous ways membership of one or other sort of private association helped to give the individual a sense of place in society, of status, of role, of security, a familiar and human framework for his existence, and an interest, perhaps instinctive rather than conscious, in the maintenance of a customary social environment.

On the whole none of these forms of connection touched the lives of the very poor. But the very poor derived at least a measure of support from two different sources: private charity and the public Poor Law.

Whatever the defects and inadequacies of the Poor Law—and these should be neither minimized nor exaggerated—it had both moral and practical implications of considerable importance. In the first place a secular authority, in the hands of people of property, acknowledged an obligation to sustain those who were potential victims of complete material deprivation. The very poor had a right of survival guaranteed by the state. Secondly, in practical terms, numbers of unfortunate people were supported by public authority which deliberately, by force of law, took resources for this purpose out of the pockets of the prosperous. Throughout the later years of the eighteenth century, of set purpose, the scope of this support was being extended, from a mixture of humanitarian and practical political motives. Limited though it was, it was a significant contribution to social stability—a fact readily apparent if English (and to some extent Scottish) experience is compared with that of Ireland or France, which lacked effective secular poor-law systems. With the public Poor Law as a first line of defence, private charity—elsewhere a sole resource under constant debilitating requisition—could more effectively be summoned in aid on a massive scale in times of crisis.

On balance intellectual and religious factors also played their part in securing social and political stability. The influence of the Churches was both more limited and more subtle than has sometimes been suggested. Undoubtedly a large part of the population—on the whole the most politically inert portion of it—had little or no contact with any Church and remained unaffected by religious influence. Many other people were swayed more by the secular than the spiritual aspects of the religious organizations to which they gave adherence. For them their Church formed part of an established, familiar, and at times sustaining social environment, contributing to their satisfaction with the status quo. The members of those minorities which were caught up by spiritual zeal, especially the evangelicals, experienced a sense of fulfilment and satisfaction, and felt an optimism about this world and the next far removed from any 'Chiliasm of despair'. Such men believed in the power of God to regenerate human character: they did not believe in the power of men effectively to improve their lot by political means. Their attitude was thus at the first remove non-revolutionary; and at the second remove it became anti-revolutionary because of the atheistic tone increasingly taken by the French Revolution.

Marginally religion overlapped with political philosophy. In the view of at least some speculative thinkers, belief in divine dispensation was carried over as an essential premiss of conservative political thought. The preservation of life, liberty, property, and justice was seen as inherent in the

natural law underlying God's creation, and forms of government were good if, by maintenance of a corresponding rule
of law, they successfully secured these basic principles.
Other thinkers, who did not start from that premiss, nevertheless took the utilitarian view that established institutions,
which had secured the welfare of the people in these ways,
had proved their worth over the generations. Since
judgements about governmental performance were subjective and liable to change, utilitarianism was hardly an
adamantine basis for any unchallengeable political theory;
but for the time being the material circumstances of a
sufficient number of people in the country seemed to
support the conservative emphasis placed upon it.

A number of considerations can thus be listed in seeking to
account for the British escape from revolution at the end of
the eighteenth century. Imponderables remain. The factors
making for stability were multifarious, and it is certain that
at least some of them defy identification or analysis. It is
likely, for instance, that there were emotional undercurrents
involved in the equation, such as the inveterate prejudice of
many British (especially Englishmen) against foreigners,
reckoned to be of inferior breed and defective experience,
whose example, on principle, was to be scorned. Authors
have sometimes written of the contagion of revolution, as
if the French experience were bound to create in other
countries a disposition to follow French example. But
contagion also creates fear and revulsion, and this was very
much the British response. There was also that deep isola-
tionist English love of country, the sense of solidarity of a
people set apart, an instinct better conveyed by poetry, the
language of the heart, than by philosophic prose.[1] Shakespeare
had expressed it as none other could:

> This royal throne of kings, this sceptred isle,
> This earth of majesty, this seat of Mars,
> This other Eden, demi-paradise,
> This fortress built by nature for herself
> Against infection and the hand of war,
> This happy breed of men, this little world,

[1] W. Shakespeare, *Richard II*, Act II, scene i.

This precious stone set in the silver sea,
Which serves it in the office of a wall,
Or as a moat defensive to a house,
Against the envy of less happier lands,
This blessed plot, this earth, this realm, this England.

Index